JORGE LUIS BORGES

MODERN LITERATURE MONOGRAPHS

GENERAL EDITOR: Lina Mainiero

In the same series:

(*continued on last page of book*)

JORGE LUIS BORGES

George R. McMurray

FREDERICK UNGAR PUBLISHING CO.
NEW YORK

Library of Congress Cataloging in Publication Data

McMurray, George R   1925-
   Jorge Luis Borges.

   (Modern literature monographs)
   Bibliography: p.
   Includes index.
   1. Borges, Jorge Luis, 1899-   —Criticism and
interpretation.
PQ7797.B635Z774   1980   868   78-20939
ISBN 0-8044-2608-2

To my father

Contents

Chronology

1899   Born on August 24 in Buenos Aires, Argentina.

1914   Travels to Europe with his family. During World War I they live in Geneva, Switzerland, where Borges completes his *baccalauréat*.

1919–21   Lives in Spain. Joins the ultraist literary movement. Publishes several poems.

1921   Returns to Buenos Aires. Collaborates on *Prisma*, a "mural" magazine pasted on walls of the city. Publishes the manifesto "Ultraísmo" in the literary journal *Nosotros*.

1922   Founds the journal *Proa* with several friends, including Macedonio Fernández.

1923   Travels to Europe with his family. Publication of his first collection of poetry, *Fervor of Buenos Aires*.

1924   Founds the second *Proa* with other writers, including Ricardo Güiraldes. Contributes to the important literary journal *Martín Fierro*.

1925   Publishes *Moon Across the Way* (poems) and *Inquisitions*, his first collection of essays.

1926   Publishes *The Extent of My Hope* (essays).

1928   Publishes *The Language of the Argentines* (essays).

1929   Publishes *San Martín Notebook* (poems). Receives second prize in Municipal Literary Contest.

1930   Publishes *Evaristo Carriego* (essays).

1931   Begins contributing to *Sur*, the literary journal founded by Victoria Ocampo.

1932   Publishes *Discussion* (essays).

1933 Begins to contribute to the literary supplement of the newspaper *Crítica,* which he will later edit.

1935 Publishes *A Universal History of Infamy,* his first collection of narrative prose.

1936 Publishes *History of Eternity* (essays).

1937 Publishes *Classical Anthology of Argentine Literature* in collaboration with Pedro Henríquez Ureña. Takes post in a small municipal Buenos Aires library.

1938 His father dies. Borges suffers accident and is hospitalized for several weeks.

1940 Publishes *Anthology of Fantastic Literature* in collaboration with Silvina Ocampo and Adolfo Bioy Casares.

1941 Publishes *The Garden of the Forking Paths* (stories); *Anthology of Argentine Poetry,* in collaboration with Silvina Ocampo and Adolfo Bioy Casares.

1942 Special issue of *Sur* dedicated to Borges to protest his not being awarded the National Prize of Literature. Publishes *Six Problems for Don Isidro Parodi* (humorous detective stories) in collaboration with Adolfo Bioy Casares, under the joint pseudonym, H. Bustos Domecq.

1944 Publishes *Ficciones* (stories). Receives the Prize of Honor from the SADE (Sociedad Argentina de Escritores).

1946 Publishes *Two Memorable Fantasies* (stories) and *A Model for Death* (stories) in collaboration with Adolfo Bioy Casares under the pseudonym of H. Bustos Domecq. Publishes *The Best Detective Stories* (anthology) in collaboration with Bioy Casares under the pseudonym B. Suárez Lynch. Is relieved of his post as municipal librarian for purely political reasons. Edits *Los Anales de Buenos Aires,* a monthly journal.

1947 Publishes *New Refutation of Time* (essay).

1949 Publishes *El Aleph* (stories).

1950 Publishes *Aspects of Gaucho Literature* (essays).

1950–53 Serves as president of the SADE.

1951 Publishes *Death and the Compass* (stories); *Ancient Germanic Literatures,* in collaboration with Delia Ingenieros; *The Best Detective Stories* (second series), in collaboration with Adolfo Bioy Casares.

1952   Publishes *Other Inquisitions* (essays).

1953   Publishes *Martín Fierro* (essay) in collaboration with Margarita Guerrero.

1955   Named Director of the National Library and member of the Argentine Academy of Letters. Publishes *The Shore Dwellers* and *The Believers' Paradise* (unproduced screenplays) and *Brief and Extraordinary Stories* (anthology) in collaboration with Adolfo Bioy Casares, *Sister Eloise* in collaboration with Luisa M. Levinson, and *Leopoldo Lugones* in collaboration with Betina Edelberg.

1956   Appointed Professor of English Literature at the University of Buenos Aires. Awarded the National Prize for Literature. Receives honorary doctorate from the University of Cuyo.

1957   Publishes *Book of Imaginary Beings* (short prose) in collaboration with Margarita Guerrero.

1960   Publishes *Dreamtigers* (poetry and short prose); *Book of Heaven and Hell* (anthology), in collaboration with Adolfo Bioy Casares.

1961   Publishes *Personal Anthology* (prose and poetry). Shares International Publishers Formentor Prize with Samuel Beckett. Teaches at the University of Texas and lectures at several other universities in the United States.

1962   Publishes *Ficciones* and *Labyrinths* (stories) in English.

1963   Travels and lectures in England, France, Spain, and Switzerland. Receives honorary degree from the University of Los Andes in Colombia.

1964   *Dreamtigers* published in English.

1965   Publishes *For the Six Strings* (poetry); *Ancient German Literature,* in collaboration with María Esther Vásquez. *Other Inquisitions* published in English.

1966   Publishes *Poetic Works (1923–1966)*.

1967   Publishes *Chronicles of Bustos Domecq,* in collaboration with Adolfo Bioy Casares; *Introduction to American Literature,* in collaboration with Esther Zemborain de Torres; *The Book of Imaginary Beings* (short prose), in collaboration with Margarita Guerrero. Marries the former Elsa Astete Millán. *A Personal Anthology* published in English.

1967–68   Occupies the Charles Eliot Norton Chair of Poetry at Harvard University.

1968   Publishes *New Personal Anthology.*

1969   Publishes *In Praise of Darkness* (poetry and short prose) and *The Self and the Other* (poetry). *Book of Imaginary Beings* published in English. Attends conference in his honor at the University of Oklahoma. Travels and lectures in Israel. Receives Inter-American Literary Prize in Brazil.

1970   Publishes *Dr. Brodie's Report* (stories). *The Aleph and Other Stories* published in English. He and his wife separate.

1971   Publishes *The Congress* (story). Awarded honorary degrees by Columbia University and the University of Oxford. Receives Jerusalem Prize in Israel.

1972   Publishes *The Gold of the Tigers* (poetry). *Dr. Brodie's Report, Selected Poems,* and *A Universal History of Infamy* (stories) published in English. Travels to the United States.

1973   Publishes *Borges on Writing,* based on tape-recorded transcripts of seminars on creative writing at Columbia University. Awarded Alfonso Reyes Prize in Mexico. Travels to Spain at the invitation of the Institute of Hispanic Culture.

1974   Publishes *Obras completas* in a single volume. *The Congress* and *In Praise of Darkness* published in English.

1975   Publishes *The Book of Sand* (stories) and *Prologues* (essays). Travels to the United States. His mother dies.

1976   Publishes *The Iron Coin* (poetry); *Libro de sueños* (prose); *What Is Buddhism* in collaboration with Alicia Jurado. *The Gold of the Tigers* published in English. Lectures at Michigan State University and other institutions in the United States.

1977   *The Book of Sand* and *The Gold of the Tigers* published in English.

1979   Now lives in Buenos Aires.

Key to Collections

The following initials are used after the first mention of Borges's stories, essays, and poems in order to indicate the collections in which they are found.

A	*The Aleph*
D	*Discussion* (not translated)
PA	*A Personal Anthology*
BOS	*Book of Sand*
DT	*Dreamtigers*
DBR	*Dr. Brodie's Report*
F	*Ficciónes*
FBA	*Fervor of Buenos Aires* (not translated)
HE	*History of Eternity* (not translated)
IPD	*In Praise of Darkness*
L	*Labyrinths*
MAW	*Moon Across the Way* (not translated)
OI	*Other Inquisitions*
SAO	*The Self and the Other*
UHI	*A Universal History of Infamy*

Introduction

Prior to 1950, the vast majority of Latin American novelists relied on traditional realism to depict life in their native lands and convey messages of social protest against adverse conditions afflicting much of their continent.* During the 1950s and 1960s, however, this regionalist fiction underwent a series of drastic changes that transformed it into one of the present-day world's most dynamic, avant-garde art forms. The spiritual "father" of this "revolution" in contemporary Latin American letters is the Argentine Jorge Luis Borges, whose metaphysical themes and stylistic innovations inspired the younger generation of writers to explore the realities of their rapidly evolving societies with far greater concern for universal and esthetic values than their predecessors. Thus, it is often said that Borges not only liberated Latin American literature from documentation but also restored imagination as a major fictional ingredient. Although he is a respected poet and essayist, it is his ingenious, highly original short stories—the most important written during the 1940s and early 1950s—that have made him one of the most widely acclaimed writers of our time.

Jorge Luis Borges was born in Buenos Aires on August 24, 1899, to a prominent upper-class Argentine family of Spanish, Portuguese, and English blood. His

* Though technically incorrect, the term *continent* is commonly used by critics referring to Latin America as a geographical entity.

grandmother was English, a circumstance that explains his early knowledge of that language and literature. Both of Borges's grandfathers were high-ranking military officers who had served their country during the nineteenth-century civil conflicts, and his maternal great-grandfather led a charge in the famous battle of Junín during the wars for independence from Spain. Although his father was a lawyer by training, he was also a man of letters, having published a novel as well as the first translation into Spanish of the *Rubáiyát* by Omar Khayyám. Thus he guided his son's literary tastes and encouraged his youthful aspirations of becoming a writer. Like his father and various members of four preceding generations on that side of the family, Borges was born with a congenital eye defect. This led to blindness in the mid-1950s.

A frail child, Borges was raised in a sheltered environment and encouraged to follow intellectual pursuits. He did not attend school until he was nine years old, his initial education having been entrusted to an English governess. During this time he spent many hours reading in his father's extensive library, where he became acquainted with a number of his favorite authors, including Stevenson, Kipling, Dickens, Wilde, Wells, Poe, James, and Twain. When he was seven years old, he wrote his first story; at the age of nine he translated Oscar Wilde's "The Happy Prince" and published his translation in a Buenos Aires newspaper. His readings in Spanish at this time included *Facundo,* by Domingo Faustino Sarmiento, and the novels of the popular Argentine gaucho writer Eduardo Gutiérrez. He recalled later that he first read *Don Quijote* in English and that when he reread it in Spanish, it seemed to him like a poor translation.

Borges's mixture of English and Spanish ancestry was destined to affect both his life and works. For him English would come to represent culture, while Spanish would represent courage and the more primitive side of life. Although the rational Borges prefers his English heritage, his works at times reveal a strong subconscious yearning to relive the glories of his Argentine ancestors. Indeed, in "An Autobiographical Essay"(A) he states, "I felt ashamed, quite early, to be a bookish kind of person and not a man of action. Throughout my boyhood, I thought that to be loved would have amounted to an injustice. I did not feel I deserved any particular love, and I remember my birthdays filled me with shame, because everyone heaped gifts on me when I thought that I had done nothing to deserve them—that I was a kind of fake. After the age of thirty or so, I got over the feeling."

In 1914, Borges's parents took him and his younger sister Norah to Europe where, because of World War I, they spent four years in Geneva. Here Borges completed the *baccalauréat* at a French-speaking school while immersing himself in the works of Hugo, Flaubert, Daudet, Maupassant, Verlaine, Rimbaud, and Mallarmé. At this time he also came to revere the writings of Thomas Carlyle, Thomas De Quincey, G. K. Chesterton, and Walt Whitman. And equally important were his readings in German philosophy and poetry, including books by Schopenhauer, Nietzsche, Heine, and the expressionist poets. The impact of German expressionism on the youthful Borges made itself visible not only in his enthusiasm for the Russian Revolution but also in his early poetry.

After the war Borges and his family spent two years in Spain, where he became involved in the short-lived poetic movement of the day called *ultraísmo*. The ultraists reacted against the ornate, self-conscious artistry of modernism* and found inspiration in avant-garde sources such as expressionism, dadaism, cubism, and futurism. They preferred free verse, concentrated on contemporary themes, and injected absurd humor into their works.

---

* Modernism was an important movement in Spanish and Latin American poetry between the 1880s and 1916, when its leader, Nicaraguan poet Rubén Darío, died. It is characterized by its perfection of form, symbolic imagery, and escape from reality.

Although they placed great emphasis on the elimination of connecting phrases and decorative adjectives, the most salient feature of *ultraísmo* was its cult of the metaphor, often used, so it seemed, solely to startle the reader or demonstrate verbal agility. The result was an unfortunate tendency toward incoherence.

Borges published his first poems in ultraist journals in Spain and, back home in Argentina, became the leader of his country's ultraist movement. But he seldom succumbed to its excesses and, unlike some of his colleagues, utilized the metaphor mainly to reinforce thematic content. He also differed from other ultraists by his nostalgic yearning for the past and by his preoccupation with metaphysical questions.

When Borges returned to Buenos Aires in 1921 after seven years of absence, he was so amazed at the many changes brought about by the economic boom and the influx of European immigrants that his homecoming turned out to be a kind of journey of rediscovery. In the course of the next ten years he helped to found two literary journals and contributed regularly to almost a dozen others. He also published three collections of poetry and four collections of essays during this time, and, although he now dislikes the majority of these works for what he considers their excess of local color and Argentinisms, they contain in embryonic form many fundamental elements of his future writings. His most memorable book of these years and perhaps the best example of Argentine *ultraísmo* is *Fervor of Buenos Aires* (1923), the poems of which convey his preoccupation with time ("Patio"), philosophical idealism ("Daybreak"), and dramatic moments from the Argentine historic past ("General Quiroga Rides to His Death in a Carriage").

During the 1930s Borges concentrated almost exclusively on the essay and short fiction. His book entitled *Evaristo Carriego* (1930) was first conceived as a critical biography of a poet friend of the Borges family and the first Argentine writer to discover the literary possibilities of the run-down outskirts of Buenos Aires. However, Borges's interest in Carriego—a comparatively minor poet—gradually gave way to fascination with the old-time city and its colorful inhabitants, especially the hoodlums, or *compadritos,* who played the guitar, sang improvised verses, and engaged in knife fights.

In 1931 the well-known literary figure Victoria Ocampo founded the prestigious journal *Sur,* to which Borges contributed regularly. Prior to this time he had been a political leftist and an admirer of liberal President Hipólito Irigoyen. When the latter's regime was overthrown by a military coup, Borges began to express his disenchantment with Argentine politics and his criticism of Argentine society, attitudes that emerge from his book of essays entitled *Discussion* (1932). Other pieces in this collection reveal his increasing interest in esoteric subjects such as Gnosticism, the cabala, and the paradoxes of the ancient Greek philosopher, Zeno of Elea. And Borges also discusses some of the literary ideals that will shape his fiction, namely, his appreciation for the well-structured plot, the possibilities of magic as a literary ingredient, and his repudiation of the psychological novel.

A Universal History of Infamy (1935) represents a landmark in Borges's career, not only because it is his first collection of narrative prose, but also because it reveals some fundamental elements of his subsequent fiction. Based on factual material and written in a tongue-in-cheek, straightforward style, these amusing tales parody the lives of a whole gamut of villains, from killers, pirates, and outlaws to slave dealers, impostors, and swindlers. The most significant pieces include the intriguing "Streetcorner Man," which is discussed below; the carefully wrought "Tom Castro, the Implausible Impostor"; and "The Masked Dyer, Hakim of Merv," an early example of "magical realism" in Latin American letters.* In 1936 Borges published *History of Eternity,* an important book of essays that also contains "The Approach to Al-Mu'tasim," the first story in which he achieved the amalgamation of fiction, pseudoerudition, and metaphysical symbolism so characteristic of his later works.

Shortly before his father's death in 1938, Borges was obliged to take an obscure post in a Buenos Aires municipal library, where he was employed for nine unhappy years. On Christmas Eve in 1938, while ascending a poorly lighted staircase, he struck his head against a recently painted open window. Soon thereafter, blood poisoning developed in the wound, and Borges hovered on the brink of death for several weeks. Upon recovering, he found himself obsessed by the fear of having lost his creative powers and decided to write a short story, reasoning that failure in a genre for which he was less known would be less humiliating. The result of his efforts was "Pierre Menard, Author of *Don Quijote,*" one of his most memorable works.

The decade of the 1940s is probably the most important of Borges's career, for it was during this time that he published the meticulously contrived and splendidly honed tales destined to earn him his international reputation. Collected in *Ficciones* (1944) and *The Aleph* (1949), they emerge as polished artifacts dramatizing the collapse of rational certainties in a world fraught with contradictions. Because of their classical purity and playful humor, they also represent the triumph of art over the chaos of reality. During the early 1940s Borges began his many years of collaboration with his friend Adolfo Bioy Casares, with whom he has written humorous detective tales and edited anthologies. In 1941, when the National Literary Prize was awarded to a writer of infe-

* "Magical realism" is a fusion of "fantasy and objective reality," usually aimed at expanding fictional dimensions and creating poetic effect.

rior merit, Borges's supporters dedicated an entire issue of *Sur* to him in protest of the jury's "error." Three years later he received the Prize of Honor established by the SADE (Sociedad Argentina de Escritores).

The Perón years (1946–55) were not easy for Borges because of his unequivocal opposition to the dictator's repressive regime.[1] Almost immediately after Perón's rise to power, Borges lost his post in the library for having signed an antigovernment resolution, and to add insult to injury, he was offered the title of Poultry Inspector for Fairs and Exhibitions. Needless to say, he turned it down. In 1950 he was elected to the presidency of the anti-Peronist SADE, a position he held for three years. During this time he taught English literature at several private institutions and also began a series of lecture tours throughout Argentina and Uruguay, speaking on such varied topics as Swedenborg, the Chinese mystics, Buddhism, gaucho poetry, Martin Buber, the cabala, medieval German poetry, the Icelandic sagas, Heine, Dante, Cervantes, and expressionism. Once he overcame his terror of public speaking, Borges actually began to enjoy his new career, which earned him a better income than he had received from his post in the library. And despite the harassment of the police, who followed him on his long walks about the city and even attended his lectures (Borges still recalls with amusement the bewildered expession of an agent during one of his talks on the Persian Sufis), he published some of his best stories as well as his most important volume of essays, *Other Inquisitions* (1952).

Perón's fall from power brought about a sudden change in Borges's fortunes, for in less than two years he was named director of the National Library, professor of English literature at the University of Buenos Aires, and a member of the Argentine Academy of Letters. Soon thereafter, international recognition came to him as a result of the growing number of translations of his works. In 1961 he shared the prestigious International Publishers'

Formentor Prize with Samuel Beckett, and was invited to lecture on Argentine literature at the University of Texas. Two years later he traveled to England, France, Spain, and Switzerland as a guest of these countries and in 1967 held the Charles Eliot Norton Chair of Poetry at Harvard University.

Prior to this time Borges's aged mother had been his constant companion, accompanying him on his travels, serving as his secretary, and managing his personal affairs. Thus it came as somewhat of a surprise when shortly before his arrival at Harvard he married Elsa Astete Millán, a widow whom he had met in his youth. The couple separated approximately three years later.

In 1970 Borges published *Dr. Brodie's Report,* his first fictional endeavor in more than a decade. Although the stories of this collection display many characteristics of his early fiction, they are more realistic and, as he suggests in the preface, more "straightforward." In his latest collection of tales, *The Book of Sand* (1975), Borges sustains his straightforward style but veers once again toward fantasy in his subject matter.

Despite his blindness and advancing age, Borges still maintains a busy schedule writing and lecturing both at home and abroad. In the past decade he has also continued to publish poetry and short prose sketches, all the while receiving an increasing number of honors and awards. Although his more recent poems deal with metaphysical themes somewhat similar to those of his youth, he has tended to utilize a simpler, more conversational vocabulary and syntax. Since his blindness, he has shown a preference for classical meters, which are easier for him to memorize than the blank verse he used previously. One also detects stronger pessimistic overtones in his mature poetry, as, for example, in the well-known "Mateo, XXV, 30," which ends with the following lines:

> In vain have oceans been squandered on you, in vain
> The sun, wonderfully seen through Whitman's eyes,

> You have used up the years and they have used up you,
> And still, and still, you have not written the poem.

Here Borges gives vent to his feelings of despair resulting from his inability to achieve the artistic perfection he has sought for decades.

Alicia Jurado, a long-time friend of Borges, has written one of the most illuminating personal portraits of him.[2] According to her, the lucidity and rigorous logic of his mind are masked by his most dominant characteristics, namely, his timidity and modesty. She also describes him as a labyrinth because of the virtual impossibility of penetrating the complex network of barriers he has erected around his inner self. Thus, when he is interrogated by interviewers about his personal life, he invariably becomes evasive and changes the subject to his books or other related matters. And Jurado recalls that during the many years of their friendship the topics of their innumerable conversations have been limited almost exclusively to literature and philosophy. Borges's distaste for personal praise and his tendency to make light of it emerge from the following anecdote. One day he and Jurado were crossing the Plaza San Martín in Buenos Aires when a woman who had recognized him approached and professed at great length her admiration for his works. Borges's discomfort increased steadily until her departure, when he remarked, "Of course you know that I hire these people. She played her role rather well, don't you think?"[3]

Borges has been described as a brilliant conversationalist, although out of shyness he tends to prefer talking with a single individual or small groups of people. His keen sense of humor stands out in his works, but he is also able to laugh at himself, as illustrated by an incident he has described to his friends. It seems that once during carnival season he was blissfully strolling through one of his beloved old districts of Buenos Aires, admiring its quaint dwellings and meditating on the charming aspects of tradition when he was drenched by a bucket of water thrown from a bal-

cony by a "traditionalist child." Borges added that he
deserved what he got for indulging in such sentimental rub-
bish.[4]

Borges's life story is less that of a man than that of a
dedicated writer, his consuming interest in literature and
philosophy having molded his day-to-day existence as well
as his career. On the subject of his childhood he once
wrote, "For years I believed I had been brought up in a
suburb of Buenos Aires, a suburb of dangerous streets and
conspicuous sunsets. What is certain is that I was brought
up in a garden, behind lanceolate iron railings, and in a
library of unlimited English books." And in his autobiographical essay he states, "If I were asked to name the
chief event in my life, I should say my father's library. In
fact, I sometime think I have never strayed outside that
library." He also writes that he has always viewed life
through books and that at the age of ten, when he visited a
ranch for the first time, the countryside and the workers
took on "a certain glamour" from the moment he learned
he was looking out over the *pampa* and associating with
gauchos.

Somewhat surprisingly, Borges has never been fond
of painting, and music bores him except for the popular
Argentine folk melodies, such as the tango and the
milonga, which he has interpreted symbolically. Despite
his powerful intellect and vast, cosmopolitan culture, he
retains an engaging, almost childlike nature. For him
literature and esoteric philosophies are not to be taken
seriously, but rather represent amusing artificial
labyrinths more artistically designed and more readily
understood than the unintelligible universe mankind
attempts in vain to decipher.

Because Borges has repeatedly come under attack in
Latin America for his aloofness from social concerns and
for his cultural elitism, a word should be said in his
defense on the subject of his political beliefs. During
World War II, when many Argentines sympathized with
the Axis powers, he publicly supported the Allies and

expressed his strong dislike of all forms of totalitarianism, including fascism, communism, and, as stated above, Peronism. In his works he has on occasion implied dismay over the horrors of man's inhumanity to his fellow man, notable examples being "The Library of Babel," "Deutsches Requiem," and "Dr. Brodie's Report." Still, due to his fundamental skepticism and intellectual bent, he is essentially apolitical. Unlike most social reformers, Borges sees reality as so ambiguous, chaotic, and unfathomable that he is reluctant to put his faith in absolute values or dogmatic ideological solutions. In recent years, however, his fear of communism combined with the ever-increasing threat of anarchy in Argentina have induced him to make unfortunate political pronouncements such as his praise of General Pinochet, the head of Chile's repressive right-wing regime.

Borges has also been accused by his fellow Latin Americans of having denied his Argentine heritage in favor of foreign values, an unjustifiable judgment probably prompted by his literary sophistication, which makes him incomprehensible to some readers. Indeed, his works reveal a deep affection for, and fascination with, the realities of his native land. His mathematically designed plots involving esoteric metaphysical subjects are not only poetized by nostalgic resonances of Buenos Aires but also are dramatized by scenes of raw violence drawn from his nation's mythical past. The important theme of the machismo cult in his writings also contributes to his identity as an Argentine man of letters. This unique mixture of universal and native elements has more than likely enhanced Borges's appeal to his wide reading public throughout the world. His symbolic, hallucinatory visions of the absurd human condition are so hauntingly real and so artistically conceived, moreover, that he has often been mentioned as a candidate for a Nobel Prize.

Because of the extreme density of Borges's style, any criticism of his work is fated to appear inadequate or pleonastic. Indeed, faced with his awesome task, this critic finds himself in a situation somewhat similar to Borges's archetypal characters attempting to decipher the labyrinthine universe. The present study represents an attempt to decipher the formal and thematic aspects of a man-made universe that rivals reality in its almost overwhelming complexity.

1

Borges and the Absurd
Human Condition

1. THE PHILOSOPHY OF THE ABSURD

Much European and New World literature of the twentieth century has depicted the absurdity of human existence, a theme perhaps best elucidated in the philosophical essays and fiction of such existential writers as Jean-Paul Sartre and Albert Camus. Although Borges differs from the existentialists in a number of important respects, he does share some of their basic concerns, an understanding of which may serve to illuminate his work. For both Sartre and Camus the absurd stems from modern man's loss of God; the denial of absolute values in a meaningless, chaotic world; and the overwhelming threat of death and nothingness. Man's freedom to act according to his convictions, his feelings of responsibility for his actions, and his terror in the face of his unknown destiny have led to solitude, despair, and metaphysical anguish, important by-products of absurdity.

Camus states that neither man alone nor the world by itself is absurd, but rather that the absurd arises from the clash between reasoning man, on the one hand, and on the other, the silent, unreasonable world offering no response to his persistent demands. The absurd man is one who recognizes a void or lack of purpose in life and resolves to commit himself to the lifelong conflict between his intentions and the reality he encounters. Like Sisyphus in Greek mythology, who was condemned by the gods to roll a huge stone up a hill again and again for eternity and whom Camus considers the epitome of the absurd hero, the absurd man can attain heroic proportions by rebelling against his torment and by demonstrating that the struggle itself gives definition and joy to his existence. The absurd, then, is the metaphysical state of conscious man fully aware of inevitable death and nothingness; it is lucid reason pitted against chaos; it is the only certainty linking man with an alien world devoid of absolutes. Camus believes that once one has recognized the absurd, one must keep that awareness permanently alive by maintaining a constant attitude of revolt against ultimate defeat, this being the only means of achieving self-fulfillment and of transcending the tragedy of existence. Sartre denies the existence of a fixed human nature, pointing out that man strives incessantly for absolute Being, i.e., an unattainable equivalent to what Sartre calls the missing God,[1] and that an individual's essence is not determined until the moment of his death. The existentialist revolt against the absurd often takes the form of commitment through action to political and social justice.

Both Sartre and Camus demonstrate an admiration for the human faculty of reason, but at the same time they recognize its limits and, consequently, the impossibility of reducing the unintelligible world to rational principles. Language in particular is deemed inadequate as a tool for depicting reality and bridging the gulf between the reasoning mind and the unreasoning universe. Nevertheless, they exalt the art of fiction, Sartre viewing it as a possible means for gaining immortality, and Camus as an absurd endeavor but one that serves to enrich the meaningless world. In their quest for a better understanding of their fellow man, they often reinterpret old myths by placing their protagonists in contemporary settings and confronting them with archetypal situations of a social or existential nature. Although both writers have coherently analyzed and illustrated the absurd in their essays and fiction, subsequent practitioners of absurd literature have utilized antirational devices such as fantasy, farce, black humor, and inane dialogue to represent life without purpose in a disintegrating world. Some of these writers, including Samuel Beckett, Eugene Ionesco, Kurt Vonnegut, Thomas Pynchon, John Barth, Joseph Heller, Ken Kesey, Julio Cortázar, and Carlos Fuentes, have attacked reason and conventions more forcefully, and probably more effectively, than either Sartre or Camus.

As indicated above, a comparison of Borges's works with those of Sartre and Camus reveals significant similarities and differences. Borges does not share the strong commitment to social justice so evident in the French authors, nor does he display their anguished preoccupation with freedom of choice or responsibility. Although Borges's characters, like those of the existentialists, are the sum of their actions, unlike Sartre's and Camus's characters they are subordinate to plot and remain psychologically undeveloped. Indeed, they emerge not as real people but as archetypal figures created solely to illustrate ontological situations or philosophical ideas. The absurdity conveyed by Borges's works derives principally from three basic themes: the distrust of language as a means of depicting reality, the failure of human reason to unveil the mysteries of the universe, and the rejection of absolute moral or philosophical values. Thus, like the typical absurd hero, his protagonists are usually engaged in a vain quest for knowledge, power, or salvation, a quest roughly equivalent to the Sartrean will to replace the missing God. Borges's fundamental skepticism emerges from his confession that he tends to "evaluate religious or philosophical ideas on the basis of their aesthetic worth and even for what is singular and marvelous about them." Somewhat like the existentialists, who stress man's never-ending search to define himself, Borges views each philosophical school as "provisional," i.e., a chapter in the history of ideas that will inevitably be replaced by another school. He further reasons that since God's order is inaccessible to man, language represents a tool for creating a more comprehensible but subjective and totally fictitious version of reality.

For Borges, then, philosophy does not constitute a mirror of reality, but rather an artificial system of thought superimposed on the real world. Still, as a sensitive man of letters, he marvels at the creative ingenuity of the world's philosophers, whose "inventions"—together with those of the artist—represent man's best weapons against chaos and nothingness. And considering esthetic perfection just as elusive as absolute knowledge, Borges likens the vain quest of the artist and philosopher to the absurd but heroic efforts of Sisyphus. As D. P. Gallagher states, "For Borges there is something splendid in the spectacle of men striding out to explain the universe. That they do so is a measure of their spirit, indomitable against overwhelming odds."[2] In order to capture this absurdity of the human experience, Borges seeks to disintegrate objective reality by weaving paradoxical situations, esoteric philosophical theories, and disconcerting symbolic motifs into the fabric of his fiction. The end result is the emergence of a fictional universe fraught with contradiction and ambiguity.

Borges's inherent distrust of language as a vehicle for thought is treated with absurd overtones in "The Analytical Language of John Wilkins" (OI). This essay describes a seventeenth-century English bishop's endeavor to devise a universal language in which the names of things are determined by the nature of the things named, his ultimate aim being to eliminate the arbitrary nature of language. Wilkins divides the universe into forty categories, which in turn are divided into subcategories he calls differences and species. To each category he assigns a monosyllable of two letters, to each difference a consonant, and to each species a vowel. For example, *de* means element; *deb* means the first of the elements, fire; and *deba,* a portion of this element, or flame. The eighth category deals with stones, which are classified as ordinary (flint, gravel, slate); intermediate (marble, amber, coral); precious (pearl, opal), etc. Borges alludes to several other artificial languages, some or all of which are probably apocryphal, and then concludes that all classifications of the universe must be arbitrary for the obvious reason that "we do not know the universe," nor can we understand the definitions in "God's secret dictionary," if indeed there is such a thing. Nevertheless, he adds, the impossibility of penetrating the divine order "cannot dissuade us from outlining human schemes, even though we are aware that they are provisional." Borges ends his essay with a quotation by Chesterton that he considers "the most lucid words ever written on the subject of language."

Man knows that there are in the soul tints more bewildering, more numberless, and more nameless than the colours of the autumn forests: . . . Yet he seriously believes that these things can every one of them, in all their tones and semi-tones, in all their blends and unions, be accurately represented by an arbitrary system of grunts and squeals. He believes that an ordinary civilized stockbroker can really produce out of his own inside noises which denote all the mysteries of memory and all the agonies of desire.

The gulf between language and the world is poetically illustrated by "A Yellow Rose" (DT). In this philosophical vignette, the dying Italian poet Giambattista Marino gazes at a rose in a goblet beside his bed and, in a kind of mystic revelation, sees it "as Adam might have seen it in Paradise." Suddenly he realizes that a rose can be "mentioned" or "alluded to" by the poet, but it can never be "expressed" in words. Then, contemplating the volumes of his treasured works, he no longer considers them "a mirror of the world, but rather one thing more added to the world."

The reasoning mind's inability to understand the scheme of the divinity emerges as the subject matter of "Inferno, I, 32" (DT), another philosophical vignette in which God reveals to a sleeping tiger that its purpose in life is to become a symbol in a poem. Upon awakening, however, the tiger no longer comprehends its destiny, "for the machinery of the world is far too complex for the simplicity of a wild beast." Similarly, God reveals to Dante in a dream the secret purpose of his life, but upon awakening he too is unable to recapture the revelation, "for the machinery of the world is far too complex for the simplicity of men."

2. THE NEGATION OF REASON

The task of organizing Borges's short stories according to subject matter is extremely complex because most of them interweave two or more themes. Thus, many works not treated in this section do indeed suggest the negation of reason. What I have attempted to do in this and subsequent sections is to discuss the stories that best illustrate the theme in question. However, this has not precluded the allusion to, or discussion of, secondary themes.

The Library of Babel   (1941) (F) (L)*

"The Library of Babel" conveys the nightmarish boredom and despair Borges felt while working as a library clerk between 1937 and 1946. It is also one of Borges's best illustrations of man's inability to decipher the meaningless world. At the beginning of this story it is suggested that the Library, an immense structure comprising an infinite number of identical hexagonal galleries, represents the universe. Communication between the different levels is provided by a spiral staircase that "plunges

* The date after the title of each story indicates the year it was first published in Spanish. The initial indicates the English collection in which it appears.

down into the abyss and rises up to the heights." In the
building's entrance hangs a mirror, "which faithfully
duplicates appearances." The narrator, whom the reader
is tempted to identify with Borges the librarian, has spent
his life vainly searching for a certain book, but he is now
growing old. He realizes that once he is dead he will be
thrown into the abyss of the staircase where his body will
dissolve in the wind engendered by the infinite fall. Other
librarians believe in the "superstition" of the Man of the
Book, i.e., a volume that is "the cipher and compendium
of all the rest." Each gallery of the Library contains the
same number of shelves and books, each consisting of 410
pages with forty lines on each page and eighty letters in
each line. It has been determined, moreover, that the
number of orthographic symbols is twenty-five, including
twenty-two letters, the comma, the period, and the space
sign. The language in which the books are written,
however, is unknown to anybody and thus meaningless.
(One mysterious volume is thought to have been written in
a Samoyed-Lithuanian dialect of Guaraní, with classical
Arabic inflections.)

From the preceding summary of the first pages of this
tale, it seems evident that, like so many of Borges's works,
it can be interpreted allegorically.[1] The systematically
designed Library does indeed represent the universe, but
not the real universe. Rather it is a metaphor of reasoning
man's perception of a universe, whose laws have been
established by philosophers and scientists. The mirror
hanging in the entrance portends the futility of the narrator's quest for a certain book, i.e., elusive, ultimate reality.
The abyss of the spiral staircase brings to mind the
existentialist void, and the "superstition" of the Man of
the Book suggests the pantheistic idea of monistic unity[2]
(one book representing all the others) as well as the
idealist theory of reality existing in a book written by
God.[3] The unidentified language, which is scientifically
analyzed but never understood, represents the divine mind

whose reason for creating man and the world remains an eternal mystery.

Eventually it is deduced that the Library is total, i.e., that its shelves contain all the possible combinations of the orthographic symbols, "whose number, though vast, is not infinite." This theory engenders limitless hope among men and inspires a feverish quest for the "Vindications," or books containing secret information. The resultant activity in the galleries, however, gives rise to bitter disputes and even physical violence. After four centuries of fruitless endeavor, a deep depression prevails among the inhabitants of the Library. About this time a "blasphemous sect" advocates the cessation of all searches and the creation of the "canonical books" by the random shuffling of letters and symbols. Alarmed, the authorities issue orders against such radical practices, and "Purifiers" begin to roam through the Library, purging it of the undesirable books.

The hope engendered by the discovery that the Library is "total" and the search for the Vindications evoke the Renaissance or the ages of Enlightenment and scientific research, which eventually led to the catastrophic destruction of World War I and the subsequent period of disillusionment. The cessation of all searches and the random creation of the canonical books recall the dadaist movement in literature during and immediately following World War I.[4] And the Purifiers of the Library bring to mind the Nazi purges in Germany during the 1930s.

The narrator also states that inasmuch as the Library contains all verbal structures in all languages, any letter combination in one language is bound to mean something else in another. (*Library,* for example, might mean "bread" or "pyramid" in another tongue.) And, we are told, the certainty that everything that has ever happened or will happen is already recorded in the Library makes phantoms of all of us. The narrator believes that, due to banditry and epidemics, the human species may be on the road to extinction, but the Library will last forever, "illuminated, solitary, infinite, perfectly immovable, filled with precious volumes, useless, incorruptible, secret."

In the final lines, Borges attempts to solve the apparent contradiction between the infinite nature of the Library and its limited number of books by stating that it is both "limitless and periodic." Accordingly, if an eternal traveler were to traverse the vast edifice in any direction, he would eventually discover that the same volumes are repeated in the same disorder which, repeated, would constitute a kind of order. The narrator concludes with the statement that his "solitude rejoices in this elegant hope."

Although absurdity pervades this entire story, in the final portion it becomes even more pronounced. The plurality of meanings expressed by all orthographic combinations is a metaphor of the linguistic confusion suggested by the story's title;* the statement that the Library contains accounts of all human activities, past, present, and future, implies once again the idealist theory of reality as an immaterial product of mental activity; the contrast between human mortality and the "solitary, infinite" Library conveys Borges's idea of twentieth-century man lost in a mysterious world in which he has become alienated; and the "limitless and periodic" nature of the Library anticipates the narrator's paradoxical hope of discovering order in the repetition of disorder, an absurd expression of man's desperate search for meaning in a world beyond his comprehension. Finally, the symmetrical design of the Library represents the labyrinth of reason that modern man has constructed in order to orient himself in the vast universe and explain its wonders. Ironically, this semblance of order has brought about his disorienta-

---

* The tower of Babel was erected by the descendants of Noah for the purpose of reaching heaven. However, Jehovah prevented them from completing the structure by confounding their language so that they could not understand one another. The tower of Babel has come to signify a visionary scheme.

tion and threatens his very survival. For Borges, then, the labyrinth of reason emerges as a modern-day version of the tower of Babel, i.e., a visionary scheme fraught with absurdity.

Funes, the Memorious* (1942) (F) (L)

"Funes, the Memorious" represents an interesting contrast to "The Library of Babel." The first-person narrator met Ireneo Funes, a young Uruguayan farm hand, fifty years prior to telling his story. Shortly before their last encounter, in 1887, Funes was crippled by a fall from a horse. The accident affected his mind in such a way that he had an infallible memory of all perceptions of the past. As he told the narrator, "I have more memories in myself alone than all men have had since the world was a world. My dreams are like your vigils. My memory, sir, is like a garbage disposal."

Since becoming crippled, Funes had undertaken two projects. The first was the development of a new system of enumeration by which every number would have a separate name. For example, for 7,013 he would say "Máximo Pérez" and 7,014 became "The Train." His second project was to catalogue all the images in his memory, but he soon realized that by the time of his death he would scarcely have finished classifying the memories of his childhood.

Funes's fantastic ability to perceive reality and its progressive changes caused him to consider language far too ambiguous. He found it difficult, for example, to understand that the generic term *dog* embraced so many unlike specimens and that a dog at 3:14 seen in profile should have the same name as a dog at 3:15 seen from the front. He remembered every leaf of every tree he had ever

---

* "Funes, the Memorious," "The South," "The Aleph," "The Intruder," and "The Gospel According to Mark" are the stories Borges has mentioned as possibly his best.

seen and could even detect the deterioration process of a decaying tooth. We are also told that he had great difficulty sleeping because "to sleep is to be abstracted from the world" and Funes was the "solitary and lucid spectator of a multiform world which was instantaneously and almost intolerably exact."[5] His prodigious memory enabled him to learn English, French, Portuguese, and Latin, but his mind was so cluttered with details that he was incapable of thinking clearly or grasping general ideas. He died in 1889 at the age of twenty-one.

"Funes, the Memorious" provides an example of fine story-telling technique. The first-person narrator's recollection of his protagonist, whom he knew many years previously, sets a factual tone likely to win the reader's confidence. Funes's renown for his eccentricity of always knowing the exact time of day and the commonplace details about his life make the reader more prone to accept the startling revelations about his mind during the narrator's final interview with him. The reference to Pliny's *Historia Naturalis,* which Funes reads but never understands, constitutes an additional link with a reality familiar to the reader. And the Uruguayan setting—for Borges a kind of primitive never-never land where his cultured Argentine narrator was vacationing—removes the strange chain of events from everyday reality to a more fictive realm.

"Funes, the Memorious" is in some respects an inverted mirror image of "The Library of Babel." In the latter, as we have seen, the Library emerges as a labyrinth of reason, a world of mental constructs separating reasoning man from the unreasoning universe. Funes's chaotic mind, on the other hand, is truly a mirror of the unreasoning world, and like the world, he is incapable of thought. Thus, his attempt to organize his myriad perceptions is just as absurd as rational man's search for the hidden meaning of the universe in "The Library of Babel." Funes's remarks on the imprecision of language, moreover, suggest that, like the Library, language represents a fictitious world created by man.

A student once asked me why Funes had to die at the end of the story. At first this question appeared trivial, but a possible answer to it seems worthy of mention. For Borges, thinking and reasoning represent two of man's most significant activities. Inasmuch as Funes is incapable of engaging in either of these activities, from Borges's point of view his continued existence would appear impossible. This might also explain Borges's choice of his protagonist's name, Funes being closely related to the Spanish adjective *funesto,* meaning "ill-fated."

Guayaquil (1970) (DBR)

"The Library of Babel" and "Funes, the Memorious" focus on the arbitrary nature of language and its defects as a means for depicting the world. "Guayaquil" casts doubt on the efficacy of language as a tool for communication because it does not necessarily convey the intention of the speaker, nor is it an accurate gauge of his strength of character. The plot of this tale evolves during the course of a conversation between two professors of Latin American history in Buenos Aires some time after World War II. It seems that a historian in Sulaco, Honduras, has discovered some of Simón Bolívar's unpublished letters, one of which deals with his famous meeting with José de San Martín in Guayaquil, Ecuador, in 1822.[6] The Argentine government has commissioned the story's narrator to travel to Sulaco in order to transcribe Bolívar's letters and publish them upon his return to Buenos Aires. Meanwhile, the University of Córdoba, Argentina, has proposed to send its Professor Zimmerman to carry out the same mission. The narrator, a highly cultured and slightly snobbish man of a traditional Argentine family, receives Zimmerman in his home to inform him of the government's decision.

Zimmerman is seen by the narrator as a somewhat brash Jewish exile from Prague and a devotee of Schopenhauer, whose belief in will as the essence of life dominates his thinking. When the narrator naively refers to his journey to Sulaco as a mission to obtain "the truth" about the meeting of the two generals, Zimmerman proceeds to dampen his enthusiasm for making the trip by reminding him that the letter in question contains only Bolívar's point of view, which may be self-serving; that the narrator's well-established reputation as a historian could be tarnished if his name were linked to an unpopular interpretation of the letter; and, alluding to Schopenhauer, that the words spoken between the two generals were far less meaningful to the course of history than the stronger will of one of them.

By the end of the story the narrator has resigned himself to defeat as Zimmerman takes from his briefcase a letter to the Minister stating the narrator's motives for not making the trip to Sulaco and the indisputable professional merits of Zimmerman. Upon signing the letter with a pen provided by Zimmerman, the narrator catches a glimpse of an airline ticket to Sulaco in Zimmerman's briefcase.

The confrontation between the two historians turns out to be ironic, not only because the complacent, condescending narrator is brought to heel by an upstart of superior will, but also because the two antagonists unwittingly become doubles of San Martín and Bolívar, thus suggesting the eternal return of an archetypal situation. A sedentary intellectual, the narrator belongs to the ideal, abstract world of words, whereas his adversary is a realist and sees reality in concrete terms. The tension between the two protagonists is enhanced by the story's structural symmetry resulting from the parallels between them and their historic counterparts. Schopenhauer's idealism—that the world is what man wills it to be—is one of Borges's favorite theories and obviously a major component of the story.[7] Still, it is the fragmentary and deceptive aspects of

...icle for expressing human reason, that
...est for truth and so create an atmosphere

...d the Compass   (1942) (F) (L) (PA) (A)

T... ...eme of the limits of reason is perhaps best
exemplified in Borges's fiction by one of his masterpieces,
"Death and the Compass." A compelling detective story
with profound philosophical implications and ironic
overtones, this tale involves a duel of wits between a clever
sleuth named Erik Lönnrot and an equally clever
gangster, Red Scharlach. The plot is set in motion by the
murder of a Talmudic scholar, Dr. Yarmolinsky, in the
northern part of an unnamed city on the night of
December 3. Lönnrot and Police Commissioner Treviranus are called to Yarmolinsky's hotel room, the scene of
the murder, where they find on a sheet of paper in his
typewriter the enigmatic sentence, "The first letter of the
Name has been spoken." It occurs to the practical, plod-
ding Treviranus that the murderer mistook Dr. Yarmolinsky's room for that of the Tetrarch of Galilee, a
known collector of sapphires whose room was just across
the hall. Lönnrot, who considers himself a "pure thinker,"
refuses to accept this explanation because it admits the
possibility of chance. Preferring to solve the crime through
the use of reason, he initiates the study of Yarmolinsky's
books on Jewish mysticism, especially the cabala.[8]

A key word in Yarmolinsky's book is the Tetragrammaton, which refers to a secret word of four letters meaning
the name of God. According to the cabalists, the person who
discovers and pronounces this secret name will achieve
omniscience and omnipotence. Lönnrot's investigation of
the cabala in order to solve the crime is referred to sar-
castically in a local newspaper.

The second murder occurs exactly a month later, on
the third of January, in front of a paint store located in the
western section of the city. The walls of the store are

covered with diamond-shaped figures, and over the figures
is scrawled, "The second letter of the Name has been
spoken." Lönnrot is, of course, increasingly intrigued
because he suspects a connection between the murders and
the Tetragrammaton.

The third crime occurs a month later, on the evening
of February third on the east side of the city. A man by the
name of Gryphius (or Ginsburg or Ginzberg) calls the
police and offers to inform them of the "sacrifices" in
return for remuneration, but before the police can reach
the hotel where the man is residing he is kidnapped by two
masked harlequins (the story takes place during Carnival)
wearing costumes with diamond-shaped designs. On the
wall of a shed next to the hotel someone has written, "The
last letter of the Name has been spoken." In addition,
Lönnrot discovers a book in Gryphius's room with an
underlined passage stating that the Jewish day begins at
nightfall. Thus, according to the Jewish calendar, the
crimes were not committed on the third of each month but
on the fourth.

On March 1, Commissioner Treviranus receives a
map of the city in the mail with an equilateral triangle
drawn using the three points of the crimes: north, west,
and east. An enclosed letter prophesies that there will be
no fourth crime on March third. Lönnrot, however, looks
at the triangle and reasons that the fourth letter of the
Tetragrammaton has yet to be spoken, and therefore there
has to be a fourth "sacrifice" on the night of March third,
the fourth day of the Jewish month. So with the aid of
calipers and a compass, he calculates on the map the loca-
tion in the southern part of the city where the fourth crime
must occur. In this way he not only traces a perfect dia-
mond design but also foresees the completion of the Tetragrammaton with the articulation of the last letter of the
Name.

The point on the southern edge of the city is an
abandoned estate known as Triste-le-Roy. Supremely
proud of his discovery and full of confidence, Lönnrot

makes his way there alone, intending to arrest the
criminal. Upon entering the gate of the estate, he
encounters an eerie atmosphere of "superfluous symmetries and maniacal repetitions." Outside the building
patios, statues, fountains, stairways, and balconies all seem
to be duplicated, but once inside, he sees himself reflected
infinitely in mirrors placed opposite each other. As he
ascends a spiral staircase leading to a rectangular
belvedere, he is grabbed by two thugs, who hurl
themselves on him and seize his weapon. At this moment
Red Scharlach appears armed with a pistol and tells
Lönnrot that he has trapped him in a labyrinth[9] to avenge
the arrest of his brother by Lönnrot three years ago. He
further explains that Commissioner Treviranus had been
correct in assuming that a thief in search of the Tetrarch of
Galilee's sapphires had murdered Yarmolinsky. Moreover,
upon reading in the newspaper that Lönnrot was attempting to solve the crime by studying the cabala, Scharlach
had deliberately planted clues to convince Lönnrot that
there was a connection between the Tetragrammaton and
the "sacrifices." The second murder was that of Yarmolinsky's assassin, a man named Azevedo who had
betrayed Scharlach and suffered the consequences. The
third "murder" was a fake (Treviranus had suggested this
possibility to Lönnrot), the roles of Gryphius and the two
harlequins having been played by Scharlach and his two
henchmen.

The fourth murder will be that of Lönnrot, but just
before Scharlach shoots him, Lönnrot speaks of a labyrinth
consisting of a single straight line and asks Scharlach to
kill him at a designated point on that line in some future
incarnation. Scharlach replies, somewhat engimatically,
that the next time he kills Lönnrot, he promises him a
labyrinth of a single straight line which is "invisible and
everlasting." Then he steps back a few paces and fires.

"Death and the Compass" dramatizes not only the
limits of reason but also its pitfalls. Lönnrot is doomed

from the beginning because, as Treviranus surmises, Yar-molinsky's murder is the result of chance. Lönnrot's efforts to solve the crimes as he would a mind-boggling puzzle lead him into an irrelevant, geometrical labyrinth that parodies the reasoning mind's fragmented view of random reality and at the same time suggest the absurdity of the confrontation between man and the irreducible world. Here, as in a number of Borges's tales, the rationalistic protagonist is drawn to the center of the labyrinth where he meets his double or alter ego and falls victim to violence or annihilation. Indeed, Lönnrot and Scharlach are more than likely meant to be doubles. Not only are their names similar (*rot* and *scharlach* mean "red" in German), but their minds function with the same rigid logic. Moreover, their antithetical natures, or inverted mirror images, are demonstrated by their roles as detective/criminal and pursuer/pursued, roles that ultimately become ironically reversed. And one might conjecture that the duplication of images on the grounds of Triste-le-Roy symbolically foreshadows Lönnrot's meeting with his double, Scharlach.[10]

"Death and the Compass' is also imbued with metaphysical irony, a concept closely related to the absurd.[11] Thus, as D. P. Gallagher has stated,[12] the story could be read as a fable about a man (Lönnrot) who attempts to explain God's (Scharlach's) deeds without suspecting that he is doomed from the beginning because God has placed him in a labyrinth, granting him limited success and then invalidating it by killing him.[13] Still, even in the face of death Lönnrot remains a prisoner of reason, plotting his future duel of wits along a straight line, a reference to the maze described by Zeno of Elea.[14] Another indication that Scharlach may represent God is his apparent omniscience, i.e., his knowledge of information such as Treviranus's conjectures (made only to Lönnrot) that a thief had killed Yarmolinsky and that the murder of Gryphius might have been a fake. Finally, when Scharlach "promises" Lönnrot his labyrinth of an "invisible and everlasting" straight line the next time he kills him, he projects the image of an omnipotent being who will continue to control man's fate for eternity.

As suggested previously, "Death and the Compass" is fraught with irony. The immaculate thinker Lönnrot pays with his life for a glimpse of truth that the dull Treviranus had hit upon from the beginning. In view of Scharlach's role as a divinity, it is ironic that the journalist criticized Lönnrot for "studying the names of God in order to 'come up with' the name of the assassin." Equally ironic is the fact that the third "victim," who in reality is Scharlach, has three possible names (Ginsburg, Ginzberg, Gryphius), which, the reader suspects, might refer to the Holy Trinity.[15] The story's title is ironic because the compass, an instrument designed to guide its user to safety, leads Lönnrot to his death. The feeling of desolation that overwhelms Lönnrot in Triste-le-Roy when he gazes into the "opposing mirrors" reflects the labyrinthine abyss of his inner self from which he has become alienated because of his excessive rationalism. "The house is not this large," he thinks. "It is only made larger by the penumbra, the symmetry, the mirrors, the years, my ignorance, the solitude." Lönnrot's climb up the spiral staircase to his death represents an ironic metaphor of his vain intellectual aspirations. And, like Lönnrot, the reader is destined to become a victim of irony because he feels compelled to follow Lönnrot through a labyrinth of reason.

This labyrinth is made more intriguing to the reader by the dialectical interplay between the numbers three and four throughout the story. The *three* series includes the name *Tre*viranus, the dates of the murders, the Third Talmudic Congress Yarmolinsky plans to attend, Yarmolinsky's three years of fighting in the Carpathians, the three men involved in the third crime, the three years that have elapsed since the arrest of Scharlach's brother, the triangle on the map of the city sent to Treviranus, and

Treviranus's remark to Lönnrot that "no hay que buscarle tres pies al gato," meaning literally, "no need to look for three feet on the cat," i.e., some complicated theory to explain the crime. The *four* series includes the Tetrarch of Galilee, the tetrarch being the ruler of a fourth part of a territory under Roman jurisdiction; the Tetragrammaton; the diamond-shaped designs on the paint store and the harlequins' clothing; Lönnrot's discovery that the crimes were committed on the fourth instead of the third of each month; the rectangle Lönnrot draws on the map of the city; and the rhomboid diamonds of the windows in the belvedere of Triste-le-Roy.

"Death and the Compass" respresents a parody of the detective story, Lönnrot recalling the brilliant Sherlock Holmes and Treviranus the simple-minded Dr. Watson. It also reveals certain similarities to the works of G. K. Chesterton, whose murder mysteries with metaphysical overtones Borges greatly admires. A more immediate influence, however, was the nightmarish atmosphere of Perón's dictatorial regime, which Borges has poetized so effectively. "Death and the Compass" might be described as a critique of pure reason demonstrating that man is his own labyrinth maker. It is a masterpiece because it deftly fuses form and content, i.e., its labyrinthine structure conveys the theme that life is an absurd labyrinth.

The Dead Man   (1946) (A)

Although different in its setting—the plains of Uruguay in the late nineteenth century—"The Dead Man" repeats the theme of metaphysical irony so skillfully developed in "Death and the Compass." The two antagonists are Benjamín Otálora, a young *compadrito* (tough) from Buenos Aires, and Azevedo Bandeira, a Brazilian smuggler and chief of a band of gauchos. After killing a man in a knife fight, Otálora flees to Montevideo where he accidentally meets Azevedo and becomes one of his hired hands. He has no trouble adapting to the rigors of gaucho life but aspires to replace Bandeira as the leader. In his efforts to undermine Bandeira's authority, Otálora makes friends with his bodyguard, ignores his orders, and takes command of his men during a skirmish with another band of gauchos. Otálora even manages to ride Bandeira's fine horse and sleep with his mistress. One night Otálora gets drunk during a fiesta and, emboldened by his recent successes, becomes boastful and boisterous. At the stroke of midnight Bandeira fetches his mistress, obliges her to kiss Otálora in the presence of everybody, and then orders his bodyguard to shoot him. But before Otálora dies, he realizes that "they have betrayed him from the start, that he has been condemned to death; that they have allowed him to make love, to command, to triumph . . . because in Bandeira's eyes he was already dead."

The reader of "Death and the Compass" should have no trouble detecting parallels between Lönnrot and Otálora, and Scharlach and Bandeira. Like Lönnrot, Otálora is granted a significant measure of success only to have it snatched away by the cruel reality of death. His fate is foreshadowed, moreover, when, shortly before he is shot, his drunken "exultation" and "jubilation" are referred to as a "vertiginous tower . . . a symbol of his irresistible destiny." This image of Otálora's rise and fall corresponds to the belvedere to which Lönnrot ascends only to meet his adverse fate. And just as Scharlach (the god figure) manipulated Lönnrot from the beginning, Bandeira appears to have played the role of Supreme Being in preparing Otálora's annihilation.

Otálora and Bandeira might also be characterized as antithetical doubles, whose identities gradually fuse. At the time of their first encounter, Otálora is a young exile in search of a job, whereas Bandeira is a mature individual already at the height of his power. Moved by ambition, Otálora not only learns all the skills of the gaucho but also "determines to rise to the rank of the contrabandist." Bandeira's illness and the mirror image of his red-haired mistress, whom Otálora sees in Bandeira's bedroom, feed Otálora's ambition to destroy the chief and assume his authority. When he takes command of Bandeira's men, rides his horse, and makes love to his mistress, Otálora, in a sense, becomes Bandeira. The final scene of his triumph and death would seem, then, to symbolize the absurd condition of all men who strive for success without suspecting that fate—often a fate of their own making—is all the while plotting their destruction.

The End of the Duel   (1970) (DBR)

One of Borges's most brutal tales, "The End of the Duel" records the meaningless lives of two nineteenth-century Uruguayan gauchos. Manuel Cardoso and Carmen Silveira have always hated each other for reasons stemming from disputes over unbranded cattle, horse races, card games, a woman, and a poisoned dog. After they are drafted into the army of the Blancos (Whites) during the civil war, they fight "shoulder to shoulder" against the Colorados (Reds) but continue to despise each other. Eventually they are taken prisoner by the Reds and condemned to death. The captain of the Red forces, Juan Patricio Nolan, knows of the rivalry between the two men and proposes a final duel "to show who's the better man." They will have their throats slit simultaneously and then run as far as possible. Large sums of money are bet on the outcome of the duel, which takes place several hours later and ends as follows: "Spurts of blood gushed from the men's throats. They dashed forward a number of steps before tumbling face down. Cardoso, as he fell, stretched out his arms. Perhaps never aware of it, he had won."

"The End of the Duel" is replete with irony, paradox, and absurdity. The two protagonists become so obsessed with their hatred for one another that it becomes their sole purpose for living and "their only claim for being remembered." They are drafted in a saloon after being harangued by a Brazilian half-breed, whose speech nobody understands. Once in the army, taking a human life holds no difficulty for them because they are already in the habit of killing cattle. Patriotism is alien to them, and they have no idea what the white badges on their hats mean, but "they found out that being companions allowed them to go on being enemies."

The narrator states that the last battle occurred in a place whose name Cardoso and Silveira never knew, because "Such places are later named by historians," a suggestion that history is lived blindly, moment by moment, and invented later by historians. The night before Cardoso's throat is cut, he asks his commanding officer to save him one of the Red prisoners the next day because until then he had not cut anyone's throat and wanted to know what it was like. When the other prisoners, who are also condemned to die, learn of the impending duel, they ask Captain Nolan to allow them to place wagers on the outcome, and Nolan, "an understanding man, let himself be convinced." Thus both contestants are urged to perform well because large sums of money and great hopes are at stake.

Cardoso's executioner is the Reds' official cutthroat, a man who always comforts his victim by patting him on the shoulder and telling him, "Take heart, friend. Women go through far worse when they give birth." Silveira, on the other hand, is executed by a mulatto, who appears delighted to be the center of attention. When Nolan gives the starting signal, the two prisoners are described as being bent forward, eager to begin.

The events of the story, together with Borges's ironic detachment, convey an overall impression of life's absurdities. This impression is heightened, moreover, if we compare Captain Nolan with Scharlach in "Death and the Compass" and with Bandeira in "The Dead Man." Just like his two counterparts, Nolan emerges as a god figure who holds the fates of his victims in the palm of his hand. And like Lönnrot and Otálora, Cardoso and Silveira are granted the opportunity to achieve an illusory triumph before they are annihilated. In this light, Borges's initial description of Nolan as a "practical joker" and a "rogue" underscores the story's metaphysical irony.

The House of Asterion   (1949) (L)

The Greek myth of the Minotaur[16] provides the basic ingredient of "The House of Asterion," but Borges's interpretation of it is both playful and original. Although the title, the epigraph, and several statements made by the first-person narrator (he refers to himself as "unique" and the son of a queen) offer clues to his identity, most readers will not guess that the Minotaur himself has been speaking until they read the words of Theseus at the end of the story: "Would you believe it, Ariadne? The Minotaur scarcely defended himself."

Asterion wistfully describes his lonely life in his "house" (the words *labyrinth* and *maze* never appear), which has an infinite number (fourteen) of galleries, doors, courtyards, and pools and which "is the same size as the world." He never goes out on the street because he is afraid of the common people, but once a dream revealed to him that seas and temples are also infinite (fourteen) in number. Although he has never learned to read and is convinced that nothing is communicable by the art of writing, his spirit yearns for "all that is vast and grand." One of his favorite pastimes is racing through the galleries of his house and pretending he is being followed. Most of all, however, he likes to imagine that the other Asterion comes to visit him, and that they wander through the long series of rooms together.

Asterion also reveals that every nine years nine men (instead of the fourteen youths and fourteen maidens of the myth) enter his house and that he runs joyfully to greet

them. Their death ceremony lasts only a few minutes.
Once one of Asterion's victims told him that someday his
redeemer would come. This knowledge makes his loneliness less painful as he waits, wondering what form his
redeemer will take and hoping to be led to a place with
fewer galleries and doors.

The story's first-person point of view and the narrator's melancholy tone are reversals of the Minotaur myth
and create sympathy for the monster. Asterion conceivably
represents modern man who, finding himself alone and
insecure in the chaotic, labyrinthine universe, builds his
own, more comprehensible labyrinth. Thus Asterion's
house becomes a metaphor of culture, that is, man's concept of reality, which turns out to be an imitation of the
real world and, at the same time, something quite different—one recalls the "infinite" number (fourteen) of
temples and seas in the outside world. Asterion's
preference for his house and his fear of leaving also evoke
the abyss between man and the blind forces of nature.

Asterion's inability to read and his conviction that the
art of writing can communicate nothing are metaphors of
man's fundamental ignorance and of Borges's belief that
language reflects only the mind of the speaker and not the
real world. The monster's yearning for "all that is vast
and grand" conveys the absurdity stemming from the clash
between human aspirations and the limited capacities of
all mortals. Theseus's words at the end of the story,
however, would seem to indicate Asterion's ultimate
resignation to death, which he sees as a welcome
deliverance from this absurdity.[17]

The Two Kings and Their
Two Labyrinths   (1946) (A)

"The House of Asterion" presents a grotesque
portrait of modern man, whose escape from the real world
into one of his own making has only accentuated his feel-

ings of alienation and ignorance. "The Two Kings and Their Two Labyrinths" demonstrates the abyss between rational man and the irreducible universe by contrasting the sophisticated king of Babylonia's man-made maze, which consists of many galleries, stairways, and doors, with that of the naive king of Arabia, whose maze is the vast desert. During a visit to Babylonia, the Arab king is allowed to wander for many hours in the maze of his host, much to the latter's amusement. Upon at last finding the exit with the aid of God, the indignant Arab returns to his homeland, declares war on Babylonia, and lays waste to his enemy's kingdom. He then leads the king of Babylonia into the desert, where he leaves him alone to die of hunger and thirst.

One of Borges's shortest pieces of fiction, this story succinctly sets forth one of his favorite themes, namely, the folly of intellectual pretensions. A metaphor of man's bid for omnipotence, the Babylonian king's "subtle," "intricate" maze is referred to by the narrator as a "blasphemy" because "confusion and marvels belong to God alone and not to man." The king's terrible fate in the desert, moreover, recalls that of Lönnrot in "Death and the Compass," both protagonists having, in a sense, met defeat in labyrinths of their own making.

Ibn Hakkan al-Bokhari, Dead in His Labyrinth   (1951) (A)

Though seldom discussed in detail, "Ibn Hakkan al-Bokhari, Dead in His Labyrinth" is one of Borges's most intriguing stories. The plot is set in motion when two young Englishmen enter a huge labyrinthine house on the English coast in the summer of 1914. As they walk toward the center of the structure, Dunraven, a poet, tells his mathematician friend Unwin that twenty-five years ago King Ibn Hakkan arrived by ship, accompanied by his black slave and a lion, and built the labyrinth. Years later, after Ibn Hakkan died under strange circumstances, the town's rector, Mr. Allaby, told the following story to the authorities investigating the death.

Ibn Hakkan had confessed to Allaby that he had been a powerful and cruel king in the Sudan until his people rebelled and he was forced to flee with his plunder, a slave, and his cowardly cousin Zaid. The three men spent the night of their flight in a holy man's tomb where Ibn Hakkan dreamed he was entangled in snakes, a dream he believed was caused by a spiderweb pressed against his flesh. Upon awakening, he felt compelled by his dream to slit the throat of his contemptible cousin. Then he ordered his slave to smash the dead man's face with a rock. Soon thereafter he and the slave fled to England where, because of his mortal fear of Zaid's ghost, he built the labyrinth as a place of refuge. One day Ibn Hakkan burst into Mr. Allaby's office in panic, announcing that Zaid's ghost had arrived, entered the labyrinth, and killed the slave and the lion. Then Ibn Hakkan dashed out of Allaby's office. The next day Allaby went to the labyrinth and found the dead bodies of Ibn Hakkan, the slave, and the lion, all three with their faces obliterated.

About the time Dunraven finishes telling Allaby's story to Unwin, the two young men arrive at the center of the labyrinth, where they spend the night. Unwin remains unconvinced by Allaby's story and proceeds to point out its defects. In the first place, he believes a fugitive would not need to build a maze to protect himself. London, for example, would be a much better maze. Then Unwin examines Allaby's story in light of the Minotaur myth. The Minotaur and the threat it poses constitute the justification for the existence as well as for the monstrous form of the ancient labyrinth of Crete, just as the spiderweb, which provoked the dream and the subsequent murder of Zaid, provides the justification for both the existence and the form of Ibn Hakkan's labyrinth. Unwin considers it likely, however, that the events of the story occurred quite differently. In his opinion the night the fugitives spent in the holy man's tomb, Zaid stole Ibn Hakkan's treasure and fled to England to wait for him in the labyrinth, and when King Ibn Hakkan arrived, Zaid killed him as well as the slave and the lion. Ibn Hakkan's face was obliterated to conceal his identity, and the faces of the slave and the lion were obliterated so that Ibn Hakkan's murder "would seem natural."

The story ends with the conjectures of Dunraven and Unwin that Zaid did not act out of greed but rather out of hate and fear. Thus, after stealing the treasure, he realized that what he really wanted was to see Ibn Hakkan dead so that he could assume his identity, so that before becoming nobody in death he could "look back on having been a king."

In order to understand this puzzling tale, one should perhaps recall that for Borges literature can be an absorbing game. Moreover, he frequently reminds his readers with great subtlety that they are being immersed in a world of pure fiction, far removed from reality. The fictitious nature of "Ibn Hakkan . . ." is obvious, given its fantastic subject matter, but a clue to its literary gamesmanship and theme are suggested at the beginning of the story when Unwin advises his friend not to multiply mysteries, adding, "They should be kept simple. Bear in mind Poe's purloined letter." Near the end of the story, Dunraven remarks that the Ibn Hakkan of Allaby's narration could well have been Zaid because "such metamorphoses are classic rules of the game . . . accepted conventions demanded by the reader." The literary nature of the tale is also implied by the final conjectures of Dunraven and Unwin regarding Zaid's motives for killing Ibn Hakkan. And Mr. Allaby, the rector, is a character borrowed from Samuel Butler's famous novel, *The Way of All Flesh*. What seems to emerge as the predominant theme, then, is the labyrinthine creative process involved in writing a *ficción*. Assuming this to be the case, we might consider Dunraven and Unwin antithetical doubles who together constitute the author's total self. Dunraven, the imaginative poet, creates the plot while Unwin, the logical mathematician, points out its implausibilities, explains the protagonists' motives, and analyzes the literary form. It will be recalled that, upon correcting the story's implausibilities, he reverses the identities of the protagonists and explains to Dunraven the analogous roles of the Minotaur and the spiderweb, both of which convey theme as well as structure.

Mr. Allaby would seem to represent the author's persona or narrative voice, creating an air of authenticity through the respectability of his office. The labyrinth emerges, then, not only as the story's major setting but also as its esthetic form and its theme, the two young men's journey to the center representing a metaphor of the author's state of mind while developing his plot. The structural design is reinforced, moreover, by the rhythmic repetition of events as well as by the movement of virtually all the characters through the labyrinthine structure. Finally, the entangled identities of Ibn Hakkan and Zaid, who represent antithetical doubles,[18] suggest the difficulties an author must deal with in creating his characters, motivating their actions, and dramatizing the complexities of their relations with one another.

"Ibn Hakkan . . ." is fraught with elements of the absurd. The existence of a labyrinth built by a Sudanese despot on the English coast defies logic. This labyrinth, which plays such a central role in the story, is a metaphor of the artist's frustrating attempt to create an esthetic order out of chaos. For Borges art, like metaphysics, is essentially an absurd endeavor, for just as the metaphysician can never attain the truth, the artist can never attain esthetic perfection. One might conclude, then, that if art is an absurd endeavor, a fantastic tale about an author writing a tale in a labyrinth, symbolizing the process of creating the tale, is an absurd product of that endeavor.

The Aleph   (1945) (A) (PA)

One of Borges's most significant *ficciones,* "The Aleph" synthesizes philosophical preoccupations, esthetic concerns, and humor. At the beginning of the story, the first-person narrator, who refers to himself as Borges, alludes to the death of his beloved Beatriz Viterbo. Since her death, Borges has paid a yearly visit to her cousin, Carlos Argentino Daneri, to commemorate her birthday. He regrets that his memory of her is fading and thus, in the entrance of Carlos's home, he gazes fondly at photographs taken at various stages of her life. During one of Borges's visits Carlos Argentino, whom Borges detests, confides in him that he is writing a long poem entitled "The Earth," in which he plans to describe the entire face of the planet.

Several weeks later Carlos calls Borges and tells him in an agitated voice that the owners of his house want to tear it down. This, he explains, would be a disaster because in the cellar there is an Aleph that is indispensable to him for the completion of his poem. He also explains to the perplexed Borges that an Aleph is a point in space containing all points, a place where all places in the world come together and can be seen from every angle. Intrigued, Borges goes to Carlos's home at once.

When he arrives Carlos tells him to go into the cellar, lie down, and look up at the nineteenth step. Then he closes the door and Borges, though at first suspecting that his "friend" is utterly mad, does indeed see the Aleph. And just as Carlos has said, the tiny sphere with a diameter of only two or three centimeters contains "the inconceivable universe." Although Borges describes the marvelous object in some detail to the reader, he refuses to discuss it with Carlos, probably because the Aleph revealed to him some obscene letters written to Carlos by Beatriz. In order to take revenge on Carlos, Borges advises him, with obvious pity in his voice, to vacation in the country for some badly needed rest. Borges somehow manages to forget the Aleph in a few days.

In the story's epilogue, supposedly written two years later, Borges speculates that the Aleph he saw was false and that the true one might be found in a mosque in Cairo. He also wonders if, when he looked at the false Aleph in Carlos Argentino's cellar, he saw the real one. If he did see it, time has eroded his memory of it, just as it is eroding his memory of Beatriz's face.

Borges's well-known irony is a major element of this tale. Carlos Argentino, a ridiculous figure, is also endowed with some of Borges's characteristics, which Borges obviously uses to poke fun at himself. "Carlos Argentino is rosy, important, gray-haired, fine-featured. He holds some subordinate position or other in an illegible library in the south side suburbs. He is authoritarian, but also ineffective. . . . His mental activity is continuous, versatile, and altogether insignificant. He abounds in useless analogies and fruitless scruples." When Carlos tells Borges about the poem he is writing, he reads part of the "Prologue Canto" aloud and then comments pompously, proclaiming its artistic merit and erudition. "I say nothing of the rare rhythm, nor of the learning which permits me—without any pedantry!—to accumulate, in four lines, three erudite allusions encompassing thirty centuries of compressed literature."

It is ironically incongruous that an object so marvelous as the Aleph should be discovered by the pedantic, unimaginative Carlos Argentino in a dark cellar beneath the trapdoor of his dining room. And in the epilogue, Borges's irony turns somewhat bitter when he reveals that Carlos won the Second Prize of the National Prize for Literature for his poem, and that Borges's book, *The Cards of the Cardsharp,* failed to receive a single vote.[19]

The story's title and its meaning contribute to the mystical aura of magic that imbues so many of Borges's works. The Aleph, we are told in the epilogue, is the first

letter of the Hebrew alphabet. For the cabalists[20] it signifies "limitless and pure divinity," or a kind of
pantheistic unity. Equally important are the story's
existentialist implications. The Aleph might be considered
a vision of the absolute sought by both the artist and the
metaphysician, a form of esthetic perfection that could only
be manifested to man by God. However, neither Carlos
nor the Borges of the story is able to depict the Aleph and
thus preserve it from destruction. Carlos's poem is an
absurd piece of pedantry, and the fictitious Borges never
bothers to publish his description of the Aleph and soon
forgets it. Implied, then, is a negation of the efficacy of
language to capture reality and achieve esthetic perfection.
Implied also is the existential tenet that truth is relative to
individual experience, as demonstrated by the fact that
Carlos and Borges both perceive the Aleph, but each in his
own very personal way. A final element of the absurd
stems from Borges's inability, in the face of time and the
ever-changing universe, to preserve the memory of his
beloved Beatriz.[21]

The Book of Sand   (1975) (BOS)

The title story of Borges's most recent collection of
short fiction, "The Book of Sand," bears a certain resemblance to "The Aleph." "The Aleph" compresses the
world into a small sphere, which becomes a metaphor of
esthetic unity and divine perfection; "The Book of Sand"
depicts infinity in the form of a mysterious book.

The first-person narrator of this story is visited by a
stranger wishing to sell him a "holy book" entitled *The
Book of Sand*. When asked to find the first and last pages
of the book, which seem to be numbered arbitrarily, the
narrator is unable to do so because pages inevitably come
between his thumb and the book's covers. The stranger
explains that the number of pages is infinite and that the
pages are numbered arbitrarily because if space is infinite,

we may be at any point in space, and if time is infinite, we
may be at any point in time.

The narrator purchases the book and soon finds
himself thinking about it constantly. Eventually he
becomes obsessed with it, suffers from insomnia, and if he
manages to fall asleep, has nightmares about it. Finally,
considering it "an obscene thing that affronted and tainted
reality itself," he takes it to the Argentine National
Library and loses it on a musty shelf in the basement.

The Book of Sand emerges as a magical image of
infinite time and space. The fact that it is a sacred text
evokes the idealist tenet that reality exists in the mind of
God, or in a book written by Him. The narrator's frustrating encounter with the enigma suggests the absurdity
of mortal man's attempt to decipher the infinite universe,
but the denouement would seem to signify an attempt to
escape from absurdity.

A major difference between "The Aleph" and "The
Book of Sand" is that in the former inexorable time erases
the narrator's memory of both the Aleph and Beatriz,
whereas *The Book of Sand* becomes an obsession that
must be relegated to the basement of the National Library.
One might speculate that for the playfully ironic Borges, it
represents the volume so assiduously sought by the narrator of "The Library of Babel."

Averroes' Search   (1949) (L) (PA)

An enigmatic tale, "Averroes' Search" is a metaphor
of man's vain quest for knowledge. In addition, Borges sets
forth in it some of his basic literary and philosophical
theories. Averroes is a medieval Arab sage residing in
Córdoba. His principal subject of research is Aristotle,
whom he considers the "fountainhead of all philosophy,"
but fourteen centuries separate him from the Greek
philosopher, and Averroes is working with a translation of
a translation of Aristotle's works. Upon reading the
Poetics, Averroes finds himself stymied by the repeated

appearance of the words *tragedy* and *comedy,* which for him have no meaning because he has never seen or heard of a theater.

That evening Averroes dines at the home of the Koran scholar Farach. Among the guests is a traveler named Abulcasim Al-Ashari, who has visted China. In the course of the conversation, Abulcasim tells of having attended a strange spectacle in China in which as many as twenty people represented a story on a kind of terrace. None of Farach's guests can comprehend the purpose of such a function, Farach himself expressing the unanimous opinion that twenty people are unnecessary because a single speaker can tell anything, no matter how complicated it might be.

The conversation then turns to the subject of poetry and the use of the metaphor. One of the guests, a poet, expresses the opinion that old metaphors tend to wear out and become useless, necessitating the search for new ones. As an example he cites Zuhair's comparison of destiny to a blind camel, a metaphor that has become commonplace after five centuries. Averroes, Borges's mouthpiece, disagrees, asserting that if the sole purpose of a metaphor is to surprise, its value would last only minutes. He believes that the true poet is less of an inventor than he is a discoverer, and fine poetry is the art of discovering metaphors that move all men. The image of a blind camel is still admirable, in his opinion, because all men throughout the ages have, at one time or another, found destiny to be clumsy, powerful, innocent, and inhuman. And nobody has expressed this concept more poetically than Zuhair. Besides, Averroes concludes, time only enriches poetry and broadens its scope. When Zuhair wrote his verse many years ago, two images were confronted: the camel and destiny; when it is repeated today, it evokes the memory of Zuhair and, in addition, fuses our misfortunes with his.

The following day Averroes is again studying Aristotle's *Poetics,* when all at once he is wracked by chills. He looks at himself in a mirror and suddenly, "as if fulminated by an invisible fire," he and everything in the story disappear. In the epilogue, the narrator—Borges himself, more than likely—explains that he has tried to relate "the process of a defeat." Averroes set for himself, we are told, an impossible goal, that of understanding the concepts of tragedy and comedy without knowing what a theater was. However, Borges believes that Averroes's search is no more absurd than his own attempt to depict it with his meager sources on the Arab scholar's life and works.

The story's absurdist theme of the vain quest for knowledge is reinforced by the parallels between the author and his protagonist. Indeed, Averroes probably represents Borges's mirror image or double, the temporal and cultural barriers between the two being just as insurmountable as those separating Averroes and Aristotle. Borges's involvement with his double is accentuated by the similarity of their literary ideals—they are both classicists—as well as by Borges's statement, in the final lines of the story, that his narration is a symbol of the man he was as he wrote it and that in order to compose his narration he had to be that man, and in order to be that man he had to compose that narration, and so on to infinity.

Averroes's search for the meaning of tragedy and comedy is treated ironically through two incidents in the story. One of these involves Abulcasim's description of the theater in China, which Averroes never identifies as the art form discussed by Aristotle. The other incident occurs when Averroes, pondering over the two arcane words in the *Poetics,* tells himself that "what we seek is often nearby" and then, by chance, observes three urchins playing a game below his balcony. One is standing on the shoulders of another, and the third is kneeling abjectly in the dust. Averroes realizes intuitively that the three children are, respectively, playing the roles of a muezzin, a minaret, and a body of Muslim worshippers.

The magical disappearance of Averroes is not only an element of the absurd but also relates to philosophical idealism. In the final line of his tale Borges informs the reader that the moment he ceased to believe in Averroes, Averroes vanished. This statement would seem to indicate that Borges, aware of the absurdity of his endeavor, ended it in an equally absurd manner. His statement also brings to mind the idealist tenet that reality exists only in the mind. Thus, when he ceased to believe in his protagonist, the latter had to disappear.

Like so many of his stories, "Averroes' Search" conveys Borges's fundamental skepticism. Ingeniously woven into the plot, moreover, is the delineation of the creative process by which the author has attempted to develop his literary and philosophical preoccupations. Thus, for example, the metaphor of destiny in the form of a blind camel suggests Averroes's destiny as a scholar in search of truth as well as Borges's destiny as an artist in search of esthetic perfection. Borges's sleight-of-hand obliteration of his protagonist conveys the absurdity of both quests.

Emma Zunz   (1948) (L)

In some of his tales Borges deliberately distorts reason in order to demonstrate the fine line separating truth from falsehood. One of these is "Emma Zunz," the account of a nineteen-year-old girl's vengeance for the death of her father. Several years before the chain of events commences, Emma's father was arrested for embezzlement, but upon leaving for his self-imposed exile in Brazil, he swore to her that his business partner, Aaron Loewenthal, had been the real culprit. Meanwhile, Loewenthal, a miserly widower, has become the owner of the factory where Emma is employed. The evening Emma receives the news of her father's suicide she immediately begins to plot Loewenthal's murder. Two days later she calls Loewenthal and tells him she has some information regarding a possible strike at his factory. It is agreed that she will come to his office at nightfall. That afternoon, despite her pathological fear of men, she goes to the waterfront district of Buenos Aires where she allows herself to be taken to a hotel and violated by a sailor. She then takes a streetcar to Loewenthal's office. In the middle of her story about the strike she asks him for a glass of water, and while he is out of the room, she takes from his desk drawer a loaded revolver he is known to keep within reach in case of thieves. When he returns, she kills him and then calls the police, claiming to have acted in defense of her honor. The reader is left with the distinct impression that her story is accepted as true.

As the action unfolds it gradually becomes evident that Emma, the calculating rationalist so typical among Borges's characters, allows herself to be violated so that her version of the crime will bear the semblance of truth and justice for her father will be carried out. However, when she goes to the waterfront district, she enters a nightmarish world in which time becomes confused and obliterated by the "perplexing disorder of disconnected and atrocious sensations." And once she is in Loewenthal's presence she forgets her carefully calculated plan to avenge her father and feels only "the need of inflicting punishment for the outrage she had suffered." Thus, at the critical moment of the crime reason is replaced by passion, and she shoots Loewenthal without forcing him to confess his guilt, as she had planned to do.

Emma's story, we are told, is substantially true. "True was [her] tone, true was her shame, true was her hate. True also was the outrage she had suffered: only the circumstances were false, the time, and one or two proper names." Her success in carrying out her own version of "divine justice"—even though the crime itself was, ironically, committed in a burst of passion—demonstrates how reason can be manipulated to camouflage truth.

Thus, Emma manages to frame Loewenthal just as he framed her father. Always the skeptic, Borges implies that truth is elusive because the evidence is never complete and human logic is easily tainted by the irrational. This would explain, at least in part, why Borges tends to reject all epistemological systems and moral codes as capricious and unreliable.

Deutsches Requiem   (1949) (L)

We recall that during World War II, although there was considerable pro-Nazi sentiment in Argentina, Borges took a strong public stand in favor of the Allies. He was convinced that Argentines knew little about Nazism and that their hopes for a German victory only masked their desire to witness the defeat of imperialistic England. He also believed that Nazism was so evil, so impossible to defend, that even Hitler and his cohorts unconsciously wanted their own defeat. "Deutsches Requiem" dramatizes this idea, but even more important, it presents a satirical justification of Nazism based on distortions of the philosophies of Schopenhauer, Nietzsche, and Spengler.

The story's first-person narrator is a Nazi, Otto Dietrich zur Linde, who is awaiting execution for war crimes. He feels no guilt but seeks understanding for the benefit of future generations. As a young man he loved music and poetry, but he was particularly interested in metaphysics and studied the works of Nietzsche and Spengler. He joined the Nazi party in 1929, believing that a new era of civilization was at hand. Ten years later, just before the outbreak of World War II, he was wounded during a "disturbance" in Tilsit, and his leg had to be amputated. During his stay in the hospital he read Schopenhauer and was impressed with his theory that everything that happens to a man has been preordained by him. Thus, according to Schopenhauer, every negligence is deliberate, every chance encounter is an appointment, and every death is a suicide.

In 1941 Zur Linde was appointed subdirector of a concentration camp. He considered Nazism an act of morality destined to purge corrupted humanity and create a new kind of man. Mercy, moreover, he viewed as a sin, thanks to his readings of Nietzsche. About this time a talented Jewish poet named David Jerusalem arrived at the camp, and Zur Linde not only showed him no mercy but even caused his madness and suicide. Now Zur Linde confesses that the real purpose of his mistreatment of David Jerusalem was to destroy his own feelings of compassion. Although the war ended with the defeat of Germany, Zur Linde is pleased with the outcome. He believes that many things had to be destroyed in order to construct a new order, and now he realizes that Germany and her Nazi leaders were necessary victims. This no longer matters, he concludes, as long as violence, and not senile Christian timidity, reigns.

Zur Linde's mind has obviously been twisted by Nazi ideology and erroneous interpretations of German philosophy. Nietzsche's theory of the superman and rejection of Christianity are visible in his scorn for prisoners and love of violence. Even more evident is Schopenhauer's pantheistic idealism, i.e., the theory that the desires of all beings constitute a single universal will and that the world is a product of this will. Thus, Zur Linde is convinced that the Nazis have chosen their glorious defeat, that they deliberately sacrificed the destiny of the Fatherland. And Spengler's cyclical theory of civilization is implied by Zur Linde's belief that Germany's destruction represents a preordained apocalypse destined to give rise to a new order.

Three Versions of Judas   (1944) (F) (L)

Borges's "Three Versions of Judas" represents a scathing parody of theological reasoning. Nils Runeberg, the story's protagonist, is an apocryphal twentieth-century

Swedish theologian, who has published two extensive treatises on Judas Iscariot. In the epigraph of his first treatise, Runeberg quotes De Quincey's* statement that everything tradition has attributed to Judas is false. Runeberg reasons that although Judas's treachery was a superfluous act, it must have been predestined because it would be intolerable to imagine an error in the Scripture or to admit "a single haphazard act in the most precious drama in the history of the world." He also believes that Judas was the only apostle to intuit "the secret divinity and the terrible purpose of Jesus," and that this knowledge induced him to accept the role of informer and welcome the punishment of eternal damnation.

As might be expected, Runeberg is denounced by other theologians on various technical grounds. He answers their refutation with his assertion that, as one of the apostles, Judas "deserves from us the best interpretations of his deeds." Runeberg is also convinced that Judas was an ascetic who, instead of mortifying the flesh, mortified the spirit. Indeed, we are told, he renounced honor, peace, and the Kingdom of Heaven by committing the most degrading offense of all: the abuse of confidence. And he willingly sought Hell for the felicity of the Lord.

Runeberg postulates in his second treatise, his masterpiece, that God's sacrifice had to be perfect in order to save man. Thus, he rejects the idea of a human but sinless Savior as a senseless contradiction. To limit Christ's sacrifice to the agony of one afternoon on the cross, moreover, to him appears blasphemous. Runeberg finds the most convincing support for his thesis in the following verse from the book of Isaiah: "He will sprout like a root in a dry soil; there is not good mien to him, nor beauty; despised of men and the least of them; a man of sorrow, and experienced in heartbreaks." To many these words

---

* Thomas De Quincey (1785–1859), a learned and imaginative English essayist, is one of Borges's favorite writers.

forecast the crucifixion of Christ, but to Runeberg they prophesy God's becoming "a man completely, a man to the point of infamy . . . all the way to the abyss." His "logical" conclusion, then, is that God chose to become Judas instead of Christ.

Readers reacted to Runeberg's second book with indifference, but he interprets this reaction as a "miraculous confirmation" of God's will. Indeed, he assumes God commanded that his book be ignored because He did not wish His terrible secret to be propagated throughout the world. And identifying himself with Elijah, Moses, Isaiah, and Saul, Runeberg senses ancient and divine curses converging on him for having discovered and divulged "the terrible name of God." He wanders through the streets, praying that he be given the grace to share Hell with the Redeemer. In the final lines it is suggested that he will no doubt be remembered by the heresiologists.

Like the protagonists of "Emma Zunz" and "Deutsches Requiem," Nils Runeberg utilizes logic to create a totally subjective reality. His interpretations of the divine mind have little to do with accepted doctrine and perhaps for this reason appear to be fraught with absurdities. Borges's skepticism toward theology is expressed ironically by his protagonist's assumption that there can be no errors in "the most precious drama in the history of the world." A similar attitude on the author's part is suggested by the preposterous debates among theologians over Runeberg's unorthodox beliefs. Borges more than likely shares his protagonist's doubts about the authenticity of Christ's role as the redeemer of mankind. However, the argument that his agony on the cross was too brief to constitute the perfect sacrifice illustrates the absurdities to which the reasoning mind will resort in order to prove a preconceived theory. Runeberg's portrait of Judas, the archetypal traitor, as the redeemer of mankind is highly amusing, but his absurd, labyrinthine logic ridicules the "inventions" of theological reasoning in general. "Three

Versions of Judas" is one of many tales that illustrate why Borges is often referred to as subversive.

The Babylon Lottery   (1941) (F) (L)

Borges's popular tale "The Babylon Lottery" is one of his most ironic statements about man's attempt to come to grips with the indecipherable universe. The unnamed first-person narrator of this tale asserts that he owes the atrocious vicissitudes of his existence to an institution known as the lottery. He then proceeds to outline the history of the institution.

The lottery of ancient Babylonia failed because it appealed only to the human faculty of hope. Thus an element of danger was introduced by the "Company" (also referred to as the secret directors), and public enthusiasm for the institution was immediately aroused. Winners were protected, losers were punished, and those who refused to participate were despised. Eventually the lottery became so popular that it was used to determine the fate of criminals. However, the logical citizenry began to criticize the system because of the unjust discrepancy between the fates of winners and losers. Disturbances broke out between rich and poor, and eventually the Company was obliged to assume complete public power. As the lottery's role in the Babylonians' lives became increasingly predominant, rituals were introduced to lend an aura of magic to the drawings, and stone lions and a "sacred privy called Qaphqa" made their appearance. And people were encouraged to express their dissatisfaction by inserting denunciations and accusations into the fissures of a "dusty aqueduct" leading to the Company.

In answer to complaints of the citizenry, the Company created "scriptures" in which it was stated that "the lottery was an interpolation of chance into the order of the world and that to accept errors is not to contradict fate but merely to corroborate it." The Babylonians accepted this

premise but considered it "desirable for chance to
intervene at all stages of the lottery and not merely in the
drawing." Thus reforms were carried out, and the lottery
became a labyrinth of infinite drawings to determine all
phases of the citizens' fate. The end result was that under
the beneficent influence of the Company the customs of
Babylon became thoroughly impregnated with chance.

"The Babylon Lottery," like "The Library of
Babel," can be interpreted allegorically. Babylon would
seem to represent the world man will never fully understand. His compulsion for order leads to the creation of the
lottery, an absurd attempt to impose structure on random
occurrence or destiny. The mysterious Company believed
to direct the lottery embodies man's perception of the
divine mind that created and controls the universe. Just as
all human institutions tend to proliferate, the lottery
gradually injects the role of chance into every phase of life
and, in fact, becomes synonymous with everyday existence.
The stone lions lend symbolic strength and ritualistic
stability to the organization; the "sacred privy called
Qaphqa" suggests a Kafkaesque element of the absurd; the
dusty aqueduct leading to the Company implies the paradoxical lack of communication between Babylonians and
the secret directors, in whom they have placed their trust;
and the scriptures drawn up by the Company serve to formalize and codify the pervasive role of chance in Babylon.

"The Babylon Lottery" and "The Library of Babel"
reveal interesting similarities and differences. Both tales
depict man's metaphysical quest for some kind of order in
a world in which disorder prevails. The basic premises of
the two stories, however, are quite different. It will be
recalled that the symmetrical Library with its unreadable
books represents the universe, whose laws have been
systematized by scientists and philosophers but whose
true meaning remains hidden. The absurd in this story
stems from the confrontation between human reason and
the unreasoning universe. In "The Babylon Lottery,"
however, the role of antirational chance is not only

accepted by the Babylonians but is even institutionalized in the form of the lottery. This illusion of order, which one might refer to oxymoronically as organized chaos, merely compounds the absurdity of man's attempt to understand the meaning of existence.

Reason is ultimately negated in both stories. The narrator of "The Library of Babel" expresses the "elegant hope" that the repetition of disorder in the stacks of the Library constitutes an order. The narrator of "The Babylon Lottery" concludes that the Company may be eternal, omnipotent, or even nonexistent, but that all this is inconsequential, "because Babylon is nothing but an infinite game of chance." "The Babylon Lottery," then, reaffirms what is implied in "Emma Zunz" and "Deutsches Requiem," namely, that all systems, whether they be moral, legal, or philosophical, are an integral part of absurd human destiny.

The Sect of the Phoenix   (1952) (F) (L)

Borges's playful nature and his view of literature as a game are evident in "The Sect of the Phoenix," a brief tale that challenges the reader to guess its meaning. The narrator first discusses the sect's controversial origin, then alludes to its possible connections with the gypsies and the Jews, and finally states that, in reality, "the sectarians are indistinguishable from the rest of the world." We are also told that, although history records no persecutions of the sect, it counts among its members representatives from all human groups, and for this reason there has never been a persecution that sectarians have not suffered.

The only thing that unites the sectarians of the Phoenix is the "Secret." There is, indeed, also an "obscure tradition of some cosmic punishment," but it has been almost completely forgotten, just as members have all but forgotten God's promise of eternity to the race "if they will only carry out a certain rite, generation after generation." This rite, which is also the Secret, is a trivial act of short duration; it is sacred but ridiculous; and its practice is furtive and even clandestine. Usage does not favor mothers teaching it to sons, nor is it performed by priests. Some devotees view the Secret as vulgar and find it difficult to admit that their ancestors lowered themselves to such conduct. Oddly enough, throughout the vicissitudes of history the Secret has never been lost, perhaps, as one commentator has asserted, because it has become instinctive.

Although some critics have pondered laboriously over the meaning of the Secret, it is not very difficult to discern what Borges himself has admitted, that the secret rite is the sex act.[22] The story's virtue lies in its irony, which remains concealed until the enigma has been solved. Then, upon recalling "an obscure tradition of some cosmic punishment" that has been almost forgotten, the reader can appreciate the veiled allusion to original sin. Equally ironic in retrospect is a certain Doctor Juan Francisco Amaro's amazement at the ease with which sectarians have become Spanish Americans.

"The Sect of the Phoenix" suggests absurdity by making sex, the most instinctive aspect of human nature, the basis for a rationally structured organization. This incongruity, together with the many clues provided for the reader's gradual enlightenment, subverts the conventional attitude toward a ritual that perpetuates the absurd human condition.

Utopia of a Tired Man   (1975) (BOS)

At least two of Borges's stories mock conventions of today's world by contrasting them with those of very different societies. The first of these tales, "Utopia of a Tired Man," describes the aging first-person narrator's visit in the home of a similar individual, who lives thousands of years in the future. (The reader suspects that they are Borges and his double or reincarnated self.) The world of the future, then, probably represents Borges's version of Utopia.

The two men speak in Latin, the only language used by the inhabitants of Utopia. Upon introducing himself, the narrator learns that his host is called "Someone" because people no longer have names. When their discussion turns to the subject of books, Someone reveals that the art of printing has ceased because the multiplication of unnecessary texts is considered evil. He himself has read only a half-dozen books in the four centuries he has lived. As far as education is concerned, facts are no longer deemed important but instead are seen as points of departure for the teaching of such subjects as reasoning, doubt, invention, and the art of forgetting. Thus history is nonexistent in Utopia.

The narrator then explains that in his world people know what happens from day to day, but each day's news is quickly forgotten because attention is focused on events of the next day. He also believes that photographs and the printed word have become more real than the things they stand for, thus inspiring his dictum, "To be is to be photographed."

In Utopia there are no cities, no personal possessions, and after the age of one hundred, an individual may devote himself to the arts until he decides to commit suicide. Space travel was abandoned long ago as was the practice of maintaining museums and libraries. Governments have also been abolished because all they did was declare wars, collect taxes, order arrests, and impose censorship. Ex-politicians have become comedians or faith healers.

Having taken up painting in his old age, the narrator's host offers him a picture that "suggested . . . a sunset and . . . encompassed something infinite." At this moment several friends arrive to help Someone pack his belongings and carry them to a nearby tower. As he enters the tower, which turns out to be a crematory invented by a philanthropist named Adolph Hitler, he waves farewell. Back in his study in Buenos Aires, the narrator discovers a canvas that will be painted thousands of years hence with substances that today are scattered over the whole planet.

In this story Borges reworks some of his previous themes and also injects elements heretofore unseen in his fiction. The appearance of the narrator's double thousands of years in the future recalls Borges's writings on circular time and the possibility of reincarnation.[23] The dissolution of individual identity, an idea Borges has connected to pantheism, is suggested by the anonymity of the inhabitants of Utopia. The narrator's discovery in his study of a canvas given to him by his future self will remind the reader of Borges's essay on pantheism entitled "The Flower of Coleridge" (OI).[24] And the idealist dictum "To be is to be perceived" is parodied by the narrator's reference to the pervasive influence of the news media, "To be is to be photographed."

"Utopia of a Tired Man," one of Borges's most recent tales, reflects the author's disillusion with today's world. The distant future as the vantage point from which he presents his weltanschauung is more than likely a metaphor of the ironic distance from which the blind, aging Borges undertakes his satire of institutions such as education and politics. Borges has repeatedly ridiculed history, considering it more fiction than fact, and in his Utopia Hitler's crematory is perceived as a philanthropist's gift to old men of the future who wish to end their lives. This distorted image of the past clearly mocks the inaccuracies of history, but at the same time, the magnitude and absurdity of the distortion suggest the impotence of human intellect against the overwhelming forces of time and change.

Dr. Brodie's Report   (1970) (DBR)

Whereas "Utopia of a Tired Man" contrasts present-day life with a future Utopian society, "Dr. Brodie's Report" describes the customs of a primitive tribe of

Indians in nineteenth-century Brazil. Both tales mock modern conventions by depicting an inverted mirror image of reality, the effect of which is to undermine traditional modes of thinking.

A Scottish missionary with a knowledge of Portuguese, Dr. Brodie was captured by the Mlch Indians, whom he calls the Yahoos (the name of a bestial people in *Gulliver's Travels*) and with whom he lived for a period of time. The Yahoos' customs, we are told, include flinging a handful of mud in order to get another's attention and concealing themselves when they eat. All other physical functions are performed in open view. They also eat the raw corpses of their witch doctors and royal family in order to partake of their wisdom.

The Yahoos' kings are chosen according to some unknown stigmata revealed at birth. So that the physical world may not lead him astray, the royal infant is immediately castrated, his feet and hands are amputated, and he is confined in a cavern. In case of war with the Ape-men, the Yahoos' traditional enemies, the king is carried into battle where he inevitably meets his death. The queen lives in a separate cavern. Once she received Dr. Brodie and promptly offered herself to him in the presence of her retinue. As a token of royal favor, she also sank a gold pin into his flesh. The Yahoos are insensitive to pain and pleasure and utterly lacking in imagination. They can count only up to four, any quantity beyond that being referred to as many.

For the Yahoos hell is a dry, sunny region where the sick, the aged, and the Ape-men go after death. Heaven, however, is a marshy, beclouded realm reserved for the royal family, the witch doctors, and those who have been merciless on earth. Dung, the tribal god, is all-powerful and usually takes the form of an ant or a serpent. Dr. Brodie decides not to try to convert the Yahoos because the words "Our Father" would have no meaning to them, that is, they see no relation between sexual intercourse and birth.

The Yahoos' language consists of monosyllabic, vowelless words that convey general concepts rather than specific meanings. *Nrz,* suggesting dispersion or spots, may stand for starry sky, a leopard, or smallpox, whereas *hrl* means something compact or dense and can be used for tribe, a stone, or a tree. The poet who succeeds in moving his audience is deified, but his deification gives anyone license to kill him. For this reason, he is likely to seek refuge in the sand dunes of the north.

The Yahoos' favorite forms of recreation are cat fights and public executions. Justice among them is carried out as follows: One accused of eating within the sight of another, for example, is brought before the king who, without listening to any testimony, renders the verdict of guilty. Then the accused is tortured and stoned to death by a mob, the queen having the privilege of casting the first stone.

When Dr. Brodie manages to escape from the Yahoos, he at first finds it revolting to eat in the presence of others and has to cover his mouth and his eyes. As he looks back on his experience, he concludes that the Yahoos are not a primitive but a degenerate nation. Indeed, there is evidence that their forefathers had a written alphabet, but they can no longer decipher it and are thus reduced to the spoken word. Still, they have some redeeming traits such as their own political and social institutions, a language based on abstract concepts, a respect for poetry, and the belief in life after death. Finally, their stand for civilization has been demonstrated by the wars they have waged against the Ape-men. Dr. Brodie hopes that the "Government of Her Majesty will not ignore what this report makes bold to suggest."

What "Dr. Brodie's Report" suggests is that the customs of the primitive Yahoos, though exaggerated for ironic effect, reflect many facets of the so-called civilized world of today. Or, more specifically, the Yahoos may represent Borges's fellow countrymen, with whom he has become increasingly disillusioned in recent years. Examples of implied comparisons abound. The Yahoos' habit of throwing handfuls of mud at each other in order to facilitate communication persists in present-day society in the form of "mud-slinging" between antagonists. The custom of eating in private and performing all other natural functions in public perhaps parodies the mores of more advanced cultures. The Yahoos' ritual of choosing their king at the moment of his birth evokes similar practice in all monarchies. His castration at birth and isolation from worldly temptations contrast ironically with the venality of many rulers, especially one Juan Domingo Perón. And the Yahoos' inability to count beyond four could constitute a metaphor of man's fundamental ignorance, one of Borges's favorite themes.

For Borges, the Yahoos' religious convictions are mere fabrications of the mind and therefore just as valid as those of any other people. The fact that their language expresses general concepts rather than specific information perhaps alludes to the imprecision that Borges finds inherent in all languages. The Yahoos' deification of their poets, and thus their right to kill them, brings to mind the precarious situation of the writer in today's violence-ridden world. The poets' flight to the "sand dunes of the north," moreover, evokes the self-imposed exile of many Latin American men of letters to Europe and the United States. The Yahoos' inability to decipher the alphabet of their forefathers and, consequently, their sole reliance on the spoken word possibly refers to the pervasive role of television in the fields of education and entertainment. And the judicial system of the Yahoos, with its emphasis on torture and executions, differs only slightly from the "justice" imposed on the citizens of many present-day societies.

The narrator's assertion at the end of "Dr. Brodie's Report" that the Yahoos are a "degenerate" rather than a "primitive" people strongly implies that they embody modern decadence. The story's implicit criticism of man-made institutions makes it Borges's most overtly satirical work.[25] Ironic overtones are also achieved through the use of the serious-minded nineteenth-century clergyman as the author's persona. But it is the absurd Swiftian descriptions of the Yahoos' way of life that, through implied juxtaposition, alter our vision and subvert our sense of values.

The Congress   (1971) (BOS)

One of Borges's longest and most diffuse tales, "The Congress" depicts an elaborate attempt on the part of a group of intellectuals to create order out of chaos. Alejandro Ferri, the narrator and only surviving member of the Congress, recalls his initiation into the secret organization in Buenos Aires in 1899. The president was a wealthy Uruguayan rancher named Alejandro Glencoe who, having failed in his attempt to win election to the Uruguayan National Congress, resolved to found a similar organization on a vaster scale, a congress of the world that would represent all men. As Mr. Twirl, one of the founders, explained, the Congress involved a problem of a philosophical nature, because planning an assembly that would represent all men was like fixing an exact number of Platonic archetypes. Thus Twirl suggested that Alejandro Glencoe might represent not only cattlemen but also Uruguayans, humanity's great forerunners, men with red beards, and those seated in armchairs. The organization's beautiful secretary, moreover, who happened to be Norwegian, named Nora Erfjord, could represent secretaries, Norwegian womanhood, and all beautiful women.*

As the Congress progressed, Twirl advocated the creation of a reference library, and this project was also undertaken. Meanwhile, the narrator visited Glencoe's

* Nora Erfjord is probably patterned after Norah Lange, a poet of Norwegian descent who was one of the founders of Argentine *ultraísmo*.

remote ranch in Uruguay, where primitive gauchos had begun the construction of a center for the Congress.[26] Soon thereafter the narrator went to London to research the question of what language the Congress should use to conduct its business. Upon his return to Buenos Aires, he learned that Twirl was expanding the library at a rapid rate, buying huge quantities of books that were piling up in Glencoe's mansion. He also learned that Fermín Eguren, a dissolute member of the Congress, was squandering large sums of money in Paris where he was supposed to be working for the organization. One evening when the narrator went to Glencoe's home to report on his trip to London, he was surprised to find the other members of the Congress also there. Suddenly Glencoe appeared, issuing orders that all the books be brought onto the patio and burned. His explanation was that the undertaking of the Congress, he had come to realize, was so vast that it embraced the whole world, that it began with the first moment of the world and would continue after they were all gone. Then he invited his colleagues, whom he would never see again, to ride through the city in his open carriage and observe the "true Congress."

That last evening together was an especially joyous occasion for the members of the Congress because, as the narrator states, they felt that their plan "really and secretly existed and was the world." When they separated, they swore never to tell anyone about their secret organization. Down through the years the narrator has sought to recapture the "taste of that night," but it has never come back to him except on one occasion—in a dream.

The interplay between the quest for order and the regression to chaos runs throughout the story and helps to illuminate its meaning. The process of structuring the Congress on the basis of Platonic archetypes, the creation of a vast library, and the narrator's trip to London represent intellectual endeavors to systematize knowledge. On the other hand, the return to Glencoe's primitive ranch in Uruguay, Fermín Eguren's bohemian life in Paris, and the book-burning episode constitute instinctual or irrational forces contrary to human logic.

Glencoe's explanation for burning the books and terminating the Congress brings to mind the clash between Platonic realism and Aristotelian nominalism, which Borges has discussed in his essay entitled "From Allegories to Novels" (OI). Philosophical realism states that universals exist outside the mind and thus stresses the abstract or the generic, whereas nominalism denies the existence of universals and emphasizes the individual or the particular. The members of the Congress are obviously realists, structuring their organization on the concept of Platonic archetypes. However, Glencoe's radical change at the end of the story indicates that he has rejected realism for nominalism, realizing that each individual is unique and thus can never be representative of a generic group. His invitation, then, to ride through the city and see the "true Congress" would seem to signify that they will observe the world itself, in all its diversity, rather than attempt to organize it into rigid categories.

The final events of the story also lend themselves to a philosophical interpretation. The joy felt by the group as they look back on their carefully planned world and the narrator's inability to recapture that joy except in a dream imply that once it was disbanded, the Congress became an ideal that existed only in the minds of its members. Inasmuch as the narrator is the only survivor, he now feels compelled to break his vow of silence and reveal the existence of the organization, thus ensuring its continuation in the minds of his readers. The philosophical idealism suggested by "The Congress" conveys an element of absurdity, for it demonstrates the impossibility of organizing the chaotic world, except, that is, in the abstract realm of human consciousness.

In certain respects "The Congress" relates to "The Library of Babel," the first story treated in this section. Both works present elaborate metaphors of an intellectually conceived, and thus fictitious, world. The Library, however, preserves a semblance of physical reality in order to convey allegorically man's absurd endeavor throughout much of history to comprehend the universe. By way of contrast, the Congress dissolves into happy, idealized memories, perhaps an indication that the aging author has all but abandoned the struggle against the absurd. (We recall that "The Library of Babel" was published in 1941, thirty years before "The Congress.")[27]

3. IDEALISM

Of all the philosophies Borges has injected into his writings, the various forms of idealism espoused by Berkeley, Hume, and Schopenhauer are probably the most visible and the most useful for depicting the fragility of things and the illusory nature of reality in general. Borges has admitted a certain predilection for idealism, as indicated by the following statement he once made in an interview. "I suppose if I had to define myself, I would define myself as an idealist, philosophically speaking. But I'm not sure I have to define myself. I'd rather go on wondering and puzzling about things, for I find that very enjoyable."[1]

The idealists maintain that to be is to be perceived; that material objects are ideas in our minds, with no independent existence; and that, therefore, the whole of reality consists of ideas in the mind of God. Given his inherent skepticism, Borges's idealism is probably more poetic than philosophical. His famous poem "Daybreak" (FOBA), for example, describes the dawn in Buenos Aires as a perilous moment for the city because it is not being perceived by its sleeping inhabitants and therefore could cease to exist. The philosophical implications of this poem are developed in many of Borges's subsequent works, his purpose being to disintegrate concrete reality and reveal the poetic and hallucinatory aspects of his visionary world. If, moreover, the existence of the material world depends solely on our mental perception of it—a perception that changes second by second and differs greatly from person to person—life emerges as unstable, insubstantial, and no more real than an absurd dream.

In his essay "On the Cult of Books" (OI), Borges refers to the tenets of various doctrines in order to reinforce his idealist theme of the world as a sacred book emanating from the mind of a divinity. For the Moslems, he states, the Koran is not merely a work of God, like the universe, but one of the attributes of God, like his eternity or his ire. According to the cabalists,[2] the *Sepher Yetzirah* (*Book of the Formation*) reveals that the universe was created from the first ten cardinal numbers and the twenty-two letters of the alphabet. Christians believe that God wrote two books: the scriptures, which convey his will, and the universe, which demonstrates his power and contains the key to the scriptures. And Thomas Carlyle espoused a form of idealism when he asserted that universal history is a sacred scripture, one that we decipher and write uncertainly and in which we also are written.

Borges's "Partial Enchantments of the Quijote" (OI) illuminates Carlyle's statement on a literary plane. In Part Two of *Don Quijote,* he recalls, the protagonist has read Part One, and in *Hamlet* the protagonist views a tragedy similar to *Hamlet.* Borges wonders why it disquiets us to know that Don Quijote is a reader of *Don Quijote* and Hamlet is a spectator of *Hamlet.* His reply is just as disquieting as the observation that provoked his question. "I believe I have found the answer: those inversions suggest that if the characters in a story can be readers or spectators, then we, their readers or spectators, can be fictitious."

"The Witness" (DT), another of Borges's many expressions of idealism, describes the death of an old Saxon, the last eyewitness of certain pagan rites in England. Because these rites no longer live in any mind, we are told, the world is "a little poorer" when this Saxon dies. Borges wonders what will disappear forever when he dies: "The voice of Macedonio Fernández,[3] the image of a roan horse on the vacant lot at Serrano and Charcas? A bar of sulphur in the drawer of a mahogany desk?"

"The Avatars of the Tortoise" (OI), which sets forth the concept of the *regressus in infinitum,* utilizes irrefutable logic to suggest the fallacies inherent in certain aspects of everyday life. Borges first reminds his readers that according to one of Zeno of Elea's famous paradoxes,[4] Achilles runs ten times faster than the tortoise and gives him a head start of ten meters. Achilles runs ten meters, the tortoise runs one; Achilles runs that meter, the tortoise runs a centimeter, and so on ad infinitum, the theoretical result being that Achilles never manages to overtake the tortoise. The principle is formulated, then, that the slower will never be overtaken by the faster because the pursuer must cover the ground the pursued has just covered, and the slower always has a definite advantage. For Borges the "vertiginous *regressus in infinitum*" illustrates the gulf that separates the reasoning mind from incomprehensible reality. It is hazardous, he asserts, to think that a coordination of words—by which he means philosophies—can resemble the universe, although he confesses his preferences for Schopenhauer's idealist thesis of the world as a fabrication of the will. Borges invites his readers to admit "what all idealists admit: that the nature of the world is hallucinatory." "We . . . have dreamed the world," he adds. "We have dreamed it strong, mysterious, visible, ubiquitous in space and secure in time; but we have allowed tenuous, eternal interstices of injustice in its structure so we may know that it is false."

Many of Borges's stories contain elements of idealism and in some of them idealism emerges as the principal ingredient. Among those discussed in the previous section, "The Library of Babel" presents a metaphor of a mentally conceived world beyond the confines of concrete, everyday reality; the protagonist of "Averroes' Search" vanishes when the narrator ceases to believe in him; "The Book of Sand" represents an image of infinity in the form of a sacred book; and in "The Congress," after an aborted attempt to create an organization based on Platonic archetypes, the entire endeavor is relegated to the cerebral realm of idealism.

Tlön, Uqbar, Orbis Tertius   (1941) (F) (L)

"Tlön, Uqbar, Orbis Tertius" is unquestionably one of Borges's most significant pieces of short fiction, not only because of its treatment of idealism, its central theme, but also because it contains many ideas developed in his subsequent works. The strange chain of events begins when "the conjunction of a mirror and an encyclopedia" causes the narrator's friend, Adolfo Bioy Casares,[5] to make an offhand allusion to Uqbar, an exotic land he has read about in his *Anglo-American Cyclopaedia*. It seems that a heresiarch of Uqbar once stated that the visible universe is an illusion and that mirrors and copulation are abominable because they multiply and extend it. Intrigued, the narrator seeks additional information on the subject, but Bioy's encyclopedia contains the only article available and, oddly, other copies of the same edition of the encyclopedia lack the entry his contains.

Some time later a book entitled *A First Encyclopaedia of Tlön* (Volume XI) makes its way into the narrator's possession. After examining it, he remains convinced that Tlön was invented by a group of scholars from different disciplines because it constitutes a complete cosmos governed by strict laws, "which . . . have been carefully formulated, albeit provisionally." The people of the planet Tlön, moreover, are "congenitally idealist." They accept the principle of isolated moments in time but not that of objects existing side by side in space. Their language has no nouns for concrete objects and only impersonal verbs. For example, there is no noun corresponding to moon, but there is a verb to moon or to moondle. In order to express "The moon rose over the sea," they would say, "Upward beyond the constant flow there was moondling." Nouns are formed by an accumulation of adjectives, the idea of moon being expressed by "airy-clear over dark-round" or "orange-faint-of-sky." And, in accordance with the laws of idealism, things tend to efface themselves when they are forgotten, a classic example being that of a stone threshold that lasted as long as it was visited by a beggar but faded from sight on his death.

Perhaps because thought is seen as the equivalent of reality and as synonymous with isolated moments of mental activity, the people of Tlön deny cause and effect. For example, instead of connecting a lighted cigar with the fire it causes, they would consider the two phenomena as an example of association of ideas. Although philosophical systems abound on Tlön, philosophers do not pretend to convey truth, but instead amazement. They realize that any system of thought is "nothing more than the subordination of all the aspects of the universe to some one of them." Metaphysics, then, is viewed as a branch of fantastic literature to be treated with artistry and imagination.

This partial summary of "Tlön, Uqbar, Orbis Tertius" illustrates not only certain facets of idealism, but also how this philosophy serves to convey absurdity. The denial of the existence of concrete objects as spatial entities, the absence of nouns in the language, and the physical disappearance of things when they are forgotten tend to make Tlön an abstract, cerebral planet devoid of material reality. The negation of reason is suggested by the rejection of cause-and-effect relationships as well as by the renunciation of the search for truth by philosophers. The paradox of a purely mental world devoid of reason assumes absurd proportions with the proliferation of "fantastic" metaphysical systems. One school of thought, for example, declares that time has already passed and our lives are only vague memories. Another school insists that the history of the universe is the handwriting produced by a minor god in order to communicate with a demon.[6] And still another school states that only the events of every 300th night are true.

The most scandalous philosophy ever to make its appearance on Tlön is materialism, the theory that physical matter is the only reality and that all being can be explained as manifestations of matter. This philosophy was disseminated by a heresiarch, who told the following anecdote to illustrate his belief: On Tuesday, X loses nine coins on a road. On Thursday, Y finds on the road four coins rusted by Wednesday's rain. On Friday, Z finds three coins and X finds two. The heresiarch concludes that the coins must have continued to exist, "albeit in some secret way," during the days that they were lost. For the people of Tlön, the heresiarch's reasoning is specious because he cannot prove that the coins continued to exist, nor can he prove that the coins lost are the same ones that were found. They admit that the coins are equal, but, in their opinion, the heresiarch's belief in the continuity of their existence is blasphemous because he is attributing to them the category of divine being. And if they do belong in this category, they would have to constitute a single coin.

Several hundred years later an orthodox thinker of Tlön sets forth the thesis that there exists only one indivisible Individual, that this Individual encompasses every being in the universe, and that these beings are the instruments and masks of the divinity itself. Accordingly, X, Y, and Z of the heresiarch's anecdote are all the same person and the coins were found because he (X, Y, and Z) remembered that they were lost. In addition, we are told, if all men are one man it stands to reason that all books have been written by the same author, who is timeless and anonymous and whose stories are variations of a single plot.

The scandal caused by philosophical materialism and the ideas set forth by the orthodox thinker several hundred years later are ironic for several reasons. Materialism is the antithesis of idealism and so, expectedly, is viewed as heresy. However, one of the reasons for rejecting materialism was the contention that if the coins continued to exist while lost, they would be a part of the Supreme Being and therefore would comprise a single coin. This idea is a manifestation of pantheism,[7] a philosophy wholeheartedly embraced several centuries later when the orthodox thinker declares that one Individual represents all men and one book, all books. Borges's point is that all philosophical theories are "provisional," and so what one generation may consider heretical, another may accept as true.

Inasmuch as idealism considers matter as a product of perception, it seems logical that in Tlön lost objects can be duplicated through memory in the minds of the people. These objects, which are called *hrönir,* range from commonplace things such as pencils to historic artifacts like earthenware urns excavated by students of archeology. As might be expected, the *hrönir* vary greatly in quality and form from generation to generation. Their development has been useful to all men, but particularly to archeologists because it has allowed them to render the past just as malleable as the future. Just as *hrönir* are mental reproductions of lost objects, *ur* are creations of hope.

The story's postscript, supposedly written several years later, clears up much of the mystery surrounding Tlön. A letter brought to the narrator's attention reveals that a secret society of scholars was founded in England during the seventeenth century for the purpose of inventing a country. George Berkeley was one of the early members. Two centuries later the organization surfaced in the United States, where a millionaire named Buckley sponsored the secret publication of an encyclopedia describing the entire planet of Tlön. The forty-volume work appeared in English in 1914, at which time plans were already being made for an expanded edition to be published in one of the native tongues of Tlön. Its projected title was *Orbis Tertius*.

Meanwhile the fantastic world of Tlön began its intrusion on the real world. In 1942 in Buenos Aires the Princess of Faucigny Lucinge received from Poitiers a crate of her silver table service with a mysterious magnetic compass bearing the letters of an alphabet of Tlön on the dial. The narrator was a witness to the second intrusion, which occurred in Cuchilla Negra, where a tiny but incredibly heavy cone-shaped object was discovered next to the body of an unknown gaucho, who had died mysteriously. The object turned out to be an image of one of the divinities of Tlön. In 1944 a set of the clandestine forty-volume encyclopedia of Tlön was discovered in Memphis, Tennessee, and hailed by the international press as a major event in the publishing world. Pirate editions of the work appeared almost immediately. People were fascinated with the "vast evidence of an ordered planet," just as they had been with other recent "symmetrical systems" such as dialectical materialism, anti-Semitism, and Nazism.

At this point in his story the narrator injects his comparison of the real world with that of Tlön, stating that if labyrinthine reality is ordered, it is "in accordance with divine laws . . . which we will never completely perceive." Tlön, on the other hand, is also a labyrinth, but one plotted by men and designed to be deciphered by men. Contact with Tlön, we are told, is gradually disintegrating this world. The languages and history of the idealist planet have made their way into the schools, and it is believed that within a hundred years the world is likely to be Tlön. Meanwhile the narrator takes no notice of these intrusions, preferring to revise his translation into Spanish of Sir Thomas Browne's *Urn Burial,* which, by the way, he never intends to publish.

The story's postscript is both humorous and profound. The gradual inroads of Tlön into the real world are treated as an absurdity because of the ease with which naive human beings, eager to establish a semblance of order, adopt any system of thought promising it. Thus the compass and cone that suddenly appear in the real world symbolize guidance and hope for the eventual creation of an ideal order.

"Tlön, Uqbar, Orbis Tertius" depicts an imaginary planet conceived according to the laws of philosophical idealism. For Borges the incursion of pantheism into the idealist realm of Tlön and, ultimately, the incursion of pantheistic idealism into the real world serve to dissolve objective reality and, as suggested by the allusion to mirrors and copulation, to convey the notion that everything perceived by human consciousness is an illusory creation of the mind. Reality, Borges demonstrates, is not what things are but how we see them. Thus mental activity can modify or recreate the past, as shown by the symbolic *hrönir* and *ur*. The encyclopedia at the beginning of the story represents the organization of reality into seemingly coherent mental constructs, but the fact that it is reflected by the mirrors alters its symbolic meaning. Tlön represents the *illusion* of a decipherable reality that is not only fictitious but just as chaotic as the real world. (It will be recalled, for example, that in Tlön causality is denied and reality consists of a random series of heterogeneous and independent phenomena.) Always in search of order, however, man prefers a fallacious design to baffling reality.

Borges's skepticism is underscored at the end of the story when the narrator, whom we are tempted to identify with the real author, ignores the intrusions of Tlön into his world and continues his insignificant intellectual pursuit of translating the works of a seventeenth-century baroque English author into Spanish. This ending implies once again Borges's conviction that all philosophies are "provisional"; therefore, the narrator will remain aloof from absurd "speculations" because eventually idealism will be replaced by another system of thought.[8]

The Zahir   (1947) (L) (PA)

The Zahir is a coin that becomes an obsession to the story's narrator and, in his disturbed mind, gradually replaces his image of the world. The plot begins with the death of Clementina Villar, a society lady who "strove for irreproachable correctness in every action." She was, we are told, in search of "the absolute," but hers was an "absolute of a moment's duration," since she was constantly altering her appearance by submitting to the shifting whims of Paris or Hollywood. After this ironic description, Borges confesses that out of snobbery, "that most sincere of Argentinian passions," he was enamored of Clementina Villar. (The first-person narrator of the story refers to himself as Borges.)

At his beloved's wake Borges recalls her many facial expressions and feels profoundly disconcerted by the realization that the vision of her "rigid among the flowers, her disdain perfected by death" will be his most lasting memory of her. On his way home he stops for a glass of brandy in a bar where he is given the Zahir as his change. Upon leaving the bar he recalls a series of fabulous coins from both the historic past and literary legends. It then occurs to him that money by nature represents an abstraction, "a repertory of possible futures and a symbol of free will." That night he has a dream in which he sees himself as a treasure of coins guarded by a griffin (a mythical monster fabled to be the offspring of a lion and an eagle).

Borges spends the Zahir the following day, but during the next few weeks he becomes increasingly preoccupied with its image and, in his efforts to forget it, even consults a psychiatrist. Meanwhile he writes a tale of fantasy about an ascetic who is obsessed with a treasure he watches over day and night. At the end of the story it becomes evident that the ascetic is the serpent Fafnir and the treasure is that of the famous medieval German epic, the *Nibelungenlied*. Borges also learns from an esoteric book that *zahir* is an Arabic word meaning "notorious" or "visible," that it can be used to describe "beings or things which possess the terrible property of being unforgettable, and whose image finally drives one mad." In another volume Borges reads that there is nothing in the world that could not take on the properties of a Zahir. Eventually he imagines that he can see both sides of the coin simultaneously, as if it were a center surrounded by his spherical vision. By 1948, he concludes, he will probably go mad, no longer perceiving the universe but instead only the Zahir. And behind it perhaps he will find God.

Like so many of Borges's tales, "The Zahir" depicts man's obsessive quest for meaning and permanence in the unfathomable, ever-changing world. Borges's bereavement at the death of his beloved leaves him momentarily adrift in a kind of existential void, which is almost immediately filled by the magical, unforgettable Zahir, a symbol of the world reduced to a more manageable proportion. Perhaps the key to the story's meaning, however, lies in the narrator's (Borges's) dream, which represents his identification with the Zahir and, more than likely, inspires his tale based on the *Nibelungenlied*. Thus "The Zahir" could be viewed as a rereading of the German epic, the "treasure" in both works causing the ruin of those who touch it. (In the *Nibelungenlied* the punishment is death; in "The Zahir" the narrator goes mad after his contact with the coin.) The potential power of the Zahir is first anticipated when the narrator perceives money as a symbol of free will. Immediately thereafter his dream, the fantastic story he writes, and his investigation of the Zahir's meaning lead logically to the denouement.

The story's symmetrical structure derives from the parallels between Clementina Villar and the coin as well as from the latter's thematic relationship with the *Nibelungenlied*. Before her death, Clementina represents the existential notion of free will and change, a notion similar to that evoked by the Zahir when Borges receives it in the bar. Clementina becomes fixed in Borges's mind when he sees her rigid in death and, likewise, the Zahir acquires its permanent essence when, in the mind of the deranged narrator, it replaces the universe. This imaginary vision wrought by a woman's death, a dream, and an epic poem would seem to embody the quintessence of the idealist tenet that reality is a product of the mind.

The Secret Miracle   (1943) (F) (PA) (L)

"The Secret Miracle" is one of Borges's most popular masterpieces. The night before the German occupation of Prague in March 1939, Jaromir Hladík dreams of a chess game in which he is one of the players. A Czechoslovakian writer of Jewish descent, Hladík is arrested by the Nazis several days later and condemned to death. During the ten days prior to the execution date he imagines the circumstances of his death many times, believing that since reality rarely corresponds to one's anticipation of it, his mental visions might somehow alter his fate.

As he looks back on his career, Hladík is well aware of his defects as a writer. His best work to date, he believes, is his "Vindication of Eternity," an essay in which he attempts to deny the passing of time.[9] When he was arrested, he was writing a drama entitled *The Enemies*, by which he hoped "to redeem himself from his equivocal and languid past." The protagonist of his drama, Baron Roemerstadt, receives in his library a series of visitors who seem to be plotting against him. In the dialogue, mention is made of a certain Jaroslav Kubin, a madman who imagines he is Baron Roemerstadt. The plot becomes confused when a conspirator killed by Baron Roemerstadt returns to life and time seems to repeat itself. Eventually it turns out that Kubin and Roemerstadt are the same person, that what has occurred is actually a circular delirium lived and relived by Kubin.

The night before his execution Hladík asks God to grant him a year's reprieve in order to finish his drama. He believes that if he exists as author of *The Enemies,* his life will be justified and he will not be just another of God's "repetitions and errata." Then he falls asleep and dreams that he is in a huge library looking for God, when a blind librarian tells him God is embodied in one of the letters of a page in one of the 400,000 volumes. Quite by accident Hladík discovers the letter in an atlas, and thereupon God grants his request. On awakening he is led into a courtyard to be shot by a firing squad, but when the sergeant gives the order to fire, time stops before the sound of the shots is heard. For a year Hladík works steadily on his drama, finishing it precisely when his reprieve comes to an end. At that moment the volley of the firing squad resounds, and Hladík dies.

"The Secret Miracle" illustrates the difficulty one encounters in classifying Borges's fiction according to theme. Time and the absurd emerge as major elements, but the encroachment of the literary world of imagination into the real world would seem to give the story its meaning and relate it to philosophical idealism. The chess game of Hladík's dream at the beginning of the story recalls Borges's poem entitled "Chess" (SAO), in which two chess players turn out to be pawns on God's chessboard and God a pawn on some other God's chessboard, etc. Similarly, Hladík's arrest and condemnation by the Nazis soon after his dream constitute a metaphor of his becoming a helpless pawn after having been a player. His repeated attempts to imagine the circumstances of his execution signify his desire to relegate death to the mental realm where it becomes insubstantial and loses its physical pain and horror. Hladík's "Vindication of Eternity," in which he rejects lineal for circular time, foreshadows the circular structure of *The Enemies* as well as that of the entire story. Thus, just as Hladík is a pawn on the Nazis' chessboard, Roemerstadt and Kubin are his pawns, i.e., his creations by which he hopes to justify his existence. The fusion of Kubin's and Roemerstadt's identities, moreover, anticipates Hladík's pantheistic union with God when he finds the divine‑letter in the library. At this point, then, Hladík, having become God, is able to finish his drama, which represents his "divine" creation. However, once his artistic world is completed, his ephemeral omnipotence is cruelly snatched away from him by God, the chess player whose pawn Hladík ultimately becomes.

The story's implication that a chess player is a pawn on the board of another player who, in turn, is the pawn of another, and so on to infinity, deprives the protagonist of material reality and creates an atmosphere similar to that of an absurd dream. Hladík's fate, moreover, recalls that of Lönnrot in "Death and the Compass," whose death was prepared in advance by the god figure, Scharlach. Like Lönnrot, Hladík is granted the illusion of success before he becomes a victim of metaphysical irony, i.e., of a cruel God who arbitrarily controls his destiny.

"The Secret Miracle" can also be read as a metaphor of the creative process, both Hladík and Borges striving to deny the passing of time through the use of imagination and art. And just as Borges is reflected by Hladík, Hladík is reflected by Roemerstadt, who lives in a kind of circular delirium symbolic of the dreamlike state the creative artist experiences as he writes. The absorption of Roemerstadt's identity by Kubin, moreover, is mirrored by Hladík's pantheistic union with God in the library when he discovers the magical letter. Hladík's destruction in front of the firing squad, however, reveals that God is his enemy, just as Kubin is Roemerstadt's enemy, and just as time is Borges's enemy. Art and the creative process, then, provide a means of escape from lineal time, but as Borges is forced to admit in his famous essay, "New Refutation of Time," this escape is illusory and temporary. "The Secret Miracle" dramatizes the marvelous ability of the mind to create its own world of art. Although Hladík is ultimately obliterated by his cruel fate, it is the miracle of mind over matter that constitutes the story's idealist theme.

The Circular Ruins   (1941) (F) (L) (PA) (A)

Another of Borges's masterpieces, "The Circular Ruins" is probably his best fictional treatment of idealism. The story's main character is a wizard who visits the ancient ruins of a circular temple destroyed by fire many years previously. His avowed purpose in coming to the deserted temple, located in a remote jungle region, is to dream a man and impose him on reality. The wizard first dreams he is in the center of an amphitheater lecturing to a large number of students, some of whom are "at a distance of many centuries and as high as the stars." Among the students the wizard proposes to tutor one soul "worthy of participating in the universe." He eventually chooses a young man whose features resemble his own and whose progress after a few private lessons is highly encouraging. Soon thereafter, however, he finds himself plagued with insomnia, unable to continue his project.

After a long rest he purifies himself in the river and then renews his efforts to create a human being from the elusive matter of dreams. Almost immediately he dreams the heart of a man and little by little all the other organs. A year later, however, the creature he has dreamed still remains inanimate, reminiscent, we are told, of the clumsy, crude Adam fashioned by the Gnostic demiurges.[10] Desperate to infuse life into his creation, the wizard prostrates himself before the statue of a horse or a tiger in front of the ruins. That night he dreams that the statue represents the fire god, who promises to animate his dreamed "son" in such a way that all creatures except the fire god and the wizard will believe him to be a man of flesh and blood. Once the dreamed youth comes to life, the wizard carries out the god's orders to instruct him in the mysteries of the universe and the cult of fire, taking great

pains to prevent him from learning of his phantom status.
When his education is complete, the phantom son is sent
downstream to another ruined temple, where "some voice
would glorify him in that deserted edifice."

Years later the wizard receives word of a charmed
man in a temple to the north who is capable of walking on
fire without burning himself. He then begins to worry lest
his son should suffer the "incomparable humiliation" of
learning that he is not a man but a projection of another's
dreams. At this moment the circular ruins are suddenly
enveloped in flames, and the wizard, believing that death
is imminent, walks toward the wall of fire. But instead of
burning his flesh, it caresses him without producing the
slightest sensation of heat. "With relief, with humiliation,
with terror, he understood that he also was an illusion,
that someone else was dreaming him."

The story's principal theme, that reality is a dream, is
inextricably linked to idealism, especially to the idealism of
Schopenhauer, who stresses the unreality of art and views
life as the manifestation of will. Thus the mysterious,
hallucinatory setting serves as a backdrop for the protagonist's determined efforts to dream a man into
existence.[11] The plot can also be interpreted as an allegory
of artistic creation. The dream of the amphitheater, where
the wizard chooses a student resembling himself to tutor,
could represent Borges's view of art as a reflection of the
artist.[12] If correct, this interpretation foreshadows the
denouement, enhancing the irony of a dreamer whose
dream reflects his own unreality. The wizard's plan to
dream a man amidst the circular ruins of a temple
destroyed by fire suggests the artist's magical regression
from rational consciousness to a prelogical, mythic state
more conducive to poetic creation and cosmic regeneration.
The travail of dreaming a man emerges as a metaphor of
the artist's arduous creative process, the product of which
becomes as real and as much a part of him as a flesh-and-
blood offspring. The startling denouement jolts not only

the wizard but also the reader into doubting his own reality.

Another significant aspect of the story is its relation to the Golem, a cabalist legend about an automaton made in the form of a human being and brought to life by means of a magic incantation. Borges treats the legend in his poem entitled "The Golem" (SAO), giving it an idealist theme similar to that of "The Circular Ruins." The creation of the Golem by a rabbi parallels God's creation of Adam, but the Adam alluded to by Borges has been fashioned by a Gnostic demiurge, whose existence depends on a superior god whose existence depends on another superior god, etc.

Just as "The Secret Miracle" applies the principle of the *regressus in infinitum* to a chess player being a pawn on a chessboard of another player, "The Circular Ruins" implies that if the world exists only as one's idea of it, then one is a mere idea in the mind of one's perceiver, and one's perceiver an idea in the mind of his perceiver, and so on to infinity. This absurd circle of futility is reinforced by the story's title and setting as well as by the fire image, which symbolizes the cyclical process of creation and destruction conveyed by the strange chain of events. Although the denial of material reality does not clearly emerge as the theme until the final lines, Borges mischievously predicts the surprise ending in the initial paragraph with his statement that the wizard climbed up the riverbank "without pushing aside (probably, without feeling) the blades which were lacerating his flesh." "The Circular Ruins" represents an esthetically balanced fusion of literary craftsmanship and philosophical idealism.

Theme of the Traitor and Hero   (1944) (F) (L)

"Theme of the Traitor and Hero" has much in common with "The Circular Ruins." Both tales display a circular structure; both contain elements of the absurd; and, most important, both dramatize the idealist tenet that reality is fictive or a dream. The action of "Theme of the Traitor and Hero" occurs in 1824 in Ireland when the heroic patriot Fergus Kilpatrick was assassinated under mysterious circumstances while plotting a rebellion against the English. The story's narrator, a man named Ryan,* is Kilpatrick's great-grandson. Approximately one hundred years after his ancestor's death, Ryan investigates the circumstances of his assassination for the purpose of writing his biography. It seems that Kilpatrick was murdered in a theater, and no trace of the killers was ever found. In the course of his research Ryan discovers striking parallels between Kilpatrick's and Caesar's assassinations, which make him "assume a secret pattern in time, a drawing in which the lines repeat themselves." He finds himself believing in the transmigration of souls and suspects that Kilpatrick existed previously as Caesar. In addition, certain words spoken by a beggar to Kilpatrick on the day of his death seem to be prefigured in *Macbeth*.

Ryan learns from documents in the national archives that one of Kilpatrick's fellow conspirators was a scholar by the name of Nolan, who had translated Shakespeare's *Julius Caesar* into Gaelic and written an article on the Swiss *Festspiele,* theatrical representations of historic episodes requiring thousands of actors. Another document reveals that Kilpatrick had signed the death sentence of a traitor, whose name had been blotted out. Ultimately it comes to light that Kilpatrick ordered Nolan to find the traitor, Nolan's investigation led to his irrefutable proof that Kilpatrick was the culprit, and Kilpatrick was obliged to sign his own death sentence. However, since Kilpatrick was idealized by the Irish as a hero of their cause, Nolan proposed a plan by which Kilpatrick would die at the

---

* Actually the story is told by a first-person narrator-author who imagines a series of events to be told by Ryan.

hands of an unknown assassin, in this way inflaming the people to revolt against their oppressors and, at the same time, allowing Kilpatrick to redeem himself.

Nolan's elaborate scheme involved his imitation of scenes from *Macbeth* and *Julius Caesar*. Thus Kilpatrick was brought to Dublin and for several days a real-life political drama reminiscent of the *Festspiele* unfolded with Kilpatrick in the leading role and hundreds of actors, all under the direction of Nolan. The climax occurred when Kilpatrick was murdered in a theater, foreshadowing, we are told, Abraham Lincoln's death.

Ryan concludes that Nolan's imitation of *Macbeth* and *Julius Caesar* were intended to make someone in the future, namely Ryan, realize the truth about Kilpatrick. Ryan also understands that he, too, is a part of Nolan's plan, according to which he is destined to publish, not the information he has uncovered about his illustrious ancestor, but instead, a book dedicated to the glorification of his role in history.

Borges states in his initial sentence that he has been inspired to write his tale by Chesterton, the ingenious author of mysteries, and Leibnitz, the German philosopher who believed in preestablished harmony. This beginning should alert the reader to the possible combination of fiction and philosophical speculation about to be narrated. Ryan, the historian, sets out in search of the truth about his heroic ancestor. What he discovers, however, is that Kilpatrick is part of a vast scheme of events that are just as much fiction as fact.

Nolan emerges as the manipulator of Kilpatrick's fate, a kind of author–god-figure who directs the series of improbable events surrounding Kilpatrick's life. In doing so, he imitates scenes from the classical English theater (*Macbeth* and *Julius Caesar*), converts fiction into contemporary reality (the *Festspiele* of Kilpatrick's death), and even foreshadows history (Lincoln's assassination). Ultimately Ryan comes to realize, like the wizard of "The Circular Ruins," that he too exists only in the mind of another or as a character in someone's great design.

Borges appears to be making two closely related points: first, history, as Ryan discovers, is as much fiction as it is fact. Thus Kilpatrick, a heroic martyr in the history books, may have been executed as a traitor. And second, history is not only contaminated with fiction but recurs in cycles that render human endeavor absurd. For example, even though Ryan thinks he has discovered the truth about Kilpatrick, he perpetuates the myth of the glorious hero, believing that, like Kilpatrick, he is a part of Nolan's orchestration of events. Thus Ryan the historian becomes, in a sense, a writer of fiction, which is what Borges really considers history to be.

For Borges there is little or no difference between acting on the stage of history and performing in a theater. Or, he seems to say, if we make the mistake of thinking we can separate fact from fiction in a world utterly lacking in absolutes, we only succeed in creating another piece of fiction. Although we cannot be certain, the absurd process of creating a cerebral, idealist universe may be what "Theme of the Traitor and Hero" is about.

The Waiting   (1950) (L)

"The Waiting" is one of Borges's more difficult tales to interpret. Its plot is reminiscent of Hemingway's famous short story, "The Killers," but its execution and philosophical implications make it quite different. At the beginning of the story a man arrives by taxi at a boardinghouse in the northwest section of Buenos Aires. When the proprietress asks his name, he answers "Villari," not his real name but that of the enemy from whom he is hiding. Although he spends most of the time in his room, he occasionally goes to a movie theater in the neighborhood where he sees gangster films. These films present episodes that resemble his past life, but it never occurs to him to make this association because the idea of a coincidence between art and reality is alien to him. In his previous confinements, "Villari" always had counted the days and the hours, looking forward to his release. The present confinement, however, has no end "unless one morning the newspaper brought news of Alejandro Villari's death." He also reflects that if Villari had died already, "this life was a dream." Whereas formerly the protagonist was a man of strong will, now he only seeks to endure. Like an old wolf-dog that lives in the boardinghouse, he exists in the present, with no memories of the past or anticipation of the future.

One night "Villari" is stricken with a toothache and is obliged to visit the dentist. On another occasion he is returning to his boardinghouse from a movie when he is accidentally pushed by a stranger. He reacts violently, shouting coarse insults at the man. When he discovers a copy of the *Divine Comedy* on a shelf in his room, he reads a canto from it every night before dinner. The punishment of hell does not seem either excessive or unbelievable to him.

At dawn every day "Villari" dreams that his enemy and two other men attack him as he leaves the movie theater. Toward the end of the dream he shoots his attackers and the noise wakes him, but he always awakens into another dream in which the attack is repeated and he has to shoot them again. Early one morning he is, in fact, aroused in his room by his enemy and a stranger, who have at last caught up with him. Instead of facing them, "Villari" turns his face to the wall "so that the murderers would be a dream, as they had already been so many times, in the same place, at the same hour." While performing this "act of magic," he is shot to death.

A salient feature of "The Waiting" is the dialectical interplay throughout the story between everyday reality on the one hand and fiction and dream on the other. In the initial lines, for example, the boardinghouse and the street on which it is located are described in realistic detail, whereas the films "Villari" attends represent a purely fictive reality. Likewise, during his previous confinements (in jails and hospitals) he had been painfully conscious of lineal time, but now he lives in an eternal, dreamlike present, savoring each momentary sensation. A possible end to his situation could be brought about by the announcement in the newspaper of Alejandro Villari's death, another example of everyday reality. The thought that his enemy might have died without his knowing it, however, makes his present life of waiting a dream. His visit to the dentist and the unpleasant incident while he is returning from the movies constitute additional examples of everyday reality that contrast sharply with "Villari's" immersion into the *Divine Comedy*. And "Villari's" recurring dream in which he kills his enemy, only to awake into another dream, finally becomes fact, except that he himself is the victim and his enemy, who perhaps represents his double or mirror image, is the killer.

Written during the Perón era, "The Waiting" would seem to represent an attempt to transform a sordid concrete reality into an immaterial idealist world of fiction and dream. Like "The House of Asterion," it could also be read as an allegory of man trapped in a world with little or no meaning and faced with the prospect of death. The two stories reveal significant differences, however. Asterión symbolizes fearful, ignorant man who, enclosed within the labyrinth of culture, anticipates death as a deliverance from loneliness; in "The Waiting" on the other hand, it is suggested that man builds a labyrinth of fiction and dreams (for Borges they are almost one and the same) as a means of escape from the horror of death. "Villari's" final "act of magic" emerges, then, as another metaphor of the triumph of mind over matter such as we have seen in "The Secret Miracle." But the triumph is ephemeral, for "Villari" has reached the fateful center of his labyrinth.

The Other Death   (1948) (A)

Borges's intriguing tale, "The Other Death," centers on the ramifications of an attempt to revoke and recreate the past. Pedro Damián, the protagonist, was a youth of nineteen or twenty years of age when he fought in the battle of Masoller in 1904. The narrator met Damián briefly in 1942 and conversed with him about the historic battle. In 1946 the narrator received a letter from his friend, Gannon,* informing him that he was translating Emerson's poem "The Past" into Spanish. In a postscript Gannon added that Pedro Damián had died of fever and that in his final delirium he had relived the battle of Masoller.

The narrator decides to write a story about Damián, who spent the last thirty years of his life as a cowhand, living alone in a cabin ten miles from Ñancay. In order to obtain more information for his story, the narrator interviews a retired colonel named Tabares, also a veteran of the battle of Masoller. Tabares remembers Pedro Damián well because he had unexpectedly revealed a streak of cowardice in the thick of the fighting. Some months later the narrator visits Colonel Tabares again to obtain more details and makes the acquaintance of Dr. Amaro, another survivor of Masoller. Dr. Amaro, however, remembers that Pedro Damián died as a hero in the battle and even recalls the details of his death. Much to the narrator's surprise, Colonel Tabares no longer remembers ever having heard of Pedro Damián. Nor does the narrator's friend Gannon, whom he meets soon thereafter, have any memory either of translating Emerson's poem or of having known Pedro Damián.

Not long after these incidents the narrator receives a letter from Colonel Tabares stating that he does indeed recall Damián's heroic death at Masoller. This information induces the narrator to seek out the cabin where Damián had spent the last thirty years of his life, but it is

---

* Patricio Gannon and the critic Emir Rodríguez Monegal are two literary friends of Borges mentioned in this story.

gone and nobody in the area remembers Damián. And the foreman under whom he worked also has died recently.

At this point in the story the narrator attempts to explain the mystery, basing his comments on a metaphysical theory of Pier Damiani, a learned cleric mentioned in Dante's *Divine Comedy*. Pier Damiani's belief "that it is within God's power to make what once was into something that has never been" leads the narrator to conclude that Damián did indeed show cowardice in the battle of Masoller, but that he spent the rest of his life preparing to set right that weakness. On his deathbed he was granted the opportunity to relive the battle. "And so," we are told, "in 1946, through the working out of a long, slow-burning passion, Pedro Damián died in the defeat at Masoller, which took place . . . in 1904."

The narrator believes that the modification of a single past incident not only nullifies the consequences of that incident but also suffices to effect the creation of a second universal history. Thus the altering of the date of Damián's death from 1946 to 1904 caused the strange contradictions in the mind of Colonel Tabares, who first recalls Damián as a coward, then forgets him altogether, and finally remembers his heroic death. The foreman also had to die, because he had too many memories of Damián. And Gannon had to forget Damián as well as his translation of Emerson's poem.

In the final lines of the story, the narrator asserts that perhaps Pedro Damián never really existed, that the entire plot may have been suggested to him by Pier Damiani's thesis regarding God's capacity to alter the past. This assertion by the narrator leads to the supposition that, like so many of Borges's tales, "The Other Death" is a purely fictional dramatization based on philosophical theories. Indeed, one might speculate that Borges's remaking of Pedro Damián's life may have been contrived to illustrate Pier Damiani's belief that it is within God's power to make what once was into something that has never been and, at the same time, to refute Emerson's thesis that the past is irrevocable, the theme of the poem Gannon was translating. Thus Borges, as the story's author, assumes the role of God, names his protagonist after a historical character who also appears in the *Divine Comedy,* and proceeds to create his *ficción.* However, as he develops his tale he discovers that the modification of a single event of the past suffices to engender a second universal history.

This discovery would seem to suggest an attitude toward history somewhat similar to that expressed in "Theme of the Traitor and Hero," namely, if the modification of a single event can change the entire course of history, we are all products of some preestablished order over which we have no control. Thus, like Ryan, Kilpatrick, and Pedro Damián, we are all actors on the stage of history or characters of a story, manipulated by Nolan, Borges, or God.

The fictive nature of "The Other Death," then, is a reflection of the fictive nature of a world whose status is as dubious as that of fiction itself. Borges's treatment of Pedro Damián may induce the reader to wonder if perhaps he too is a character in a book and, following Borges's reasoning, if the readers of that book are characters in another book, ad infinitum. This concept of reality reduced to an endless series of insubstantial perceptions implies absurdity, but it also constitutes the essence of philosophical idealism, the principal theme of this story.

4. PANTHEISM

Except for idealism, pantheism is the philosophy alluded to most frequently in Borges's works, perhaps, on the one hand, because of its implications of monistic unity and, on the other, because of the possibilities it provides for the dissolution of objective reality and the emergence of poetized fantasy. According to this doctrine, God is the essence of everything, and reality comprises a single being, of which all things are modes, moments, members, appearances, or projections. One individual, then, can represent all men, one point in space the entire universe, and one moment in time all of history.

Pantheistic themes underlie several of Borges's essays. In "Pascal's Sphere" (OI), for example, he traces the concept of the divinity from ancient Greece to the seventeenth century, the beginning of modern times when "humanity was intimidated by a feeling of old age." Six centuries before the Christian era, Xenophanes of Colophon attacked the poets who attributed anthropomorphic traits to the gods and proposed to the Greeks his belief in a single deity represented by an eternal sphere. A medieval theologian, Alain de Lille, espoused the idea, popular in his day, that "God is an intelligible sphere, whose center is everywhere and whose circumference is nowhere." A similar belief appears in Rabelais's *Pantagruel,* a literary masterpiece of the Renaissance. However, Pascal, a seventeenth-century philosopher, emerges as a kind of existential pantheist who, in his solitude and anguished quest for God, views the universe as an "abyss," "a frightful sphere, the center of which is everywhere, and the circumference nowhere." Borges concludes his essay on a more literary note with his famous statement that "perhaps universal history is the history of the diverse intonation of a few metaphors."

In a somewhat lighter vein, "The Flower of Coleridge" (OI) sets forth the pantheistic notion that the plurality of authors and literary works is illusory, one person having written a single, infinite book. To illustrate this concept, Borges alludes to similarities in three writers: Coleridge once wondered how a man would react if he dreamed he had been in Paradise and awoke with a flower in his hand proving that he had been there; in his novel *The Time Machine,* H. G. Wells depicts a man who travels into the distant future and returns with a wilted flower from that realm, and Henry James's protagonist in *The Sense of the Past* goes back in time to the eighteenth century and returns with a picture of himself from that period.

Another aspect of pantheism illustrated by Borges is the annihilation of individual identity, which becomes absorbed in the monistic unity of the world. In "From Someone to Nobody" (OI), for example, the medieval theologian Scotus Erigena draws parallels between the divinity and Shakespeare. Erigena defines God not only as the supreme creator of all things, which are revelations of the divine, but also as the primordial nothingness or the abyss in which the first archetypes and concrete beings were engendered. For Erigena, then, because God is everything and everybody, he becomes nothing and nobody. Borges believes that Shakespeare, who has been deified for his creative genius and universal characters, has ceased to be an individual man for, like Erigena's God, he, too, has become everybody and, consequently, nobody.

The dissolution of the individual personality, both human and divine, is also treated in Borges's essays entitled "Everything and Nothing" (DT) and "Note on Walt Whitman" (OI). The first of these poetically summarizes Shakespeare's life, emphasizing his many roles on the stage and the emptiness he feels once the curtain falls after each performance. Shortly before his death Shakespeare informs God that he would like to be only one man: himself. God's reply conveys both the pantheistic concept of an omnipresent divinity and the idealist denial of concrete reality. "Neither am I one self; I dreamed the world as you dreamed your work, my Shakespeare, and among the shapes of my dream are you, who, like me, are many persons—and none."

In his "Note on Walt Whitman," Borges imagines that Whitman suffers a fate similar to that of Shakespeare when he publishes his famous collection of poems, *Leaves of Grass.* Projecting an image of the ideal, convivial democrat, Whitman attempts to identify himself with all men and, in this way, to establish a personal relationship with each of his readers. As a result he has become, in Borges's words, "the eternal Whitman, the friend who is an old American poet of the eighteen hundreds and also his legend and also each one of us and also happiness."

An ambiguous mélange of pantheism, idealism, and existentialism comprise "Paradiso, XXI, 108" (DT), a poetic parable expressing Borges's awe at the mysterious universe. The theme is man's search for God, whose image has become fragmented and lost, like "an image in a kaleidoscope," down through the ages. Borges imagines that since every saint in history saw the features of God in a different light, God may still exist today in the most unexpected places under a variety of guises: the profile of a Jew in a subway; the hands that give us our change at a ticket window; the figure glimpsed in the depths of a mirror. Or perhaps God's face was erased in death so that he could become all of us. A final conjecture is that God may appear tonight "in the labyrinth of dreams" only to be forgotten tomorrow. This suggestion of a ubiquitous deity evokes the principles of pantheism. The tone of uncertainty, however, would seem to link Borges to Pascal, although the former characteristically exudes poetic ambiguity and the latter, metaphysical anguish.

Several stories discussed in sections 2 and 3 reveal elements of pantheism. These include "The Library of Babel," in which it is believed that there must exist a book comprising the perfect compendium of all the others; "The Zahir" and "The Aleph," in which the vast spatial universe is reduced to small spherical objects; "The Book of Sand," in which infinite time becomes a metaphoric moment in the form of a mysterious book; and "Tlön, Uqbar, Orbis Tertius," in which the idealists of Tlön eventually accept the concepts of one indivisible Individual being every separate individual in the universe, all books being the work of one timeless and anonymous writer, and all works of fiction being permutations of the same plot.

The Immortal   (1947) (L)

"The Immortal" is one of Borges's most complex and most fascinating tales. Like so many others, it is very difficult to classify, its treatment of elements such as time and esthetics being of considerable importance. Nevertheless, it seems to me that the pantheistic notion of one man representing all men, or more specifically, one author representing all authors, is predominant.

"The Immortal" takes the form of a manuscript found in a copy of Alexander Pope's translation of the *Iliad,* which in 1929 was sold by an antique dealer, Joseph Cartaphilus, to the Princess of Lucinge. According to her, Cartaphilus was a "wasted and earthen man" who "could express himself with fluency and ignorance in several languages." He died a short time after she made the purchase.

The narrator of the manuscript is Marcus Flaminius Rufus, a Roman tribune with Caesar's army in Egypt. Learning of a secret river whose waters grant immortality and on whose banks is located the fabulous City of the Immortals, Rufus sets out with several hundred soldiers in search of the river. They travel through strange, barbaric lands until Rufus, suspecting a mutiny among his disgruntled troops, flees into the desert. After many days of wandering, he loses consciousness and when he awakens, finds himself a prisoner of the troglodytes, a tribe of cave dwellers incapable of speech. These primitives live along the banks of a stream, on the other side of which rises the City of the Immortals.

Rufus manages to break his bindings and sets out for the walled city. Unable to locate a door, he enters a cave below the walls and then a dark, circular chamber with nine doors, one of which opens into a labyrinth leading upward to the "resplendent City." He exits into the courtyard of an ancient, chaotically structured palace which, he is convinced, must have been built by mad gods. Increasingly confused and frightened, he flees the City of the Immortals and returns to the troglodytes.

Rufus attempts to teach rudimentary verbal communication to one of the cave dwellers, whom he calls Argos because of his resemblance to Ulysses' dog by that name. His efforts are fruitless, however, until a heavy rain enlivens the troglodytes and somehow makes Argos more communicative. When Rufus asks him what he knows about *The Odyssey,* he receives the unexpected reply, "Very little. . . . It must be a thousand and one hundred years since I invented it."

That day Argos, whom we now know as Homer, answers many of the narrator's questions about the strange region in which he finds himself. The stream is the river of immortality, the troglodytes are the Immortals, and the original City of the Immortals was razed approximately nine hundred years previously. In its place the troglodytes built the chaotic city Rufus visited, a kind of burlesque monument to the "irrational gods who govern the world and of whom we know nothing, save that they do not resemble man." Since the city was leveled, the Immortals have lived as cave dwellers, dedicating their lives to "pure speculation" and ignoring the physical world around them.

Rufus then explains how "divine, terrible and incomprehensible" it is to know that one is immortal. The troglodytes, for example, as a result of their immortality, have become tolerant of, and indifferent to, almost everything. They have come to believe that since everything must eventually happen to all men, opposites such as good and evil will correct each other, making moral and intellectual values meaningless. Thus, in their eyes a single immortal man is all men: god, hero, philosopher, demon, the world. And in view of each person's multiple identities, they conclude that no one is anyone.

Rufus's identity soon fuses with that of Homer, making him one of the Immortals. Immortality causes him to realize that the prospect of death renders men "precious and pathetic" because they are constantly "on the verge of dissolving like a face in a dream." Furthermore, whereas for mortals everything has the "value of the irretrievable," the Immortals view each act as the echo of others that preceded it in the past or that will recur in the future. Eventually the Immortals reason that a river granting immortality must have its counterpart in one granting mortality. They propose to discover that river.

Meanwhile, the narrator reveals that he fought at Stamford Bridge in 1066, transcribed the adventures of Sinbad in some forgotten tongue in the seventh century of the Hegira,* professed the science of astrology in Bikaner, and in 1714 purchased the six volumes of Pope's *Iliad*, which he read "with delight." The story told in the manuscript comes to an end when the narrator, sailing for Bombay on the *Patna*, disembarked on the Eritrean coast and drank from a stream that made him mortal once again.

Like "Ibn Hakkan al-Bokhari, Dead in His Labyrinth" and "The Circular Ruins," "The Immortal" can be interpreted as an allegory of the creative process. Clues to the story's literary subject matter are provided at the close of the manuscript when the author (Cartaphilus) injects his critical commentaries on his work. What he has written, he states, lacks verisimilitude because he has had Rufus, the Roman, utter phrases in Greek that are known to have been said by Homer. Still, he does believe that esthetically the two protagonists, Rufus the warrior and

* The Hegira was the flight of Muhammad from Mecca to Medina in 622. In 639 it was decreed that the Muslim calendar would date from this event.

Homer the poet, complement each other. The reference to Bikaner, he concedes, "was fabricated by a man of letters, desirous . . . of exhibiting splendid words."

Cartaphilus represents Borges's persona and, perhaps, his double, for like Borges, he is interested in antiquities and can "express himself with fluency and ignorance in several languages." (Borges, a polyglot, enjoys poking fun at himself, his "ignorance" being of a metaphysical nature.) We know that the narrator of the manuscript read the *Iliad* "with delight," and, given Cartaphilus's professional interests, we might conjecture that for Borges, his narration is a metaphoric return to the embryo of world literature for the purpose of creating his *ficción*.

Marcus Flaminius Rufus is a man of action whose quest for eternal life frames the plot, but on a symbolic level he represents Cartaphilus's (Borges's) quest for literary immortality, which he will achieve through his identification with the immortal Homer. The process of this fusion of identities constitutes a crucial portion of the story. The chamber with nine doors that Rufus enters just prior to his arrival in the city represents the womb from which he will emerge as a would-be man of letters, the nine doors symbolizing the nine-month gestation period. The "mad" City of the Immortals evokes a vision of the chaotic world he wishes to organize and depict. The reason for his initial failure becomes evident when, immediately after fleeing the city, he attempts to communicate with Argos and discovers the defects of language and thought (note the ironic use of anaphora in the following quotation), his only tools for creating his work of art. As he explains, "I thought that Argos and I participated in different universes; I thought that our perceptions were the same, but that he combined them in another way and made other objects of them; I thought that perhaps there were no objects for him, only a vertiginous and continuous play of extremely brief impressions. I thought of a world without memory, without time; I considered the possibility of a language without nouns, a language of impersonal verbs or indeclinable epithets."

The long-awaited rain that facilitates communication between Rufus and Argos (Homer) symbolizes inspiration and perhaps intuition, elements far more useful to the creative artist than thought. Through inspiration, then, Rufus assumes the identity of Homer and, as one of the Immortals, reveals to the reader the "laws" of this strange realm. His assertions that "a single immortal is all men" and "no one is anyone" suggest the story's pantheistic theme, elucidated by the plot, that one author is all authors. The Immortals' concept of time as a series of recurring events is expressed metaphorically when the narrator reappears under new identities but in archetypal situations similar to those of either Rufus or Homer. Thus he relives Rufus's military career when he fights at Stamford Bridge in 1066 and becomes Homer again when he transcribes the adventures of Sinbad and rediscovers the *Iliad*. The last of the narrator's identities, which, we suspect, represents Cartaphilus himself, is that of a traveler on his way to Bombay in 1921, when he regains mortality. Eight years later Cartaphilus dies. The final words of his manuscript, written shortly before his death, convey the temporal anguish of an author who knows he has achieved immortality in his writings but, nevertheless, faces the disintegration of his mortal self: "When the end draws near, there no longer remain any remembered images; only words remain. . . . I have been Homer; shortly, I shall be No One, like Ulysses; shortly, I shall be all men; I shall be dead."

In the postscript, the literary nature of the subject matter is alluded to once again when the original author-narrator playfully suggests that the entire manuscript is a kind of cento,* consisting of passages plagiarized from Pliny, Descartes, Thomas De Quincey, and G. B. Shaw.

---

* A cento is a literary composition consisting of a patchwork of passages from writings of well-known authors.

He might have added the name of Joseph Conrad, who is also represented by the allusion to the *Patna,* the ship on which Lord Jim sailed. All this reminds the reader of Borges's well-known statement that originality in fiction is no longer possible, that men of letters have already expressed everything there is to say, and consequently, that literature has become a mere reworking of previous literatures. This tale of a man of action in search of immortality, then, is an ironic metaphor of a writer seeking immortality through plagiarism. His pantheistic union with the immortal Homer, a kind of literary divinity reminiscent of Shakespeare,[1] illuminates both the philosophical and literary aspects of the story.[2]

The God's Script   (1949) (L)

Another of Borges's compelling masterpieces is "The God's Script," a tale that also lends itself to multiple interpretations. Tzinacán, the first-person narrator, is an Aztec priest of the pyramid of Qaholom who was imprisoned by the Spanish conquerors many years ago when he was a young man. Now he awaits death in a circular dungeon, the other cell of which is occupied by a jaguar. He can view the jaguar only briefly each day when his jailer opens a trapdoor above in order to lower jugs of water and chunks of meat to them.

To occupy his mind, Tzinacán tries to remember everything he knew when he was a priest, including, for example, the order of stone-carved serpents on the pyramid. One night he recalls a myth of the god Qaholom who, on the first day of creation, is believed to have written a magical sentence to ward off the devastation and ruin that would threaten man at the end of time. According to the myth, a chosen individual would someday be granted the privilege of intuiting the magic script of Qaholom. Tzinacán comes to believe that he is the chosen one.

The thought that any form on earth could represent the symbol he seeks and that perhaps he has seen it many times fills Tzinacán with a kind of vertigo. He knows it must be something invulnerable, more invulnerable even than a mountain or a star. At last he recalls that the jaguar is one of the attributes of the god,[3] which convinces him that the god's script must have been written on the skin of the entire species from the beginning of time. Thus he devotes years to learning the order and configuration of the spots on the jaguar in the adjacent cell. The task of deciphering the text, however, is extremely difficult. Tzinacán cannot imagine what kind of sentence the absolute mind of a god would write when even in man's language "there is no proposition that does not imply the entire universe." For example, to say "the tiger" is to say "the tigers that begot it, the deer and the turtles devoured by it, the grass on which the deer fed, the earth that was mother to the grass, the heaven that gave birth to the earth." Therefore, he believes that in the language of a god every word would enunciate explicitly and instantaneously the "absolute fullness" of the universe.

One night Tzinacán dreams there is a grain of sand on the floor of his cell. He sleeps again and awakens to find a second grain of sand. This same dream continues until sand fills his cell and threatens to suffocate him. Then he hears a voice telling him that he has not awakened to wakefulness but to a previous dream which is enclosed within another dream, to infinity.

When he awakens from this labyrinthine nightmare, Tzinacán returns to his harsh prison cell, viewing it now as his beloved abode. Then occurs the union with the divinity, namely, his vision of a magic wheel, which seems to occupy all space. Tzinacán discovers himself as one of the fibers of the wheel's fabric, but even more important, he now understands the secret scheme of the universe as well as the script on the tiger. The latter is a formula of fourteen "random words," which, if uttered in a loud voice, would suffice to make him free, immortal, and omnipotent. Tzinacán will never pronounce these words, however, because, as he reveals, "I no longer remember

Tzinacán." And, he concludes, "whoever has beheld the fiery designs of the universe, cannot think in terms of one man, of that man's trivial fortunes or misfortunes, though he be that very man. That man *has been he* and now matters no more to him . . . if he, now, is no one."

"The God's Script" depicts a dreamlike world full of striking contrasts (darkness-light, human-divine, concrete-abstract) and symbolic motifs (circular structures, the jaguar, the grains of sand) that convey Borges's wonder in the face of the vast unknown. This enigmatic tale could represent a version of the quest for knowledge of the self. Considered within this frame of reference, it dramatizes the archetypal descent into a labyrinthine underground region, the initiation process by which humility and grace are achieved, and the final vision of truth and rebirth. The story might also be interpreted as the search for artistic perfection, that is, the author's desire to establish the ideal communication with his readers. And to attain this impossible goal, he must become united with God, a metaphor of his muse.

It seems to me that the most plausible way to read "The God's Script" is as a poetic expression of reasoning man's obsessive efforts to decipher the universe and achieve divine omnipotence. Tzinacán first attempts to recall the designs on the pyramid and then initiates his search for the god's script, a symbol of supreme knowledge and power. His nightmare is a terrifying experience for it transforms him into a phantom by thrusting him into the limbo of infinity represented by the countless grains of sand and his infinitely recurring dream. Thus, upon awakening, he is blissfully content to resume his human condition, even under the wretched conditions of his confinement. When he envisions the magic wheel and sees himself as "one of the fibers of that total fabric," he has achieved an intimate understanding of both the limitless universe and his own insignificant role in its vast scheme. This extraordinary enlightenment, then, enables him to decipher the god's script and effects his pantheistic union with the deity.

According to some critics, Borges implies that man must come to know himself and accept his human condition before he can achieve a union with God. Others have stated that Tzinacán's decision not to pronounce the fourteen words of the god's script indicates his awareness of his human condition and his responsibility to fulfill his human destiny. In my opinion, Borges is not conveying a message but merely giving free rein to his penchant for speculation, in this case about what would happen if man ever attained divine omniscience and omnipotence. The answer is that he would lose his individual identity, which would become fused with that of God and the universe, and that the fabulous revelation of the divine mind would make him forget the trivial fortunes and misfortunes of any one human being. Thus Tzinacán, who has become nobody, will not seek to realize his worldly ambitions of freedom, revenge, and immortality.

"The God's Script" imaginatively dramatizes the absorption of the individual personality by the mysterious, awe-inspiring universe. Its magical elements include the phantasmagorical image of the wheel, which like "The Aleph" represents an idealist vision of the world, and the fourteen-word god's script, which evokes the cabalistic Tetragrammaton of "Death and the Compass." Pantheistic philosophy underlies its plot and, in addition, enhances its esthetic impact by jolting the reader into new areas of awareness.

The End (1956) (F)

The loss-of-identity theme also emerges from "The End," Borges's imaginary conclusion to José Hernández's famous nineteenth-century gaucho epic, *Martín Fierro*. Toward the end of the poem, Martín Fierro encounters a black, whose brother he has killed in a brawl. Instead of

fighting, however, the two men match wits in a spon-
taneous singing bout, a gaucho custom known as the
payada.

The action of Borges's story takes place in the same
rural bar where Martín Fierro and the black first met.
Although the events are told by a third-person narrator,
they are reflected by the consciousness of the bar owner, a
man named Recabarren who, paralyzed from a stroke,
sees the action and hears the dialogue from his cot in the
next room. The black has been in the bar for several days,
having been defeated in a *payada* and having stayed to
wait for Martín Fierro. While listening to the "meager
labyrinth" of the black's guitar, "infinitely winding and
unwinding," Recabarren catches sight of a stranger on
horseback approaching his establishment. He then hears
the conversation of the two men, which gradually reveals
that the black has waited seven years since the first
encounter in order to avenge his brother's murder. As the
rivals go out on the plain, they once again enter the field of
vision of Recabarren, who witnesses "the end" of Martín
Fierro, i.e., his death in a knife duel. Ultimately the reader
learns that the black, once having accomplished "his
righteous task," "was nobody," or "more accurately, he
became the stranger: he had no further mission on earth,
but he had killed a man."

"The End" is an excellent example of Borges's ability
to create fiction from fiction, his story alluding not only to
the Argentine epic but possibly as well to *Beowulf,* the
English medieval epic. (Like Borges's Martín Fierro,
Beowulf dies from wounds received in a duel fought years
after a decisive encounter.) The reader is unaware of the
stranger's identity until the final lines, which state that
"for the first time in the dialogue, Martín Fierro heard the
sound of hate." For those familiar with *Martín Fierro,*
this revelation also explains several remarks made by the
two antagonists just before the fateful duel.

The technique of filtering the events through the mind of the prostrate, paralyzed Recabarren tends to fragment the action and dialogue, contributing to the dream-like quality of the story. This impression of a dream is enhanced, moreover, by the following description of the typical Borgesian "vertiginous moment" that portends the dramatic climax: "There is an hour of the afternoon when the plain is on the verge of saying something. It never says it, or perhaps it says it infinitely, or perhaps we do not understand it, or we understand it and it is as untranslatable as music."

Perhaps a more important aspect of this narrative point of view, however, is Recabarren's possible identity with Borges, i.e., the detached creator of fiction. (In this connection Recabarren's paralysis could represent a metaphor of Borges's above-mentioned fascination with knife fights as well as his inability to be a man of action.) The *payada* prior to Martín Fierro's arrival, then, might be read as Borges's evocation of the *payada* that ended José Hernández's poem. The infinitely winding labyrinth of the black's guitar anticipates the eternal labyrinth of fiction in which Martín Fierro, an avatar of Beowulf, will find himself trapped. And the loss of the black's identity at the end of the story could represent Borges's state of mind after having "killed" the famous gaucho hero and brought an end to the dramatic tension of Hernández's masterpiece.

The black's identity and subsequent transformation into Martín Fierro also reflects the story's underlying pantheistic philosophy. Accordingly, as Borges himself has pointed out, if one man is all men, when he kills another, he kills himself as well. We might reason then, that like the black, the hypothetical killer becomes nobody, or perhaps he becomes his victim, who is also nobody. We might reason, in addition, that Martín Fierro's death represents, pantheistically, the destiny of the two pro-

tagonists compressed into a single moment. These
pantheistic themes serve a purpose in Borges's writings
similar to that of idealism, i.e., the disintegration of objective reality and the creation of a poetic, hallucinatory
vision of the world. The fact that he utilizes fiction as well
as metaphysics to accomplish his goal makes "The End"
one of his most memorable works.

The Duel   (1970) (DBR)

Though very different in tone and setting, "The
Duel" bears a certain thematic resemblance to "The
End." The protagonists are two Argentine society ladies,
Clara Glencairn de Figueroa and Marta Pizarro, both of
whom dabble in painting out of boredom and a vague
sense of dissatisfaction with their lives. Although they
remain genuinely fond of each other, they become secret
rivals, each being the other's judge and only public.
Indeed, the relationship imposed on them by painting
gradually comes to dominate their lives. The narrator is
even convinced that he can see a mutual influence in their
works. "Clara's sunset glows found their way into Marta
Pizarro's patios, and Marta's fondness for straight lines
simplified the ornateness of Clara's final stage." When
Clara dies, Marta realizes that her life lacks meaning. She
hangs "a sober portrait" of Clara in the National Gallery
and never paints again. The narrator concludes that in this
"delicate duel, only suspected by a few close friends, there
were neither defeats nor victories nor even an open
encounter. . . . The story that made its way in darkness
ends in darkness."

Borges's tale is enriched by his ironic comments on
art critics and painters. For example, in defense of abstract
painting, a Dallas critic supposedly has written that this
school merely follows the biblical edict that man shall
make no images of living things. The iconoclasts, he

argues, are those who practice traditional painting, which was led astray by such heretics as Dürer and Rembrandt.

When Clara exhibits her abstract paintings, the moderns paradoxically condemn her "anomalous forms" because, though not representational, they do suggest "the tumult of a sunset, a tangled forest, or the sea," and do not limit themselves to "dots and stripes." Some time later Clara is awarded a prize only after the critics fail to choose between the two front-runners, one of whom has dedicated "solemn oils to the representation of awe-inspiring gauchos of a Scandinavian altitude"; the other has won both praise and indignation through "deliberate chaos." Clara is honored at a banquet attended by "a large number of society people, by almost all the members of the jury, and by two or three painters."

The analogies between "The End" and "The Duel" are evident. Like the black, who becomes nobody after the death of Martín Fierro, Marta has no purpose in life and so loses her sense of identity when Clara dies and the rivalry ends. Furthermore, the fusion of identities in "The End" is paralleled in "The Duel" by the narrator's discovery of mutual influences on the two women's paintings. Whereas the former tale is characterized by dramatic and fictive elements, the latter is ironic and more realistic. In both, however, the pantheistic dissolution of the personality emerges as the major ingredient.

The Form of the Sword   (1944) (F)

Although "The Form of the Sword" could also be classified as a dramatization of the theme of the double or the inverted mirror image, its overriding implications are, in my opinion, of a pantheistic nature. The story's original narrator, who is referred to as Borges, is obliged to spend a night on the ranch of a man known as the Englishman of La Colorada. The latter is by reputation an authoritarian, but scrupulously fair, landowner who has lived in Brazil.

He is also a heavy drinker, but his most distinctive trait is an arc-shaped scar running across his face from one temple to the other cheek. After several hours of drinking, the Englishman tells Borges that he is really Irish and then narrates the story of the terrible scar on his face.

His tale begins in 1922 when he was fighting with an army of Irish conspirators for independence from England. One evening his unit is joined by a disdainful young man named John Vincent Moon. Moon shows his cowardice when he and the narrator are ambushed by the enemy and Moon receives a superficial wound. The narrator saves Moon's life and takes him to a large country house of a certain General Berkeley. Each day the narrator joins his comrades in the campaign against the enemy, returning at dusk to find Moon, who is afraid to leave the premises, reading books on military strategy and arrogantly offering his advice on what ought to be done. One night when the narrator enters the house, he hears Moon telling the enemy on the phone how they might capture him (the narrator). Outraged, he chases Moon through the dark corridors of the house and, with one of the general's cutlasses, "sealed his face forever with a half-moon of blood." Having revealed with these words his true identity as Moon, the narrator confesses that he collected the "Judas-money" for informing on his benefactor and fled to Brazil.

The most striking element of "The Form of the Sword" is its surprise ending, which the author achieves by having his cowardly narrator don the mask of a brave man. However, this apparent fusion of opposites also serves to suggest the pantheistic theme that any man can be all men. The theme is reinforced and the ending foreshadowed by the following words of the narrator when Moon refuses to leave the general's house. "I blushed for this fearful man, as if I, and not Vincent Moon, were the coward. What one man does is something done, in some measure, by all men. For that reason a disobedience committed in a garden contaminates the human race; for that reason it is not unjust that the crucifixion of a single Jew suffices to save it. Perhaps Schopenhauer is right: I am all others, any man is all men, Shakespeare is in some way the wretched John Vincent Moon." The narrator also recalls that the nine days he and Moon spent together "form a single day." This compression of time, which parallels the fusion of antithetical identities, reinforces the story's theme of pantheistic unity.

Borges has stated that his reason for withholding Moon's true identity until the end of the story was to increase the element of pathos. Moon's final words addressed to the story's original narrator, "Despise me," would seem to serve a similar purpose. As several critics have observed, Moon's guilt complex evokes Joseph Conrad's *Lord Jim,* a favorite novel of Borges. This literary connection also evokes Borges's pantheistically related assertion that his stories are merely reworkings of books he has read and reread.

Biography of Tadeo Isidoro Cruz
(1829–1874)   (1949) (PA)

"Biography of Tadeo Isidoro Cruz (1829–1874)" dramatizes the pantheistic notion of an individual destiny reduced to a single moment in time. The protagonist, whom Argentine readers will recognize as a character in the gaucho epic poem *Martín Fierro,* is the illegitimate son of a soldier and a woman who spent a night together during a civil conflict. Cruz lives his entire life on the pampa, never knowing a mountain or a city. Once when another gaucho makes fun of him, he kills him and is forced to flee. He is captured by the police after a knife fight that lasts most of a night and, as punishment, is drafted into the army and sent off to serve on the frontier. Years later, the past rectified, he acquires a piece of land, settles down with a woman, and fathers a child. Having become a sergeant in the rural police, he thinks he is happy until, in 1870, he is ordered to capture an outlaw who has murdered a mulatto in a brothel. Cruz and his band of policemen surround the man at night in a field of tall grass, but the outlaw courageously defends himself, wounding or killing several of Cruz's men. Suddenly Cruz, feeling that he has lived this moment before, discovers his true identity and destiny mirrored in his adversary. As the dawn breaks over the plains, he throws off his kepi and begins to fight alongside the brave Martín Fierro against his own men.

The impact of this story derives from several factors. The name of Martín Fierro is not mentioned until the final sentence, when the reader familiar with the famous poem will recall in it a similar chain of events. Borges, however, has invented many details of Cruz's early life as well as the emphasis on the "luminous, fundamental night" when Cruz "saw his own face" in Martín Fierro and realized that "any destiny . . . in reality consists *of a single moment.*" At this moment Cruz also understands that his destiny is "that of wolf and not of gregarious dog" and that "the other man was himself." Thus he cries out that "he would not be party to the crime of killing a brave man" and at this moment seals his fate.

"Biography" reveals Borges's fascination with the concept of doubles and the cult of courage, subjects treated in subsequent sections, but his depiction of Cruz's moment of destiny illustrates his adroit use of philosophy to reinterpret other literary works and enhance dramatic effect.

As indicated above, Borges utilizes pantheism to nullify the unity of the individual personality and the traditional concepts of time and space, thus creating the impression of a world fraught with mystery and threatened with disintegration. This may strike the reader as paradoxical, given the fact that the pantheistic belief in the omnipresence of God should supposedly unify the vast universe and strengthen man's faith in an overall purpose.

Paradox, however, is a fundamental element of Borges's work.

5. THE TREATMENT OF TIME

Critics generally agree that time is a major theme in Borges's works. In his essays and fiction time and its many ramifications provide the subject matter for the expression of playful speculation, serious philosophical investigation, and profound ontological anguish. "Time and J. W. Dunne" (OI) presents a series of ideas from the books of the English philosopher John William Dunne, whom Borges finds more amusing than erudite. Dunne believes, on the basis of premonitory dreams, that the future already exists and that each individual must move toward it, but that this postulate suffices to convert time into space, thus making it multidimensional. He also believes that after death we shall enter eternity, from where we shall be able to arrange all the moments of our lives as we please. Skeptical but delighted, Borges is moved to exclaim, "With such a splendid thesis as that, any fallacy committed by the author becomes insignificant."

As indicated by "Circular Time" (HE), Borges is intrigued with the concept of the eternal return, i.e., the idea that time moves in a never-ending circle and that all events have occurred in the past and will recur in the future. In this essay he examines various facets of the subject, including those set forth by Plato, Nietzsche, and Hume, after which he indicates his personal preference for the idea of similar, rather than identical, temporal cycles. However, he demonstrates a special interest in the writings of Schopenhauer and the stoic Marcus Aurelius, both of whom see cyclical time as a negation of the past and future and the affirmation of a continuous present. In

"The Nightingale of Keats" (OI) Borges finds echoes of the eternal return in Keats's "Ode to a Nightingale," which contrasts the fugacity of human life (the poet's mortality and awareness of it) with the permanence of a bird's life (that of the species). Thus the imperishable nightingale emerges as a Platonic archetype "whose voice, now, is the same heard by Ruth the Moabite on the fields of Israel one ancient afternoon."

In "The Dream of Coleridge" (OI) and "The Enigma of Edward FitzGerald" (OI), both of which have strong overtones of pantheistic idealism, Borges's poetic speculations on reincarnation bear witness to his fascination with circular time. The first of these essays tells of the thirteenth-century Mongolian emperor, Kubla Khan, who dreams a palace and then builds it according to his dream. Five centuries later Samuel Taylor Coleridge, without knowing that the structure was derived from a dream, reads a description of the palace and dreams a poem about it. By way of explanation of this phenomenon, Borges theorizes that the emperor's soul penetrated Coleridge's, enabling the latter to rebuild the destroyed palace in words more lasting than stone. Similarly, in "The Enigma of Edward FitzGerald," the soul of the eleventh-century Persian poet Omar Khayyám is reincarnated in an Englishman eight hundred years later when Edward FitzGerald publishes his famous translation of the *Rubáiyát*. Often regarded as more English than Persian, this lengthy poem describes universal history as a spectacle that God conceives, represents, and contemplates, which causes Borges to speculate that "the Englishman could have recreated the Persian, because both were, essentially, God—or momentary faces of God."

One of Borges's oft-quoted vignettes, "The Plot" (DT), suggests cyclical time by connecting history and fiction with Argentine local color. The subject is Caesar's assassination by Brutus, which is revived in the works of Shakespeare and Quevedo, and the murder of an Argentine gaucho by his adopted son. As he expires, we are told, "he does not know he is dying so that a scene may be repeated."

Reincarnation in a more personal and contemporary setting is also examined in "Delila Elena San Marcos" (DT), in which Borges speculates on the implications of saying goodbye. One day he takes leave of a friend and shortly thereafter learns that she has died. This leads him to reason that if, as Plato suggests, the soul escapes from the body at death, one "should not make much of saying goodbye." Indeed, "to say goodbye . . . is to deny separation . . . because man somehow knows he is immortal." Thus, Borges predicts that at some time in the future he and his friend will resume their "uncertain dialogue."

The changes wrought by time constitute the theme of "Mutations" (DT) and "Dead Men's Dialogue" (DT), two pieces that also contain magic elements of idealism. In "Mutations" Borges probes the dramatic historic connotations of three objects: an arrow, evoking fierce battles; a lasso, the rapid movement of horsemen pursuing a bull across a prairie; and a runic cross,[1] the gallows where "a god suffered." With the passing of time, however, these three objects have been reduced to the status of mere symbols. Borges concludes that everything on earth eventually is either altered or erased, and "no one knows into what images he himself will be transmuted by the future."

"Dead Men's Dialogue" records an imaginary conversation between two of Argentina's most famous historical figures: José Manuel Rosas (1793–1877), the dictator who tyrannized Argentina from 1835 until 1852; and Juan Facundo Quiroga (1793–1835), a ruthless provincial governor who was assassinated, probably on the orders of Rosas.[2] The principal topic of the dialogue, which occurs immediately after the death of Rosas, concerns the legends the two men will become. Quiroga has already been immortalized by "a worthy citizen of San Juan,"[3] but he is convinced that both he and Rosas will be given "another face and another destiny." On the other hand, Rosas, whom Quiroga accuses of cowardice in 1852,[4] is satisfied to remain unchanged for posterity. To him, the entire dialogue seems like a dream dreamed by somebody other than himself. Borges appears to suggest that the so-called concrete realities of the past are phantoms constantly reevaluated by human imagination. The end result is the idealist concept of history as a purely mental and, according to Borges, fictional reality. This metamorphosis results in part from the corrosive influence of time.

The most comprehensive and profound statement by Borges on the subject of time appears in his famous essay entitled "New Refutation of Time" (OI), whose purpose, as the title suggests, is to deny that time exists. Basing his arguments on idealism, he first explains Berkeley's rejection of matter and space (objects exist only in the perceiving mind) and Hume's rejection of spirit (the mind is nothing more than a series of perceptions). He then quotes the two philosophers' definitions of time, Berkeley viewing it as a succession of ideas and Hume as a continuum of indivisible moments. Borges reasons that "having denied matter and spirit, which are continuities, and having denied space also, I do not know with what right we shall retain the continuity that is time. Outside of each perception (actual or conjectural) matter does not exist; outside of each mental state the spirit does not exist; nor will time exist outside of each present instant."

Borges reinforces his negation of time with the tale of a Chinese emperor, Chuang Tzu, who dreamed he was a butterfly. According to the idealists, who admit no other reality than that of the mental processes, there was a dreaming, a perceiving, but not a dreamer or even a dream. It follows, then, that since each psychic state consists of a momentary act of perception without a connecting circumstance or ego, we have no right to impose on it (the psychic state) a place or a time. Therefore, the chronological determination of any event would seem to be alien and exterior to the event.

Borges also reasons that the chance recurrence of identical moments suffices to nullify time, and by way of example, he relates a strange episode from his own life during the 1920s. One evening as he was walking through a lower-middle-class district of Buenos Aires he experienced the mysterious sensation of having been transported back to the nineteenth century. At the same time he felt dead and imagined that he was imbued with supreme metaphysical knowledge enabling him to understand the meaning of the "inconceivable word *eternity.*" As he continued to gaze at the street, he suddenly recognized that the scene he was witnessing was an exact repetition of the same scene on the same street many years before. Such recurring moments, he is convinced, not only disrupt time but also dissolve it and make it a delusion. The final lines of this essay, some of the most compelling Borges has written, reveal that his refutation of time is in reality a vain appeal to philosophical logic to suppress his temporal anguish. But, inevitably, the unreasonable universe reasserts itself, and he is forced to acknowledge the irreversible flow of time and thus his own mortality.

And yet, and yet—To deny temporal succession, to deny the ego, to deny the astronomical universe, are apparent desperations and secret assuagements. Our destiny (unlike the hell of Swedenborg and the hell of Tibetan mythology) is not horrible because of its unreality; it is horrible because it is irreversible and ironbound. Time is the substance I am made of. Time is a river that carries me away, but I am the river; it is a tiger that mangles me, but I am the tiger; it is a fire that consumes me, but I am the fire. The world, alas, is real; I, alas, am Borges.

Many of Borges's tales deal with time as an important, but secondary, theme and therefore have been treated under different thematic categories. Of the works discussed in previous sections, time is a central issue in the following: "The Library of Babel," in which the repetition of chaos becomes, ironically, evidence of temporal and spatial order; "The Secret Miracle," in which time is stopped for a year; "The Other Death," which involves the remaking of the past; "The Circular Ruins," "Theme of the Traitor and Hero," and "The Immortal," all of which evolve circular temporal structures; "The Aleph," which confronts the esthetic problem of depicting an instantaneous vision of the world through language, a lineal art form; "The God's Script," in which a magic wheel contains all time and space simultaneously; "The Book of Sand," which presents a metaphoric book of infinity; "Utopia of a Tired Man," in which Borges ironically contrasts the present with an imaginary future; and "Biography of Tadeo Isidoro Cruz (1829–1874)," which compresses an individual destiny into a single moment.

The Garden of the Forking Paths   (1941) (F) (L)

Although critical appraisals of "The Garden of the Forking Paths" vary considerably, it is one of Borges's most popular stories and, in my opinion, one of his masterpieces. Its themes include the absurd and the double or inverted mirror image, but the treatment of time dominates. The initial lines reveal that, according to a history of World War I, an offensive planned by the British in July 1916 was postponed for five days. A deposition signed by a certain Dr. Yu Tsun supposedly casts "unsuspected light" on this postponement. Yu Tsun, the narrator, formerly a teacher of English at the Tsingtao *Hochschule,* is in London in 1916 serving as a spy for the Germans. His most pressing duty is to inform them of the exact site of a new British artillery park before Captain Richard Madden, an Irishman working for British intelligence, can arrest him. Yu Tsun's hastily contrived plan leads him to a name in the telephone directory that will convey the information to the German chief of operations. He will take a train at once to the home of Dr. Stephen Albert, who lives in Ashgrove, a suburb of London. Just as the train is pulling out of the station, Madden appears in hot pursuit of Yu Tsun, but he is too late to board the train.

When Yu Tsun arrives in Ashgrove, some children indicate the way to Albert's house, telling him he should turn left at every crossroad. This reminds Yu Tsun that turning always to the left is also the common formula for reaching the center of a labyrinth. And he should know something about labyrinths because he is the great-grandson of Ts'ui Pên, once the Governor of Yunnan, who gave up political power to create a maze and write a novel. Thirteen years later he was murdered by a stranger, leaving a rough draft of his novel, titled *The Garden of the Forking Paths,* but his maze was never found.

As he walks through the countryside toward Albert's house, Yu Tsun senses an air of mystery caused in part by the sound of Chinese music. Upon reaching an iron gate, he is greeted by Albert, who invites him to visit "the garden of the forking paths." Yu Tsun recognizes the title of his great-grandfather's novel and informs Albert of his relationship to Ts'ui Pên. Albert then leads his guest along a zigzagging garden path to a summer house containing many Chinese books and art objects. Albert, it turns out, is a sinologist who has studied Ts'ui Pên's life and translated his chaotic novel into English. He informs Yu Tsun that his ancestor's book, which was written in a summer house located in an "intricate garden," is also the maze he intended to construct. The basis for this discovery is a letter left by Ts'ui Pên, the most important sentence of which is, "I leave to various future times, but not to all, my garden of the forking paths." This sentence suggests to Albert the bifurcation of time, not of space. Thus, he explains to Yu Tsun, the characters of the novel, instead of making one choice of several, at all junctures of the plot

choose all possible alternatives simultaneously, which in
turn constitute points of departure for other bifurcations
and their ramifications. He concludes that Ts'ui Pên's
novel is a parable on the subject of time. It is also, he
believes, "a picture, incomplete yet not false, of the
universe," for Ts'ui Pên does not see time as absolute or
uniform, but as an infinite series, an ever-spreading network of diverging, converging, and parallel times embracing "every possibility." This intricate temporal design
explains the many contradictions in Ts'ui Pên's novel. It
also induces Albert to remind Yu Tsun that, according to
Ts'ui Pên's concept of time, he (Albert) and Yu Tsun are
friends now, but in the future they may be enemies.

At this moment Yu Tsun senses a kind of invisible,
intangible pullulation around him and, looking down the
garden path, sees Captain Madden approaching. Yu Tsun
shoots Albert, is arrested by Madden, and is condemned to
death. Yet, the account of his crime in the newspapers
conveys to his chief in Berlin that Albert is the name of the
English city to be bombed. Yu Tsun's feeble voice has been
heard above the tumult of war, but he believes that he has
triumphed "abominably" for no one can know his
"infinite penitence and sickness of heart."

"The Garden of the Forking Paths" is a spoof of the
spy story just as "Death and the Compass" parodies the
murder mystery. Another aspect the two tales have in common is their presentation of doubles, Yu Tsun and
Lönnrot both meeting their inverted mirror images, Albert
and Scharlach, at the center of a labyrinth. Yu Tsun is a
Chinese in England and Albert an Englishman whose
home simulates a Chinese ambience; Yu Tsun is a spy
determined to commit acts of violence in England and
Albert a peaceful man, formerly a missionary in China;
and in their discussion of Ts'ui Pên's novel, Yu Tsun
emerges as the student who knows little about the subject
and Albert, as the professor and expert.

The garden of the forking paths is a metaphoric image of bifurcating time that provides both the form and content of the story. Yu Tsun's deposition, which comprises all but the first and last paragraphs, not only contains a discussion of Ts'ui Pên's novel but also reflects its labyrinthine plot and structure. Albert spends years in a summer house at the center of a labyrinth interpreting and translating Ts'ui Pên's novel, which was written in a similar setting over a long period of time. Both Albert and Ts'ui Pên are assassinated by strangers. And Yu Tsun's intricate maneuvers to impart information to the Germans might be seen as a metaphoric temporal labyrinth because the only plausible explanation for the series of absurd events in his deposition is that they are contained in Ts'ui Pên's *Garden of the Forking Paths,* which embraces "every possibility" and which has been left "to various future times." These absurdities include the following: Yu Tsun, a Chinese teacher of English in a German school, hates the Germans but nevertheless serves them as a spy in order to prove to his superior that "a yellow man could save his armies." He is being pursued by an Irishman in the service of England who cannot possibly know where Yu Tsun is going or what he intends to do. By pure coincidence, the name of the city to be bombed coincides with that of a sinologist and translator of a novel by Yu Tsun's ancestor. And at the end of the story, Yu Tsun triumphs "abominably" and feels "infinite penitence" for having killed a highly cultured man he admires in order to enhance the cause of the barbarous Germans.

Borges demonstrates that time has many threads, of which we discern only one. Moreover, if, as suggested in "Theme of the Traitor and Hero," history constitutes a web of preordained and cyclical circumstances determining each individual destiny, Yu Tsun and Albert might be viewed as mere puppets caught up in an absurd chain of events destined to recur. This postulated "order" in the repetition of disorder recalls the "elegant hope" expressed by the narrator in "The Library of Babel." It might also be designed to mock the reader who, in his search for a rational explanation of this absurd story, becomes a victim of irony.

"The Garden of the Forking Paths" is Borges's most intriguing fictional expression of complex existential time. The denouement, however, like the river, the tiger, and the fire in "New Refutation of Time," indicates that in the end, at the center of the labyrinth, inexorable lineal time prevails.

The Man on the Threshold   (1952) (A)

In "The Man on the Threshold" Borges attempts to bring time to a halt through the repetition of dramatic events. The story is told by Christopher Dewey, a British counsel in Buenos Aires who worked as an official in India between the two World Wars. During his tour of duty there was a series of disturbances in a Muslim city, prompting the English government to appoint a brutal army officer named Glencairn as judge in charge of the city. The disturbances ceased because of the fear Glencairn inspired, but soon thereafter he disappeared. Dewey was sent to investigate the disappearance.

From the beginning Dewey senses the "invisible presence of a conspiracy" among the people to keep Glencairn's fate hidden. One day he receives an envelope with an address, which turns out to be a house with a series of inner courtyards where some sort of ceremony is taking place. In front of the house is an extremely old man whom Dewey asks about the missing judge. The old man answers evasively that many years ago the British government had sent out a judge to restore order to the divided city but hopes for improvement were in vain because the judge showed himself to be wicked. For this reason he was kidnapped and tried by a group of conspirators. (As the old man speaks, he is constantly interrupted by people entering the house to attend the ceremony.) Because the conspirators were unable to find an upright man to judge the official, someone hit upon the idea of engaging a madman as judge so that God's wisdom would speak through his mouth and shame human pride.

At this point in the old man's story large numbers of people begin to leave the ceremony, and a passerby shouts something to him. He then turns to Dewey and joyfully informs him that the defendant had received the death sentence and died bravely. When Dewey asks him where the trial took place, he is told, "in a house like any other, like this one. One house differs little from another." Dewey then forces his way through the exiting crowd to the inner courtyard where he discovers a naked man, crowned with yellow flowers, holding a bloody sword in his hand. Glencairn's mutilated body is found in a stable behind the house.

The grotesque image of the mad judge-executioner at the center of the labyrinthine house is crucial to the denouement for esthetic and philosophical reasons. It creates the surprise ending by bringing the stories of both Dewey and the old man to a dramatic, simultaneous climax. In addition, by making the two stories one, it implies that the repetition of identical moments in time and place suffices to nullify temporal progression and produce an eternal, timeless present. Thematically, "The Man on the Threshold" is Borges's fictional expression of an episode in his essay, "New Refutation of Time," in which two identical moments many years apart reveal the meaning of the word *eternity*. The story differs from the essay, however, in its suggestion of the absurd, i.e., that the characters are archetypal figures in a drama whose ending has already been written. In its fusion of two plot threads at the center of a labyrinth, "The Man on the

Threshold" resembles "The Garden of the Forking Paths," but the latter's treatment of time is more complex and its plot more compelling.

The Gospel According to Mark   (1970) (DBR)

"The Gospel According to Mark" is one of Borges's few stories based on biblical myth. The action occurs in 1928 on a ranch where Baltasar Espinosa, a kindly, thirty-three-year-old medical student is spending the summer vacation. While his cousin, the owner of the ranch, is in Buenos Aires on business, a severe rainstorm causes a flood, isolating Espinosa, the foreman Gutre, and Gutre's son and daughter. Espinosa finds an English Bible in the house containing a family chronicle of the Gutres (originally Guthries), which reveals that they are a mixture of Scottish and Indian blood, their Scottish ancestors having arrived in Argentina early in the nineteenth century. The chronicle ceased in the 1870s when the Gutres no longer knew how to write. The foreman and his children are illiterate, know no English, can barely speak Spanish, and have no religious faith. We are told, however, that the rigid fanaticism of the Calvinist and the superstitions of the pampa Indian survive in their blood.

Because of a leak in the roof of their house, the Gutres move into the main house with Espinosa for the duration of the storm. Every night after dinner Espinosa, who is an eloquent speaker, reads to them a portion of the Gospel according to St. Mark, a story that holds mysterious fascination for them. When he finishes reading it the first time, they ask him to repeat it so that they can understand it better. It occurs to Espinosa that through the ages men have always told and retold two stories: "that of a lost ship which searches the Mediterranean seas for a dearly loved island, and that of a god who is crucified on

Golgotha." The respect and affection Espinosa has earned from the Gutres is enhanced when he cures a pet lamb injured on a strand of barbed wire.

One night Espinosa dreams of the Flood and imagines he hears the hammer blows of carpenters building the Ark. Upon awakening, he learns that the rain has damaged the roof of the toolshed, which the Gutres supposedly set about to repair. The next day Gutre asks Espinosa if Christ allowed himself to be crucified for the sake of all men and, though a freethinker, Espinosa feels obliged to answer in the affirmative. That afternoon, while taking a nap, Espinosa again imagines he hears a persistent hammering. When he gets up, the Gutres ask for his blessing, then spit at him and push him toward the back part of the house. Through the open door to the toolshed, Espinosa can see that it is without a roof, because the Gutres have taken down the beams to make a cross.

"The Gospel According to Mark" presents a biblical theme transferred to a modern setting and imbued with irony. The thirty-three-year-old protagonist emerges as a Christ figure, the name *Baltasar* recalling one of the three Magi and *Espinosa* ("thorny" in Spanish) Christ's crown of thorns. The pet lamb Espinosa cures recalls the miracles Christ performed as well as the sacrificial lamb Espinosa will become. And Espinosa's dream of the Flood and the construction of the Ark foreshadow his act of redemption for the Gutres.

The allusions to the *Odyssey* and the Bible, the two stories men have always told and retold, have a direct bearing on the lives of the Gutres. Indeed, the history of the Gutres family represents a kind of odyssey, their having abandoned a civilized country for a remote, barbarous land where they lost their religion, forgot their native tongue, and regressed to ignorance and superstition. For them, ironically, the crucifixion represents a metaphoric return, a means of redemption and regeneration, for by sacrificing their redeemer they will assume his virtues.

Borges's reinterpretation of biblical myths suggests that although specific circumstances change, archetypal situations reflecting the essence of human behavior will be repeated ad infinitum. One is reminded of the author's essay "Circular Time" (HE), in which he expresses his preference for similar, rather than identical, temporal cycles. The evocative motifs and climactic ending of this tale, which might be described as a parable of persuasion, enhance its esthetic impact and illuminate its theme of the eternal return.

The Unworthy Friend   (1970) (DBR)

Another of Borges's works based on biblical myth, "The Unworthy Friend" is a reworking of Judas's betrayal of Christ. Santiago Fischbein, the protagonist, is a Jewish shopkeeper who recalls an incident from his youth. Raised in a low-class district of Buenos Aires, he felt himself sneered at, perhaps because of his Jewish ancestry and physical cowardice, and thus had little self-esteem. When he was fifteen years old, his hero was not San Martín, Argentina's liberator from the Spaniards, but rather a neighborhood hoodlum named Francisco Ferrari. The tough, handsome Ferrari for some inexplicable reason took a liking to Fischbein, making the timid youth a member of his gang. Once when Fischbein was asked if Ferrari was a friend of his, he said no, not wishing to brag. Soon thereafter, Ferrari planned a burglary of a textile mill and assigned Fischbein the job of lookout. Two days before the date set for the burglary, Fischbein informed the police of the plan. Then, following their advice, he went to the mill with the rest of the gang but did nothing to warn them when the police arrived. During the ensuing melee, Ferrari and one of his cohorts, though unarmed, were killed by the police "to settle an old score."

Fischbein was arrested along with the others and released within a few days.

In this tale Borges not only revises the biblical theme of betrayal but also examines the mysteries of friendship, which he believes can be just as complicated as love. Fischbein obviously represents a Judas figure. Moreover, his attitude toward Ferrari ("to me he was a god") and his perfidious actions cause Ferrari to emerge as a kind of subverted Christ figure, who is first denied (Fischbein refuses to admit they are friends), then sold out to the police, and finally sacrificed "to settle an old score."

One can only speculate on the reasons for Fischbein's treachery. A clue to the cause, however, would seem to lie in his lack of ego, which makes him feel unworthy of Ferrari's friendship and leads him to betray his "god" in order to punish himself for his cowardice and, like the Gutres in "The Gospel According to Mark," to appropriate the virtues of the sacrificial victim. Indeed, there are indications that he wants to be punished even before he commits his betrayal. For example, just before the burglary he asks Ferrari if he is sure that he can trust him (Fischbein). Similarly, when he informs the police of Ferrari's plan and they warn him to be careful because of what happens to "stoolies," Fischbein replies, "I wish they would lay their hands on me—maybe that's the best thing that could happen."

Borges's revision of the Judas episode, like his reworking of the crucifixion and the *Odyssey* in "The Gospel According to Mark," suggests that time moves in similar but not identical cycles. This, of course, is only one of his ways—perhaps the one he prefers—of treating the crucial metaphysical question of time. He has also depicted it as a chaotic labyrinth ("The Garden of the Forking Paths"); an eternal present ("The Man on the Threshold"); an instrument of change ("Mutations"); a phenomenon to be manipulated by the mind ("The Secret Miracle"); a human destiny compressed into a single instant ("The End"); a sequence of moments to be revised ("The Other Death"); a regressive, branching current ("An Examination of the Work of Herbert Quain")[5]; and an enemy he attempts to destroy before its emergence as a river that carries him away, a tiger that mangles him, and a fire that consumes him ("New Refutation of Time").[6]

6. THE DOUBLE AND THE MIRROR IMAGE

With the explosion of knowledge in the field of psychology during the present century, the mind in conflict with itself and individual identity crises have been the subjects of much fiction. Like many authors, Borges is fascinated with the concept of the double, which emerges as a major theme in his work. However, unlike those writers who stress the psychological motives of their divided protagonists and, seemingly, elicit Freudian or Jungian interpretations, Borges depicts psychic fragmentation primarily for esthetic effect and, on occasion, to convey irony or ontological anguish. Closely related to the double in his writings is the mirror image, which he often finds esthetically superior to material reality because it projects an illusory, dreamlike quality. And like the mirror, the dream in his stories reflects hallucinatory, protean visions destined to render the concrete abstract and the objective world of reason empty, ambiguous, or absurd.

Borges has, on several occasions, alluded to his fear of mirrors which, as he states in his parable "The Draped Mirrors" (DT), dates back to his childhood. "As a child, I felt before large mirrors that same horror of a spectral duplication or multiplication of reality. Their infallible and continuous functioning, their pursuit of my actions, their cosmic pantomime, were uncanny then, whenever it began to grow dark. One of my persistent prayers to God and my guardian angel was that I not dream about mirrors. I know I watched them with misgivings. Sometimes I feared they might begin to deviate from reality; other times I was afraid of seeing there my own face, disfigured by strange calamities."

His famous poem "Mirrors" (DT) likewise imparts his fear, the reason here being that they make the world incomprehensible and everything in it, including man, fictitious.

> I ask myself what whim of fate
> Made me so fearful of a glancing mirror.
>
> . . .
>
> I see them [mirrors] as infinite, elemental
> Executors of an ancient pact,
> To multiply the world like the act
> Of begetting. Sleepless. Bringing doom.
> They prolong this hollow, unstable world
> In their dizzying spider's-web;
>
> . . .
>
> God has created nighttime, which he arms
> With dreams, and mirrors, to make clear
> To man he is a reflection and a mere
> Vanity. Therefore these alarms.

In his parable "Everything and Nothing" (discussed in section 4), Borges describes Shakespeare's lack of identity as a man, which he hides by simulating other identities on the stage. In a somewhat similar vein, another of Borges's parables, "Borges and I," treats his own identity problem resulting from the predominance of his role as an author ("the other," his double) and his subordinate role as a man. ("I allow myself to live, so that Borges may contrive his literature and that literature justifies my existence.") However, what he writes belongs to the Spanish language and posterity, not to Borges the man, who is destined to disappear forever. Meanwhile, he is condemned to live on in "the other," even though he has spent his life trying to escape from him. For this reason, he states, "I passed from lower-middle-class myths to playing games with time and infinity [Borges abandoned poetry for the short story], but those games are Borges' [the other's] now, and I will have to conceive something else." And so Borges the man's life is a constant flight in which everything is lost to oblivion "or to the other one." His concluding sentence merely underscores his confusion. "I do not know which of us two is writing this page."

This beautifully written piece expresses the existential dilemma of the sensitive artist trapped in the inexorable flow of time; it also reveals the dichotomy that exists between the author and the man when the latter discovers he is nobody and searches vainly for the identity he has lost or, perhaps like Borges's Shakespeare, has never had. The explanation for Borges's problem may lie in his personal life, as some critics have maintained. It is also true, however, that the artist by nature tends to be a protean being whose instinctive, creative side may control his rational ego, leading him to identify more with his creations than with his true self. I am reminded of Borges's remark that during the days he spent writing his phantasmagorical tale "The Circular Ruins," he lived in a dream world, completely apart from reality.

Many of the stories discussed in previous sections contain various types of doubles or mirror reflections. The protagonist of "Biography of Tadeo Isidoro Cruz (1829–1874)" discovers his identity—and his destiny—during a fight with his mirror image, Martín Fierro. Similar, though not identical, doubles appear in "The Duel" and "The End of the Duel," the former depicting two women painters vying with one another for public recognition and the latter a race between two gaucho prisoners of war after they have had their throats slit. In both of these tales, the characters emerge as doubles because their identities depend solely on their personal rivalry.

Far more common in Borges's fiction are his inverted mirror images or opposites such as Lönnrot and

Scharlach, the all-too-human pursuer-detective and the pursued-criminal god figure in "Death and the Compass." Others in this category include the gauchos Otálora and Bandeira in "The Dead Man"; the two history professors in "Guayaquil"; the Babylonian and Arab kings in "The Two Kings and Their Two Labyrinths"; Dunraven and Unwin and Ibn Hakkan and Zaid in "Ibn Hakkan al-Bokhari, Dead in His Labyrinth"; Christ and Judas in "Three Versions of Judas"; and Yu Tsun and Albert in "The Garden of the Forking Paths." Antithetical alter egos are ingeniously fused into one individual in "Theme of the Traitor and Hero," in which Kilpatrick dies a hero after betraying his fellow conspirators, and "The Form of the Sword," in which the cowardly John Vincent Moon narrates his tale as if he were a courageous man.

Occasionally Borges's protagonists or narrators stand for doubles of himself, the best example being Averroes, the Arab Aristotelian scholar in "Averroes' Search," whose attempts to understand the meaning of comedy and tragedy parallel Borges's attempt to portray Averroes on the meager information available to him. Cartaphilus, the narrator of "The Immortal," also shares certain characteristics with Borges such as his interest in literature and ancient civilizations.

Borges has repeatedly stated that his fiction represents a reelaboration of other works, thus suggesting that, in a sense, his writings are mirror reflections of books he has read. For example, "The House of Asterion" is a reworking of the Minotaur myth; "The End" and "Biography of Tadeo Isidoro Cruz (1829–1874)" add imagined literary and philosophical elements to *Martín Fierro*; "Theme of the Traitor and Hero" bases much of its plot on plays by Shakespeare and the historic *Festspiele*; "The Immortal" utilizes the *Iliad* and Homer as key elements in its composition; "The Zahir" includes a tale based on the legend of the Nibelungs; and biblical myths are reinterpreted in "Three Versions of Judas," "The Unworthy Friend," and "The Gospel According to Mark."

Borges gives us mirror reflections of the world in a wide variety of forms, all distorted by human reason or imagination. These include "The Zahir," "The Aleph," and "The God's Script," describing circular microcosmic images; "The Library of Babel" and "The House of Asterion," in which man-made structures symbolize his view of the world; "The Babylon Lottery," "Funes, the Memorious," and "The Garden of the Forking Paths," which depict reality as pure chance or chaos; "Tlön, Uqbar, Orbis Tertius" and "Utopia of a Tired Man," idealized versions of the world; and "Dr. Brodie's Report," a veiled satire of present-day society.

In other tales structural patterns serve as reflecting mirrors to reinforce theme and enhance compositional unity and esthetic effect. One of the best examples of this technique is "The Man on the Threshold," in which two stories first seem to mirror each other and then, unexpectedly, become one. Other notable examples are "The Garden of the Forking Paths," whose plot repeats that of the novel by the same title; "The Secret Miracle," whose protagonist writes a play paralleling many of the events in the story; and "The Circular Ruins," "The Immortal," and "Ibn Hakkan al-Bokhari, Dead in His Labyrinth," three works that allegorically reproduce the creative process.

Occasionally dreams are utilized as mirror structures in order to undermine concrete reality and create the kind of fictive world Borges relishes. The best example of this technique is "The South," a masterpiece discussed in section 6. Others include "The Circular Ruins," in which the wizard dreamer discovers that he is the dream of another; "The Waiting," whose dreamlike atmosphere foreshadows the protagonist's murder; "The Other Death," which depicts a man who dreams his heroic death in order to nullify an act of cowardice; and "The End," an imagined account of how the fictional hero Martín Fierro might have dreamed his own death.

*The Approach
to Al-Mu'tasim*   (1936) (HE) (F) (A)

"The Approach to Al-Mu'tasim" is very significant
within the framework of Borges's *oeuvre* because it is the
first of his tales in which we encounter the curious blend of
ingredients so characteristic of his subsequent *ficciones*: the
pseudoerudition, the playful humor, the metaphysical symbolism, the exotic setting, and the fusion of fiction and
essay. The basic subject matter is a review of an apocryphal
novel (*The Approach to Al-Mu'tasim*) written by a
Bombay lawyer named Mir Bahadur Ali and published in
two editions (1932 and 1934). The second edition bears the
subtitle, *A Game with Shifting Mirrors*.

Bahadur was influenced by the detective novel as well
as by the twelfth-century mystic Persian poet, Farid ud-
din Attar; consequently, his book is a kind of mystery
story with an undercurrent of mysticism. The main
character is a Bombay law student and freethinker who
kills—or thinks he kills—a Hindu during a dispute
between religious factions. He flees from the city and jour-
neys throughout India, becoming involved with the most
evil people, but adjusting to their way of life. One day
while conversing with a despicable man he unexpectedly
perceives in him a sign of tenderness that seems to mitigate
the infamy around them. The student reasons that this
goodness, which could not originate with his interlocutor,
must be a reflection of a friend, or of a friend of a friend.
Thus, some place in the world there must exist a person
from whom this "clarity" emanates, who is this clarity.
The student resolves to dedicate his life to finding him.

The plot, then, consists of the search for a man, referred to as Al-Mu'tasim, through the reflections he has
left in others. As the student draws nearer to his goal, he
discovers that though "they are mere mirrors," those
closest to Al-Mu'tasim reveal a greater proportion of the
divine attributes of reason, imagination, and goodness.

Eventually the student, having returned to Bombay, finds himself in a gallery at the end of which a curtain screens a radiant light. He claps his hands and asks for Al-Mu'tasim. The novel concludes when, at the request of "a man's voice—the incredible voice of Al-Mu'tasim"—the student opens the curtain and enters.

The remainder of Borges's story consists of literary and philosophical comments on the novel in question. The 1932 edition, for which the narrator has expressed a preference, treats the characters as real people. The second edition, however, slips into allegory, Al-Mu'tasim emerging as a symbol of the divinity and the student's itinerary as the progress of the soul in its mystic ascent. It soon becomes evident that this second version of the novel is of greater significance to the overall meaning of Borges's story. Al-Mu'tasim assumes the guises of various divinities, all of which represent a "unitary God who accommodates Himself to human 'diversities.'" But the narrator prefers to conjecture that Al-Mu'tasim, like the student, is in search of Someone, and *that* Someone is in search of some superior Someone, and so on.

Borges concludes his story with several additional allusions to literary influences on Bahadur's novel. These include Kipling, the sixteenth-century cabalist Isaac Luria, and the previously mentioned Persian, Farid ud-din Attar. Attar's allegorical poem, "Colloquy of the Birds," which is discussed in a footnote, has a direct bearing on the story's meaning and structure. In this poem, the birds initiate a search for their king, the Simurg. They know that the king's name means "thirty birds," and they also know that his palace stands on a circular mountain surrounding the earth. Their task, however, becomes so arduous that eventually only thirty persevere; these, purified by their labors, are the ones that reach the mountain of the Simurg. As they contemplate it, they realize that they are the Simurg, and that the Simurg is each one of them and all of them.

"The Approach to Al-Mu'tasim" is obviously an allegory of life, the student-protagonist representing man, India the labyrinthine world, and the student's search for Al-Mu'tasim rational man's quest for truth or the missing God. The circular frame of the plot is reflected by structural and stylistic devices that also serve to reinforce the thematic content. For example, at the beginning of Bahadur's novel the student climbs to the top of a circular tower via a ladder with several missing rungs. The circular tower symbolizes the direction his search will take and the defective ladder the arduous nature of his task due to the missing link between man and God. (We recall that the student is a freethinker.) The reflections of goodness that guide the student to his goal reinforce the novel's structure, leading logically to the climactic conclusion that Al-Mu'tasim is the student's mirror image. This mirror structure is again suggested by the footnote on the "Colloquy of the Birds," the thirty birds and the Simurg corresponding to the student and Al-Mu'tasim. And the story's introduction and conclusion also reflect each other symmetrically through their allusions to literary influences on Bahadur: the detective novel and Farid ud-din Attar at the beginning and Kipling and the cabalist Isaac Luria at the end.

Borges has enriched the texture of his allegory with references to Gnosticism (the view of Al-Mu'tasim as a demiurge in search of a superior god) and to pantheism, which, through analogy with "Colloquy of the Birds," conveys the notion that each man is Al-Mu'tasim, and Al-Mu'tasim is each man and all men. These philosophical systems illustrate Borges's taste for playing with ideas, but they are injected only to heighten ambiguity and esthetic effect. The story's meaning, in my opinion, lies in its existential implications, namely, that truth lies within the individual. The tale's mirror structure, then, also conveys its absurdist theme: that rational man's search for the missing God inevitably takes him back to himself.

The Theologians   (1949) (L)

"The Theologians" is another of Borges's tales that defy thematic classification. It parodies theological systems, has strong overtones of pantheism, and depicts antithetical doubles. Aurelian and John of Pannonia are prominent theologians of ancient Rome whose duties include the refutation of heretical doctrines in order to preserve orthodoxy. When a heretical sect called the Monotones appears on the shores of the Danube professing the doctrine of circular time, horrified orthodox believers take heart upon learning that John of Pannonia will publish a treatise denouncing it. Aurelian is jealous of John of Pannonia's reputation and resolves to write his own refutation of the Monotones. The day after completing his treatise, he receives a copy of John of Pannonia's, which, he must admit, is brilliantly conceived. And as might be expected, John of Pannonia's work is used in Rome to impugn the errors of the Monotones and condemn one of their heresiarchs to the stake.

Aurelian continues his efforts to surpass John of Pannonia in a kind of invisible duel. Many years after the suppression of the Monotones, another heretical sect, known as the Histriones, appears in the eastern provinces. These people of wild customs believe in asceticism, self-mutilation, and purification through evil. More significant, however, is their rejection of circular time, which has become orthodox since the Monotones professed it. In preparing his denunciation of the Histriones, Aurelian refers to the heresy of lineal time in a sentence of twenty words coined by John of Pannonia years before when it was an orthodox doctrine. He adds to his treatise, "What the heresiarchs now bark in confusion of the faith was said in our realm by a most learned man, with more frivolity than guilt."

When Aurelian is obliged to reveal the source of his quotation, John of Pannonia is arrested, found guilty of heresy, and burned at the stake. Some years later Aurelian dies in a fire caused by lightning. In Paradise he learns that in God's mind, he and John of Pannonia (the orthodox believer and the heretic, the abhorrer and the abhorred, the accuser and the accused) form one single person.

"The Theologians," like "Three Versions of Judas," mocks theological reasoning by alluding to the absurd conflicting beliefs of various religious sects. The Histriones, for example, replace the image of the Lord with a mirror and, altering the cabalist idea that the higher world is a reflection of the lower, assert that the earth has influenced heaven. They also believe that every man is two men, the real one being the one in heaven, and that when we die we will join this other and assume his identity. Their belief in lineal time, moreover, convinces them that the world will come to an end when the finite number of possibilities is exhausted. Since there can be no repetition, they advocate that the righteous commit the most infamous acts so that these will not soil the future and will hasten the return of Christ.

The fact that the Monotones' heretical doctrine of circular time eventually becomes orthodox illustrates Borges's well-known dictum that all philosophical systems are "provisional," i.e., subject to change according to the whims of human reason. The ingeniously conceived absurdities comprising these systems also illustrate why Borges considers philosophy a branch of fantastic literature. Several clues in the story suggest that Aurelian and John of Pannonia are opposite facets of the same person. Their duel is said to be "invisible"; in the many volumes written by Aurelian the name of "the other" does not figure once; and only twenty words (those copied by Aurelian) of John of Pannonia's writings have survived. When John of Pannonia is burned at the stake, his face in the midst of the flames reminds Aurelian of someone (probably himself), but he cannot remember who. And the Histriones' belief that the "higher world is a reflection of the lower" could indicate that the two men's fusion of identities in heaven is a continuation of their life as doubles on earth.

"The Theologians" may be viewed as a literary game of constantly shifting, inverted mirror images: the accuser and the accused, orthodoxy and heresy, theology and fiction, reason and absurdity. At the end of the story, the magical fusion of opposites into a kind of pantheistic unity imparts an ironic view of man's search for absolutes and enhances the esthetic ambiguity Borges finds in mirror reflections.

Story of the Warrior and the Captive   (1949) (L)

"Story of the Warrior and the Captive" and "The Theologians" have much in common, both presenting inverted mirror images, which together form a single entity. However, "The Theologians" concentrates on character opposites, whereas "Story of the Warrior and the Captive" juxtaposes antithetical plots or destinies. This narrative was inspired by an allusion to a Lombard warrior named Droctulft in a book by Croce. When the Lombard barbarians of the north laid siege to the Roman city of Ravenna in the sixth century, Droctulft abandoned his companions and died defending the city they had attacked. After his death he was honored by the citizens of Ravenna.

The legend of Droctulft kindled Borges's memory of an anecdote told by his English grandmother who in 1872 was living in Junín, an outpost on the frontier where his grandfather, an Argentine army officer, was stationed. Borges's grandmother thought she was the only English woman in that remote region until somebody informed her of an "Indian" girl living nearby who was also of English origin. Some months later the blond, barefoot woman, dressed like an Indian, appeared in Junín, and Borges's grandmother arranged a meeting with her. It had been fifteen years since she had spoken English, but somehow she managed to convey that her family was from Yorkshire, that she had been kidnapped during an Indian raid, and that she was married to a chief. Although Borges's grandmother offered to help her return to civilization, she refused, saying that she was happy.

Borges concludes that thirteen hundred years and an ocean lie between the two antagonistic destinies: that of a barbarian who embraces civilization and that of a European woman who chooses a life among savages. He believes that both individuals were "swept away by a secret impulse . . . more profound than reason" and that their fates may comprise one single story because "the obverse and the reverse of this coin are, for God, the same."

These contrasting tales illuminate each other through the montage technique of juxtaposition and the inclusion of parallel details that reinforce the mirror structure. For example, Borges imagines Droctulft's feelings of awe upon arriving from the dark, barbaric north to an orderly, symmetrically designed city of stone buildings, gardens, and statues. Suddenly all this beauty moves him to renounce the pagan gods and marshes of his homeland. Borges's grandmother, on the other hand, recalls that some months after seeing the "Indian" girl for the first time, she was visiting a ranch where they had just butchered an animal, and "as if in a dream, the Indian woman passed by on horseback . . . threw herself to the ground and drank the warm blood." This metaphoric act signifies the woman's instinctive acceptance of barbarism. Each of the protagonists, moreover, is reflected in other destinies. Droctulft is the first of his fellow countrymen to become an enlightened, civilized Italian, and the Indian woman, Borges conjectures, is perhaps perceived by his grandmother as "a monstrous mirror of her own destiny," that of a woman "held captive and transformed by the implacable continent."

Since Borges was inspired by Croce to create this story, it, like so many of his writings, reflects literature rather than real life. Nevertheless, he has shed new light on an episode of Roman history by relating it to a comparatively recent occurrence of the Argentine past. For the reader the end result is an esthetic experience enriched by Borges's imaginative manipulation of the inverted mirror image.

Pierre Menard, Author
of Don Quijote   (1941) (F) (L)

"Pierre Menard, Author of *Don Quijote*" recalls "Averroes' Search," for the protagonists of both stories are in many respects Borges's doubles. Pierre Menard is an apocryphal French symbolist poet whose recent death has prompted the narrator, a friend of Menard, to publish an essay on his writings in order to correct some misconceptions. He first presents Menard's bibliography, which includes articles and books on a variety of esoteric subjects, some real and some invented. His most important work, "possibly the most significant of our time," consists of the ninth and thirty-eighth chapters of Part I of *Don Quijote* and a fragment of the twenty-second chapter (of which part we are not told).

According to the narrator, Menard's ambition was not to compose another *Don Quijote,* but rather *the Don Quijote.* He did not wish to copy *Don Quijote,* but to produce pages that would coincide, word for word and line for line, with those of Cervantes. His initial method was to attempt to become Cervantes by learning Spanish well, by fighting the Moors and the Turks, and by forgetting all history between 1602 and 1918. But he rejected this plan because it was too easy and because to approach *Don Quijote* through Cervantes seemed to him less arduous and less interesting than to approach the novel through the experiences of Pierre Menard. Cervantes's task, Menard reasoned, was less arduous than his because Cervantes wrote his book spontaneously. Menard, on the other hand, had the "mysterious duty" of reconstructing it literally. He also believed that writing *Don Quijote* at the beginning of the seventeenth century was a "reasonable undertaking," but in the twentieth century it is almost impossible because of the many changes during the intervening three hundred years.

According to the narrator, Menard's version of *Don Quijote* is more subtle than that of Cervantes, which "indulges in a rather coarse opposition between tales of knighthood and the meager, provincial reality of his country." Menard proscribes local color from his work; there are no gypsies, no conquistadors, no mystics, no autos-da-fé. Moreover, Cervantes's preference for arms to letters in Chapter 38 of Part I is attributed to his previous military career, whereas Menard's preference for arms may be due to one of three factors: the psychology of his hero, the influence of Nietzsche, or his sense of irony, which induces him to express the opposite of what he believes. Thus, the narrator contends that although the two versions of *Don Quijote* are identical, that of Menard is more ambiguous and, therefore, "infinitely richer."

Borges and Menard resemble each other in several important respects, causing the reader to suspect that in presenting his protagonist Borges is creating a self-portrait. Menard's bibliography reflects Borges's interests, which comprise such arcane subjects as the creation of a poetic language of concepts, ways to enrich the game of chess, and possible solutions to the paradox of Achilles and the tortoise. Menard's reworking of *Don Quijote* recalls Borges's well-known belief that a book is a manuscript undergoing infinite change because each reader gives it a different meaning and, in a sense, creates another book. For Borges, then, reading a book is the equivalent of rewriting it, which is precisely what Menard does. For this reason Menard's "originality" lies not in the creation of a new text, but in demonstrating how an old text can convey new meanings.

The passage the narrator chooses in order to prove this point is one dealing with history, which Cervantes eulogizes as the mother of truth. For a twentieth-century intellectual like Menard, however, historical truth is not necessarily what took place, but what we *think* took place. Another difference between Cervantes's *Don Quijote* and Menard's is the style of the two authors. Cervantes writes in a flowing language typical of his day, whereas Menard's style is archaic and, because he is a foreigner, "suffers from a certain affectation." Thus, in order to enrich the art of reading, Menard utilizes "deliberate anachronism" and "erroneous attributions," techniques that evoke those of Borges, who reworks old texts and injects new life into them. Menard's technique, the narrator concludes, would fill the dullest book with adventure, perhaps even a book as dull as *The Imitation of Christ* (a treatise on mysticism by Thomas à Kempis, 1379–1471).

Although "Pierre Menard, Author of *Don Quijote*" might be described as a poetics of reading, it can also be read as a parody on the creative process. Borges has repeatedly stated that literature in general, and his own works in particular, are mere reworkings of texts by other authors such as Chesterton, Stevenson, and Kipling. Thus Menard's absurd project of "rewriting" *Don Quijote* emerges as an ironically conceived method of literary composition, a method also utilized by Borges.

The Other (1975) (BOS)

One of Borges's most recent stories, "The Other" reinterprets three of his fundamental themes: the double, time, and the idealist tenet of life as a dream. Borges recalls an incident that occurred in 1969 when he was lecturing at Harvard University. One morning while he was seated on a bench next to the Charles River watching the ice floes "borne along on the gray water," he suddenly felt he had lived that moment before. A young man seated beside him began to whistle an Argentine song, leading to the revelation that he, too, was Borges, i.e., Borges's double of the year 1918, when he was living in Geneva. Borges tries to convince the youth that it is 1969 and that they are in Cambridge, but the youth implies that he is dreaming Borges. Borges then tells him what he can expect from the future, including facts about his family and world politics. A literary discussion ensues, during the course of which the differences between the two become increasingly apparent. Finally, seeking to prove to himself, as well as to his double, that he is not a dream, Borges shows him an American dollar bill dated 1964. The youth, for his part, has in his possession some Swiss francs. Before they say goodbye, Borges suggests they meet the following day, adding that if the supernatural occurs twice, it ceases to be terrifying. They both know, however, that they will not see each other again.

"The Other" is the first tale in which Borges's doubles meet face to face and confront the problem of their identities. It is also his first presentation of protagonists who have split as a result of the passing of time. Time as a thematic preoccupation emanates from Borges's allusion to historic events between 1918 and 1969—World War II, the Perón era in Argentina, and the Cold War—and from his literary discussion with his youthful counterpart. Thus when the young man reveals that he is writing a book of poems destined to unite the oppressed masses (Borges's early poetry had a similar goal), Borges replies that the masses are an abstraction, that only individuals exist. The topic of metaphors is another source of disagreement, "the other" insisting on the search for new metaphors and Borges relying on the revision of old ones. When the two cannot agree on an interpretation of a verse by Walt

Whitman, Borges realizes that "the man of yesterday is not the man of today," that the fifty years between them has made each one a "caricature copy" of the other.

Borges's double also represents a mirror image that, though unreal, casts doubt on the reality of Borges, making him fear that he, too, is an image or a dream in the mind of "the other." For this reason, when the youth implies that he is dreaming Borges, Borges reaffirms his identity by describing his life during the last fifty years. His ontological anguish recalls the denouement of "The Circular Ruins," when the terrified wizard discovers that, like the son he has dreamed, he, too, is a mere phantom.

The story's ending exudes ambiguity. Borges believes that the meeting was real, that he was awake and for this reason cannot forget it. Still, he states that his double was dreaming when he conversed with him, making Borges a dream of "the other." Perhaps the key to this paradox lies in Borges's words to his young counterpart at the beginning of the story: "If this morning and this meeting are dreams, each of us has to believe that he is the dreamer. . . . Our obvious duty . . . is to accept the dream just as we accept the world."

"The Other" dramatizes the disunity of the personality that has been split by the ravages of time and rendered unreal by the confusion between dream and dreamer. The mysterious episode narrated by Borges would seem to indicate his desire to deny the flow of time evoked by the river he is watching. The confrontation with his youthful double, nonetheless, makes him aware that although life is a dream, it is a dream that must come to an end.

Borges's treatment of the double and the mirror image encompasses a wide variety of examples ranging from the portrayal of alter egos to the utilization of plot and structural reflecting patterns. He uses these motifs primarily as devices to enhance the esthetic worth of his stories and to capture the wonders of a world he never expects to comprehend. His most poetic reference to the mirror image and its significance to the artist appears in the following lines of his "Epilogue" (DT): "A man sets himself the task of portraying the world. Through the years he peoples a space with images of provinces, kingdoms, mountains, bays, ships, islands, fishes, rooms, instruments, stars, horses, and people. Shortly before his death, he discovers that that patient labyrinth of lines traces the image of his face."

These words are provocatively ambiguous. A possible interpretation of them is that art is a process of self-discovery for the artist. Another is that art is a voyage of self-creation, a kind of initiation during which the man creates his identity as an artist. Or, and this is what I believe, these lines could represent a poetic repetition of what Borges has implied so many times elsewhere, that art is essentially an absurd activity because the artist, naively attempting to depict the world, merely creates a labyrinthine reflection of his own mind. Art, then, is a mirror image, or perhaps an idealized double, of the artist.[1]

7. THE MACHISMO CULT

Because of Borges's treatment of metaphysical themes and archetypal motifs, his works have frequently been viewed as more universal than Latin American or Argentine. His *ficciones* of the 1940s and 1950s are, indeed, far more universal in themes and literary techniques than the fiction published by most other Latin Americans of that period. Nevertheless, Borges's outlook on life makes him very much a part of his native land. As we have indicated previously, he is fascinated with the Argentine past, has written extensively on various aspects of Argentine culture, and his poems, stories, and essays are sprinkled with allusions to the Argentine setting. One of the themes in

Borges's writings that contributes to his identity as a Latin American is the machismo cult.* His attitude toward this psychological phenomenon is ambivalent, perhaps because of his family background and upbringing. It will be recalled that several of his ancestors were men of action, participating prominently in the Argentine civil wars of the nineteenth century, whereas his father was an intellectual who exercised much influence on his son. It will also be recalled that, because of Borges's frail health and poor eyesight, he was raised in a sheltered atmosphere, surrounded by books, and encouraged to follow intellectual pursuits. Thus at times he appears to be captivated by the vibrant display of courage, passion, and raw violence of the gaucho and the knife-wielding *compadrito* or city tough, his antithetical opposites, while at other times he parodies the treachery and hollow glory of the braggart and pseudohero.

Given his mild, intellectual nature, Borges's fascination with knives and brutality may seem paradoxical to his readers. Alicia Jurado, his friend and biographer, attributes this strange fascination to something irrational in his complex psychological makeup. She also recalls "the attraction Borges felt for a dagger . . . I had on my desk; he kept playing with it, unconsciously clutching it all the time he was dictating to me the gentle doctrine of Buddhist philosophy."[1]

Of the stories treated in the previous sections, the machismo cult is prominent in four: "The Other Death," whose protagonist spends much of his life attempting to relive heroically a moment of cowardice; "The Dead Man," in which a young *compadrito* of Buenos Aires becomes a gaucho and strives to replace the leader of his gang; "The End"; and "Biography of Tadeo Isidoro Cruz (1829–1874)." The last two are particularly significant

* Machismo is a characteristic often associated with the Latin American male (the macho). It manifests itself in an overt display of valor and masculinity.

because of their portraits of Martín Fierro, the fictitious gaucho embodying the mythical macho image in the mind of the Argentine. In "The End," the action is seen through the eyes of the paralyzed bar owner, "habituated to living in the present, like an animal." This static point of view, which is reinforced by the setting ("the plain seemed almost abstract, as if seen in a dream"), creates an aura of timeless myth. In contrast to the epic poem, which ends with Martín Fierro's refusal to fight the black because he (Fierro) has become "civilized," Borges imagines how the mythical macho ought to end his life—in a knife fight.

"Biography of Tadeo Isidoro Cruz (1829–1874)" also mythicizes the machismo cult by its portrait of a courageous man, whose life of violence in many respects parallels that of Martín Fierro. Tadeo Isidoro Cruz's father died with "his skull sliced open by a saber from the Peruvian and Brazilian wars." Cruz, we are told, lives his entire life in "a world of monotonous barbarity." Like Martín Fierro, he kills a man with a knife, fights bravely against a band of policemen, and is drafted into the army and obliged to serve on the frontier. The story's denouement, which is similar but more dramatic than the same occurrence in the poem, emphasizes the valor and independence of Martín Fierro.

The South   (1953) (F) (PA)

An undisputed masterpiece, "The South" synthesizes several major themes, including the double, time, and the fusion of reality and dream. But upon finishing this story, the reader is most likely to be impressed by its romantic idealization of the machismo cult, an impression produced by the plot, the protagonist, the structure, the symbolic motifs, and even the title.

Juan Dahlmann, the main character, is employed in a municipal library of Buenos Aires. His paternal

grandfather was a German clergyman who arrived in
Argentina in 1871; in contrast, his maternal grandfather
served in the Argentine army on the frontier, where he
died heroically fighting against the Indians. Dahlmann
prefers the romantic past of his military ancestor, relating
it in his mind with the gaucho epic *Martín Fierro*.
Perhaps for this reason he has managed to keep in his
possession a family ranch in the South, but the property
seems more dream than reality because he is seldom able
to go there.

One evening in 1939 Dahlmann is hurrying up a
poorly lighted staircase with a special edition of *The
Thousand and One Nights* when he strikes his head on an
open window. Because the window was recently painted,
he develops blood poisoning and, gravely ill, is taken to the
hospital where, in the operating room, a masked man
sticks a needle into his arm. After the operation Dahlmann
undergoes painful treatments that only make him more
aware of his wretched physical condition. One day his doctor dismisses him with the joyful news that he can go to
his ranch in the South to convalesce. The following morning he takes a carriage to the railroad station. Having time
to spare, he enters a nearby café, where he orders a cup of
coffee and caresses an enormous black cat. It occurs to him
that, unlike man who experiences lineal time, this
"magical animal" lives in an eternal present.

On the train Dahlmann glances at his copy of *The
Thousand and One Nights,* but he is so grateful to be alive
and so captivated by the countryside that he puts the book
aside to enjoy the scenery. The solitude of the plains suggests that he is traveling not only south, but also into the
past. As he draws near his destination the conductor
informs him that he will have to get off at an earlier stop.
Upon arriving at the unfamiliar station, he learns that he
can probably rent a carriage at a general store, the archi-
tecture of which reminds him of an engraving he has seen
in an edition of *Paul et Virginie* (a French romantic

novel). The shopkeeper, moreover, reminds him of a male nurse in the hospital.

Dahlmann orders a carriage and sits down at a table to take his evening meal. Three drunken ranch hands are seated nearby, and squatting next to the bar is an old man who seems "outside of time, situated in eternity." Dahlmann, noticing his quaint garb, reflects that gauchos like this one no longer exist outside the South. Suddenly a spitball of crumbs brushes against his face and lights on the table. He opens his copy of *The Thousand and One Nights* by way of suppressing this unpleasant reality, but a few moments later another ball of crumbs falls in front of him, and the three men at the other table laugh mockingly at him. Dahlmann gets up to leave, wishing to avoid a scene, but at this moment the storekeeper, calling him by name, advises him not to pay any attention to the "lads," who he says are "half high." Now that he is no longer an unknown face but a name, Dahlmann feels he must defend his honor and, pushing the storekeeper aside, confronts his mockers. One of the three, who looks Chinese, insults him in obscene language and then, flashing a long dagger, challenges him to a fight. The storekeeper hastily intervenes, pointing out that Dahlmann is unarmed, but at that moment the "old ecstatic gaucho" next to the bar throws him a dagger. Dahlmann picks it up "almost instinctively," realizing that this act will only justify his murder. Fearlessly he accompanies his adversary out onto the plain.

Borges has obviously projected many aspects of his own life into that of his protagonist, suggesting that they are doubles. Dahlmann's family background is similar to Borges's, although Borges has given his protagonist German, rather than English, blood; both men are librarians by profession; and both have similar accidents, followed by bouts with blood poisoning, at approximately the same time. The significance of doubles, however, does not lie in the similarities between Borges and Dahlmann but rather emerges from the story's plot and structure. "The South" can be divided into two parts, the first consisting of real events that come to an end, probably during Dahlmann's stay in the hospital, and the second constituting a dream. Thus Dahlmann the librarian-intellectual of the first part more than likely dies in the hospital, perhaps on the operating table, but he dreams his trip to the South and his romantic death as a man of action, his inverted mirror image.

This mirror image effect is reinforced structurally by tension-producing, symmetrically arranged parallels and contrasts between the protagonist's reality and dream. Examples abound. Eager to examine his copy of *The Thousand and One Nights,* Dahlmann walks up the stairway instead of waiting for the elevator, an act that results in his accident and subsequent death; similarly, upon his arrival at the station in the South, he walks to the country store where he will meet his death; Dahlmann is taken to the hospital in a hackney coach and to the railroad station in the same type of conveyance; the hospital is located on Ecuador (Equator) Street, a symbol of the division between Dahlmann's reality and dream; the storekeeper of Dahlmann's dream reminds him of a male nurse in the hospital; the spitball of crumbs that strikes his face while he eats reflects the blow he received when he ran into the open window; and the knife his Chinese-looking adversary wields at the end of the story recalls the needle the masked man inserted into Dahlmann's arm before his operation.

The literary works mentioned in the story also trace parallels and contrasts between Dahlmann's real world and his dreamworld. The protagonist of *Martín Fierro,* which is alluded to in the initial lines, represents the archetypal hero Dahlmann becomes in his dream. Dahlmann's memory of *Paul et Virginie* as he approaches the store takes him back to his world of books, just when his moment of destiny is at hand. *The Thousand and One Nights* is a more ambiguous symbol. The fact that it is an incomplete edition possibly alludes to Dahlmann's subconscious feelings of "incompleteness" as a man. The fantastic nature of the book suggests Dahlmann's desire to escape from his dull urban existence. But as a literary classic it could also symbolize culture and intellect as opposed to primitive instinct. Thus, while traveling southward on the train, Dahlmann puts the book aside and "allowed himself to live," looking out the window at the countryside. And at the first moment of danger in the store, "he opened the volume . . . by way of suppressing reality."

Although the entire story is narrated in what appears to be a direct style, certain rhetorical devices in the second part create a dreamlike atmosphere that prepares the dramatic denouement. For example, after despising his weakened body in the hospital, Dahlmann boards the train where he senses that he is "two men at a time: the man who traveled . . . across the geography of the fatherland, and the other one, locked up in a sanitarium." His view of the vast expanse of plains is conveyed by anaphoric repetition evoking the obsessive quality of the dream coupled with the movement of the train. "He saw unplastered brick houses, long and angled, timelessly watching the trains go by; he saw horsemen along the dirt roads; he saw gullies and lagoons and ranches; he saw great luminous clouds that resembled marble; and all these things were accidental, casual, like dreams of the plain." The sharply defined colors of the sun (white, yellow, and red) as the day progresses and the "limitless," "intimate," and "secret" landscape somehow seem more subjective than real. And the occasional solitary bull on the vast plain anticipates the final expression of the machismo cult. When Dahlmann confronts the three toughs, the one who challenges him shouts insults "as if he had been a long way off." Moments later the dreamlike atmosphere dominates the story's ending as Dahlmann clutches the knife, anticipating his fate: "he felt that to die in a knife fight, under the open sky, and going forward to the attack, would have been a liberation, a joy, and a festive occasion,

on the first night in the sanitarium, when they stuck him
with the needle. He felt that if he had been able to choose,
then, or to dream his death, this would have been the
death he would have chosen or dreamt."

As in so many of Borges's tales, time plays a major
role. The South represents a past era of instinctive feedom,
this part of Argentina being associated with the primitive
life of the gaucho. (The analogy with the cowboy's life in
the American Wild West is valid.) The cat[2] in the café and
the old gaucho in the general store are related motifs, the
former symbolizing the eternal present in which the
animal lives and the latter an idealized, literary archetype
of Argentine myth. (The old gaucho is described as having
been "polished . . . as water does a stone or generations of
men do a sentence"; Dahlmann sees him as a "summary
and cipher of the South.") These two motifs serve to
illuminate Dahlmann's withdrawal from the lineal present
into the legendary past where he will encounter the macho
destiny for which he has subconsciously yearned all his
life.

"The South" is one of Borges's most successful stories
for a variety of reasons. To the Latin American it evokes
the conflict between civilization and barbarism, of which
Sarmiento wrote so convincingly well over a century ago.[3]
The plot fascinates because of its climactic denouement
and its harmonious fusion of reality and dream. The
inverted mirror structure creates a degree of symmetry and
balance seldom achieved in fiction. Dahlmann's dream of
dying in a knife fight would seem to emanate from the
Argentine collective unconscious (he picked up the knife
"almost instinctively"), but Borges's artistic treatment of
man's yearning for the epic elevates the story to the realm
of universality.

Streetcorner Man   (1935) (A) (UHI)

Idealized and mythicized in "The South," the
machismo cult is parodied in "Streetcorner Man," a tale

designed to recapture the slum atmosphere of Buenos Aires in the early twentieth century. The first-person narrator, an unnamed hoodlum, recalls a dramatic incident that occurred many years ago. Rosendo Juárez was a handsome tough known as the Slasher, whom everybody respected because of his prowess with a knife. One night when he and his friends were enjoying themselves at the local dance hall, Francisco Real, also called the Butcher, arrived from another section of the city with several of his men. Real confronted Rosendo, challenging him to a knife fight, but Rosendo shocked all those present by rejecting the challenge. Indeed, when his girl friend, La Lujanera, handed him his knife, he tossed it out the window into the Maldonado, the river next to the dance hall. Disgusted, La Lujanera left with Real.

At this point the narrator also left, feeling that Rosendo had betrayed the entire neighborhood by his cowardice. Shortly after he returned to the dance hall, La Lujanera entered with Real, who had been mortally wounded in the chest. As he was dying, she explained that somebody had stabbed him, but it was not Rosendo and she did not recognize the assailant. When Real's men accused La Lujanera of the killing, the narrator defended her and challenged them to a fight. Before anybody could accept the challenge, however, the sound of the police riders was heard outside. Hastily they threw Real's body out the window into the river and resumed the dance. At dawn, upon returning to his shack, the narrator found La Lujanera waiting for him. The story ends when, addressing Borges by name, he states that after leaving the dance, he took out his knife to examine it. "It was as good as new, innocent-looking, and you couldn't see the slightest trace of blood on it."

Borges's parody of the machismo cult is conveyed principally by the narrator, who stands out as a braggart and, as revealed in "Rosendo's Tale," a liar. Considered from a psychological point of view, the narrator suffers from a lack of identity, wearing the mask imposed on him by the code of behavior young males are supposed to follow. When Rosendo, through whom he lives vicariously, is discredited by his refusal to fight, the narrator expresses his emptiness as he stands outside the dance hall and views his miserable slum surroundings. "The thought that we were a bunch of nobodys really had me burned up . . . it came to me that in the middle of this ragweed and all these dump heaps and this whole stinking place, I'd grown up just another weed myself. What else was going to come out of this crap but us—lots of lip but soft inside, all talk but no standing up to anyone? . . . I just couldn't get over Rosendo's yellow streak and the newcomer's plain guts." Thus the narrator must kill Real in order to reaffirm his own macho image, which in a sense has been destroyed by Rosendo.

Real's character also parodies the machismo cult, his challenge to Rosendo being as senseless as it is theatrical: "Word's going around there's someone out in these lousy mudflats supposed to be pretty good with a knife. They call him the Slasher and they say he's pretty tough. I'd like to meet up with the guy. Maybe he can teach a nobody like me how a man with guts handles himself." Only a short time later Real's macho image is reduced to "that worn-out look dead men have." And one of the girls present expresses what the entire story suggests: "A man's so full of pride and now look—all he's good for is gathering flies."

Borges has been very outspoken about his personal dislike for "Streetcorner Man," calling it "stagy," "operatic," and "sheer choreography." It does, indeed, depend heavily on visual and audio effects—gaudy costumes, melodramatic action and dialogue, music and dancing—and perhaps for this reason has been adapted for ballet, the stage, and the movies. The characters emerge as stereotypes who, like actors in a musical comedy, alternately claim the spotlight and deliver their somewhat artificial speeches. And when Rosendo refuses the challenge to fight, Real's exit with La Lujanera evokes an episode from a folkloric ballet. "Then wrapping his arms around her like it was forever, he calls to the musicians to play loud and strong. . . . The music went like wild fire from one end of the hall to the other. Real danced sort of stiff but held his partner up tight, and in nothing flat he had her charmed. When they got near the door he shouted, 'Make way, boys, she's all mine now!' And out they went, cheek to cheek, like the tango was floating them off."

Borges has subtly foreshadowed the story's surprise ending, one of its esthetic virtues, through the narrator's veiled allusions to the daring crime he has committed. In the initial lines he states that that night La Lujanera, who is first Rosendo's and then Real's woman, "got it into her head to come around to my shack and bed down with me." When he returns to the dance hall following Real's and La Lujanera's exit, the narrator remarks, "I was on the lookout for something," and after Real's death, when La Lujanera is accused of the murder by Real's men, the narrator defends her, "forgetting [he] had to be careful."

Although the language of "Streetcorner Man" imitates the speech of the *compadrito*, by Borges's own admission it is highly stylized for poetic effect. For this same reason the story is symmetrically structured through the use of repetitions and contrasts. For example, the first time Real enters the dance hall he is a blustering braggart; the second time he is bleeding and dying. And the narrator reveals his macho vanity by alluding to La Lujanera's presence in his shack on both the first and last pages.

In spite of Borges's dislike of "Streetcorner Man," I must admit I find it rather appealing. Its fictive, artificial, and burlesque qualities enhance its demythification of the machismo cult that rules the lives of the protagonists. With the exception of "The Approach to Al-Mu'tasim," this tale stands out as Borges's best *ficción* prior to 1939, when he began his career as a serious writer of short stories.

Rosendo's Tale   (1969) (DBR)

A sequel to "Streetcorner Man," "Rosendo's Tale" is narrated by Rosendo Juárez, the man who refused to fight Francisco Real in "Streetcorner Man." Because Borges deliberately imbued his earlier story with a kind of "stagy unreality"—due primarily to the boastful, unreliable narrator—he was embarrassed by its wide popularity and by the fact that his readers mistakenly considered it realistic. Thus thirty-six years later he wrote "Rosendo's Tale" as a kind of antidote to, in his words, "the romantic nonsense and childish vanity of dueling."

Rosendo narrates his story to Borges in a bar many years after the events of "Streetcorner Man." He was born and raised in a rough section of Buenos Aires. After killing a man in a knife fight he was arrested and released in the custody of a political boss who used him as a strong-arm man to organize and control elections. Rosendo soon earned a reputation as a tough and acquired a fancy sorrel and a woman, La Lujanera. One day a friend of Rosendo, Luis Irala, told him that Casilda, Luis's woman, had left him for a man named Rufino Aguilera. Irala felt compelled to avenge the insult, although he admitted that he cared nothing about Casilda, and did not even know Rufino. He was only afraid people would say he was a coward. Rosendo knew Rufino was an expert knife fighter and warned Irala that it would be foolish to risk his life for a woman he did not care for and a man he did not know. The next day Rosendo learned that Irala had challenged Rufino to a fight and that Rufino had killed him.

Rosendo then tells Borges about the night Real was killed, but his story differs in several respects from what we have been told in "Streetcorner Man." According to Rosendo, Real died of a wound in the back, not in the chest. When Real challenged Rosendo to a fight, Rosendo refused because, as he explains, "In that big loudmouth I saw myself, the same as in a mirror, and it made me feel ashamed. I wasn't scared; maybe if I'd been scared I'd have fought with him." After Rosendo's brief exchange of words with Real, La Lujanera took Rosendo's knife from his vest and handed it to him, but he let it drop to the floor and walked out. To make a clean break with the past, he went to Uruguay for a while; upon returning to Buenos Aires, he settled down in a respectable neighborhood.

As a result of his friend Irala's death, Rosendo realizes that he is a pawn of the machismo code, which has all but destroyed his identity by compelling him to project the stereotyped macho image. Thus in a moment of illumination (when he sees Real as his double), he rejects the code's absurd tyranny and escapes to anonymity and prosaic respectability. Although both stories condemn the machismo cult, "Streetcorner Man" and "Rosendo's Tale" are antithetical. The former parodies the cult by creating a false aura of romantic myth—which many readers mistakenly have accepted as reality—and the latter demonstrates that the cult produces no heroes, only treachery and victims. The protagonists, moreover, contrast strikingly with one another, Rosendo transcending his macho fate and his counterpart embracing it wholeheartedly. Although "Rosendo's Tale" is intended to correct some misconceptions about "Streetcorner Man," the latter emerges as the more exciting and artistically structured of the two stories.

The Challenge   (1952) (A)

In a commentary on "The Challenge," Borges states that the reader will find in it "a full explanation of my feelings for the subject of knives, knife fighters, courage, and so on, as it has concerned me over the past forty or forty-five years." This story hardly provides a "full explanation," but it does lend interesting insight into Borges's thinking on the subject. Though very different in tone, "The Challenge" is a reworking of "Streetcorner Man," both being based on an archetypal situation that Borges calls the disinterested duel, i.e., a duel fought by total strangers for no apparent motive except the need to prove their courage.

The action of "The Challenge" occurs during the 1870s. Its main character is Wenceslao Suárez, a harness maker in his forties who has earned a reputation for bravery. He has probably killed a man or two, but we are told these killings have been in fair fights and for this reason have not tarnished his good name. One day he receives a letter from a stranger in another province who, having learned of Suárez's renown, extends to him the hospitality of his humble home. The illiterate Suárez dictates his reply, explaining that he cannot leave his aging mother alone, but inviting the man to visit him. Some months later the man appears and Suárez prepares a barbecue for him. After they have eaten and drunk a considerable amount, the stranger suggests that they engage in a bit of harmless knife play. Suárez accepts, but he soon realizes that the man intends to kill him. The stranger's knife slices through Suárez's wrist, and Suárez, jumping back, lays his bleeding hand on the ground, clamps it down under his foot, and tears it off. He then feints a thrust to the stranger's chest and rips open his belly. We are told that in one version of the story the stranger dies, but in another Suárez gives him first aid and he returns to his home.

Borges's rather lengthy conclusion makes "The Challenge" as much an essay as a story. He believes that details such as Suárez's honest trade, his qualms about leaving his mother, and the polite exchange of letters render the "barbarous tale" more effective. Also, the fact that the challengers in both "Streetcorner Man" and "The Challenge" are defeated indicates a tacit disapproval of aggression or perhaps the idea that man is the cause of his own downfall. Most illuminating, however, is Borges's reference to the "blind religion of courage," which was forged by the gauchos and rediscovered by the rough workers and outlaws living on the edges of the city. This "religion," Borges believes, is not a form of vanity but rather "an awareness that God may be found in any man."

Borges's presentation of the machismo cult in "The Challenge" differs markedly from what we have seen above because Wenceslao, unlike the other protagonists discussed in this section, is a complex mixture of respectability, courage, hospitality, brutality, and compassion. Here Borges clearly expresses his fascination with physical prowess and his awe over the possession of blind faith in the individual self. For him, these virtues represent a rediscovery of the "age-old cult of the gods of iron," but this religion of courage is only one of many aspects of the machismo cult in Borges's works.

The Intruder   (1966) (A) (DBR)

"The Intruder" dramatizes another facet of the machismo cult, namely, the attitude of the *compadrito* toward the emotions of love and friendship. The action occurs on the outskirts of Buenos Aires toward the end of the nineteenth century. The two Nilsen brothers, Cristián and Eduardo, work as drovers or teamsters and like to drink, gamble, fight, and carouse in brothels. Tall and red-haired, they are feared by people in the neighborhood because of their skill as fighters. The close ties between them have made it general knowledge that to fall out with one of them is to reckon with two enemies.

Once Cristián brings to the rambling old house occupied by him and his brother a pretty, likeable woman named Juliana Burgos, and before long, with his consent, Eduardo is sharing her favors. This situation does not last because, although they never admit it, they both fall in love with her and thus become jealous of one another. Fearing for their friendship and eager to resume their

former way of life, they take Juliana to a whorehouse some
miles away and sell her to the owner. Soon thereafter the
two brothers begin—each on his own—to be unac-
countably absent, until one night they meet in the place
where Juliana works. They decide to take her back with
them, but within a short time the old enmity between them
is inevitably revived.

One evening when Eduardo returns home, he finds
Cristián loading some hides on a cart. Together they drive
to a lonely spot in the country where Cristián informs his
brother that he has killed Juliana so that she will not cause
them any more harm. He adds that they must bury her
immediately, before the buzzards take over. The brothers'
reaffirmation of their friendship brings the story to its
close. "They threw their arms around each other, on the
verge of tears. One more link bound them now—the
woman they had cruelly sacrificed and their common need
to forget her."

Borges once said that he was inspired to write "The
Intruder" by the following statement of an acquaintance:
"Any man who thinks five minutes straight about a
woman is no man—he's a queer." This attitude toward
women, typical of the machismo code, is clearly integrated
into the story's plot. For example, for Cristián, Juliana
"was no more than an object." And when friction develops
between the brothers, we are told that "in tough neigh-
borhoods a man never admits to anyone—not even to
himself—that a woman matters beyond lust and
possession, but the two brothers were in love. This, in
some way, made them feel ashamed."

The Nilsens' behavior is governed by this strict
machismo code, which must be preserved at all cost. Thus,
when their feelings for Juliana pose a threat to the code,
she becomes an ironic Christ figure, sacrificed to atone for
their "sin" of love. Her symbolic role is underscored,
moreover, by the "tiny crucifix" she carries first to the
house of prostitution and then to her grave.

Borges has referred to "The Intruder" as "perhaps the best [story] I have ever written." His mother, on the other hand, thoroughly disliked it. In my opinion, it is indeed a well-written evocative tale, but I am puzzled by Borges's enthusiasm for it. I suspect that it is due in part to his fascination with the machismo cult and in part to the paradox—one of his favorite devices—of committing murder to preserve friendship.

The Meeting   (1969) (A) (DBR)

"The Meeting," somewhat like "The South," treats the machismo cult as a myth that lives on in the so-called civilized twentieth century. The first-person narrator recalls an incident that happened many years ago, in 1910, when, at the age of nine or ten, he was taken by his cousin to a fiesta on a country estate outside of Buenos Aires. The other guests were young adults, all well versed in such sophisticated matters as cars, race horses, the best tailors, and expensive women. During the elaborate meal someone played the guitar and sang songs about gauchos and knife fights.

After dinner the narrator wandered alone through the many rooms of the dark house, until the owner came to find him and led him to a display cabinet filled with a collection of knives that had belonged to famous fighters. As they are discussing the history of the different weapons, they overhear angry voices coming from the game room where two men, Uriarte and Duncan, are involved in a poker game. Uriarte accuses Duncan of cheating and eventually challenges him to a duel. When somebody remarks that weapons are not lacking, they go to the display cabinet and each man chooses a knife, Uriarte, a long dagger with a U-shaped crosspiece in the hilt, and Duncan, a shorter, wooden-handled dagger with the stamp of a tiny tree on the blade. Upon picking up their weapons, the hands of both men begin to tremble. The duel takes place outside on the lawn. At first, the two adversaries fight clumsily, obviously not knowing what they are doing, but before long they resemble experts, fencing with skill and boldness. Suddenly Uriarte wounds Duncan mortally in the chest, and it is all over.

Many years later the narrator relates this episode to a retired police captain, stressing his belief that Uriarte and Duncan had never fought with knives before. The captain reveals that there were only two daggers with a U-shaped crosspiece that became famous, one of which belonged to a man from the southern part of the country named Juan Almada. He also states that the knives with the Little Tree brand were quite common, but one of these belonged to a well-known tough from the north named Juan Almanza. Because people were always confusing them, Juan Almanza and Juan Almada longed to meet and even searched for each other for many years around the turn of the century. However, the anticipated meeting never took place. The narrator concludes that perhaps the duel he witnessed in 1910 was the end of another story, that of Almada and Almanza, whose weapons awakened that night after a long sleep and, as if they had a will of their own, fought each other in the hands of their tools, the unsuspecting Duncan and Uriarte.

In "The Meeting" the elemental spirit of the machismo myth created by the gaucho erupts in the midst of sophisticated, genteel society. The story implies a metaphoric return to the past to recapture this primitive force that the characters themselves cannot comprehend. The journey to the country estate and the gaucho ballads set the stage for the subsequent series of events. The narrator's walk through the dark mansion suggests a labyrinth, the center of which is the display cabinet filled with daggers symbolizing the mythical past. The myth comes to life when the two adversaries' hands begin to shake and, outside on the lawn, the narrator senses "that an overpowering current was dragging [them] on and would drown [them]." At the moment Duncan dies, he seems to have lost touch with reality, uttering in a low voice, "How strange. All this is like a dream." And after Duncan's death, Uriarte weeps and begs to be forgiven because "the thing he had done was beyond him." The fact that the spectators of Duncan's death agree "to elevate this duel with knives to a duel with swords" in order to mollify the authorities suggests the mythification of the event. Another mythicizing element is the name of the victim, probably an allusion to King Duncan, who is murdered in *Macbeth*. Engulfed by forces beyond their control, Borges's two protagonists become pawns of fate, a fate mysteriously determined by the primitive instincts lurking in the collective unconscious. As demonstrated by "The South," Borges has felt similar stirrings within himself.[4]

Borges's treatment of the machismo cult varies from romantic idealization ("The South") to outright parody of the role-playing macho ("Streetcorner Man"). Between these two extremes are a reformed *compadrito* ("Rosendo's Tale"), two hard-bitten men who prefer friendship to love ("The Intruder"), civilized antagonists manipulated by knives embodying spirits of the past ("The Meeting"), and a respectable tradesman who bravely defeats his challenger ("The Challenge"). Borges's attitude toward the cult seems ambivalent and even contradictory. He clearly expresses his dislike for knife fighting in "Rosendo's Tale," but he admires the courageous protagonist of "The Challenge." Aside from the brutality inherent in the machismo code, Borges's condemnation of it is based on its tyranny over his victimized protagonists, who lack individual identity because they are forced to don masks and prove their manliness. This false role imposed on the male is so pervasive, so much a part of the collective unconscious, that it become synonymous with irrevocable fate. As we have seen in "The Meeting," this fate is expressed by metaphorical knives that make instruments of the two protagonists. It would seem, then, that the gaucho and the *compadrito* are symbols of primitive valor to be held in awe but, at the same time, to be debunked.

In "The Challenge" Borges equates the machismo cult with a "religion of courage," with "its ethic, its mythology and its martyrs." Given his skepticism of all philosophies and all attempts to formulate absolute values, an objective Borges could only view the rigid rules of this "religion" as absurd. In a sense, then, virtually all of Borges's fiction contains strong elements of absurdity. On the one hand, the world is presented as incomprehensible, chaotic, or phantasmagorical while on the other, the systems devised to mirror and decipher it are presented as nothing but creations of the human mind and, therefore, separate and provisional realities.

2

Some Aspects of
Borges's Esthetics

1. THE ESTHETIC IDEAL

The preceding chapter dealt primarily with the thematic
contents of Borges's prose fiction, special emphasis having
been given to the absurdity of man's uncertain position in
an alien world. Nevertheless, formal aspects of the stories
were occasionally treated, especially those structural techniques having a direct bearing on theme. The present
chapter constitutes a broader and more systematic analysis
of Borges's esthetic ideas and practices. Here stress will be
placed on esthetic form and its relation to the content
already discussed.

One of the consummate literary artists of our time,
Borges is a disciplined, cosmopolitan man of letters who, it
is often said, has taught a generation how to write. As
indicated above, he has revitalized the Spanish language
and restored imagination to Latin American fiction. Also
indicated above is the relative absence of social and moral
preoccupations in his stories. Rather, as we have seen, he
dramatizes intellectual propositions within a seemingly
abstract, cerebral universe, all the while viewing philosophical and scientific pursuits as mere provisional reflections of the mind, not of the real world. The fact that his
characters tend to be faceless individuals set in archetypal
situations is probably due to his belief that neither
philosophy nor psychology have succeeded in defining
man. Borges sees reality as a chaos of fleeting perceptions

so incomprehensible that for him life takes on the unreal, hallucinatory nature of a dream. As he states in "The Gauchos" (IPD), "They [the gauchos] lived out their lives as in a dream, without knowing who they were or what they were. Maybe the case is the same for all of us." And in Borges's eyes, if life is a dream, so, indeed, is the world of art.

Brief mention should be made of Borges's essays, which not only elucidate his fiction but also set forth many of his ideas on esthetics. Neither profound nor erudite, they nevertheless offer short, incisive commentaries on a wide variety of topics ranging from rare books to esoteric metaphysical theories. Borges often utilizes his subjects as points of departure for reflections that in turn lead him to the formation of intriguing insights bordering on fantasy. Not infrequently his essays emerge as symmetrically designed paradoxes consisting of a perplexing question by way of introduction, a series of plausible explanations, and an unexpected or contradictory conclusion. A case in point is his poetically conceived essay "The Wall and the Books" (OI), which attempts to illustrate what constitutes an esthetic event. In the initial sentences we are told that during his long reign the Chinese emperor Shih Huang Ti, a contemporary of Hannibal, issued two historic decrees: the construction of the Great Wall and the burning of all books written before his time. The fact that these two decrees were issued by the same man is so disturbing to Borges that he feels compelled to investigate both the emperor's motivation and his own reactions.

His numerous conjectures include the possibility that Shih Huang Ti wanted to abolish the past in order to destroy the memory of his libertine mother's dishonor; that the "wall in space" and the "fire in time" were magic barriers against death; that the emperor wanted to recreate the beginning of time in order to call himself First; and that he imagined his rule was threatened from without by enemy forces and from within by sacred books containing "what the whole universe or each man's conscience teaches." By way of conclusion Borges states that, like the pure forms of music, mythology, and certain twilights, all of which try to tell us something, the hypotheses and emotions generated by the images of the wall and the fire express an "esthetic reality." He defines the esthetic reality as "that imminence of a revelation that is not yet produced," i.e., a kind of hovering, vertiginous moment of apprehension in which an inexpressible reality is intuited.

A number of the stories discussed in the preceding chapter conclude with what might be described as an esthetic reality, a means by which Borges intensifies the emotional impact and leaves the reader with a combination of heightened awareness and ecstatic expectancy evading intellectual formulation. For example, in "The End," Martín Fierro's death and the dissolution of his killer's identity are preceded by a vibrant description of the plain, which just before sundown "is on the verge of saying something . . . as untranslatable as music." "The South" ends with the imminent death of Dahlmann and his hallucinatory encounter with his antithetical self. The protagonist of "Biography of Tadeo Isidoro Cruz (1829–1874)" experiences an illuminating moment of destiny when he discovers his identity in his mirror image, Martín Fierro. In "The Gospel According to Mark," Espinosa the nonbeliever emerges as an ironic Christ upon seeing the cross erected for his own crucifixion. "The Intruder" concludes with the paradoxical revelation that the preservation of friendship demands an innocent victim's life. The wizard of "The Circular Ruins" ultimately learns that he, the dreamer, has also been dreamed. In "The Approach to Al-Mu'tasim" the student's final act of opening the curtain implies his imminent meeting with God in the guise of his double. The absurdity of Otálora's life in "The Dead Man" is illuminated at the moment of his death when he realizes his fate was determined from the begin-

ning. Two final examples of a list that does not pretend to
be all-inclusive are "The Theologians," in which the
accuser and accused on earth turn out to be one and the
same in heaven, and "The God's Script," whose protagonist loses his human identity when he succeeds in
deciphering the script of the tiger.

The so-called esthetic reality stands out as the major
element of "Pedro Salvadores" (1969) (A) (IPD), based on
an anecdote Borges heard from his grandfather. Pedro
Salvadores was a member of the Unitarian party during
the time of Rosas.[1] One night Rosas's men broke into his
home in Buenos Aires to arrest him, but he managed to
hide in a cellar under the dining room. He lived in the
cellar until Rosas's fall nine years later, when he emerged,
pale as wax and barely able to speak. Puzzled and
intrigued, Borges ponders at length over Salvadores's long
period of imprisonment, his emotions, and his nightmares.
The unfortunate man's fate remains so tragically incomprehensible, however, that for Borges it emerges as "a
symbol of something we are about to understand, but
never quite do."

A similar anticipation of enlightenment dominates
one of Borges's shortest pieces, "The Captive" (1957) (A)
(DT). Here, we are told, a white boy in a frontier town is
carried off during an Indian raid. Years later the child's
parents hear of a blue-eyed savage, now a man living in
Indian territory, who may be their son. Somehow the man,
whom the parents think they recognize, is led back in
silence to his home. Suddenly he shrieks, runs into the
kitchen, and removes from the chimney a knife that he had
hidden there as a boy. It soon becomes clear that he cannot
adapt to life with his parents, and one day he returns to
the pampa. Borges is fascinated with that first bewildering
moment when past and present merge and the savage
rushes to the chimney. He wonders exactly what the
"Indian" felt and if "the lost son was reborn and died."
This emotion-packed, dizzying instant must be viewed as

an example of the Borgesian esthetic phenomenon, i.e., something we feel we are about to experience but never do.

Whereas "The Captive" explores the emotional impact of the esthetic reality, "The Anthropologist" (1969) (IPD) treats the same subject from an epistemological point of view. Fred Murdock is an American student in a southwestern state university. Having decided to study aboriginal languages, he is advised to live on an Indian reservation in order to observe certain rites and uncover the medicine man's secret. Upon his return to the university, he will write and publish a thesis. Murdock enthusiastically agrees to undertake the project and spends two years with the Indians. After many arduous months of adapting himself to the new way of life, he receives instruction on the interpretation of dreams from a medicine man, who eventually teaches him the secret. Soon thereafter Murdock returns to the university and tells his adviser that he has learned the secret but has made up his mind not to reveal it because it means a great deal more to him than scientific knowledge. This Indian ritual, steeped in mystery, represents a metaphor of the esthetic reality that, undisclosed, sustains a kind of ecstatic limbo of expectancy. To reveal the secret would imply a commitment to knowledge and truth, which from Borges's point of view are inferior to the esthetic ideal.

"Undr" (1975) (BOS) is another of Borges's allegories on the creative process. A fantastic tale with a medieval flavor, it is narrated by an Icelandic traveler, Ulf Sigurdsson, who describes his search for the single Word comprising all the poetry of the Urns. Sigurdsson receives a talisman in the form of a ring from the king of the Urns and then meets the poet Bjarni Thorkelsson, who tells him that nobody can teach him the Word, that he must find it for himself. Thus Sigurdsson initiates a series of incredible adventures involving every possible vicissitude of human fortune, all the while searching for the Word. Many years later he returns to the home of Thorkelsson and relates to him his adventures. Then Thorkelsson, accompanying himself on his harp, sings the magic Word, *undr,* the meaning of which is "wonder." Sigurdsson immediately discovers all of his many adventures reflected in the Word and begins to intone his own verses.

In this story Borges once again attempts to illustrate and define the esthetic reality, which derives not only from Sigurdsson's labyrinthine search but also, paradoxically, from the open-ended denouement. Thus, the word wonder does not necessarily mark the end of the narrator's quest; rather it creates an esthetically loaded situation by revealing the abstract goal of literature which the narrator now must set out to achieve.

In "His End and His Beginning" (1969) (IPD), Borges describes death as an esthetic reality and, at the same time, perhaps alludes to his own blindness. This short piece tells of an unnamed man's demise, followed by his nightmarish sensation of losing contact with time and the concrete world around him. Eventually it becomes clear that his eerie perceptions, which also contain elements of "newness and splendor," result from the fact that he has been in heaven since the moment of his death. Here the experience of death emerges as a labyrinth whose center is reached in a lucid, vertiginous moment of tension. Borges's transition to blindness is also suggested by the statement that "even the fingers of his own hands were shadows; but however dim and unreal, they were familiar, they were something to cling to." Submerged in darkness, Borges exercises his powers of imagination to alleviate his tragic condition, a condition symbolically applicable to all men.

In several of his parables Borges conveys the impossibility of attaining the esthetic ideal. Such is the case of "Dreamtigers" (1960) (DT), in which he describes his lifelong fascination with tigers. When he was a child, he would gaze in admiration at the beasts in zoos and books of natural history. As he grew older, however, his "passion" for them faded into his subconscious where, he admits, they still occasionally dominate his dreams. On these occasions Borges imagines he has "unlimited powers" to "cause a tiger," but he never succeeds. "The tiger indeed appears, but stuffed or flimsy, or with impure variations of shape, or of an implausible size, . . . or with a touch of the dog or the bird." A symbol of childlike innocence, strength, and esthetic perfection, the tiger represents ideals that, according to Borges, cannot be created ("caused") by the adult, whose rational ego has stifled the creative instinct and blurred the artistic vision.

"Parable of the Palace" (1960) (DT) dramatizes the clash between divine and artistic creation. According to a legend, we are told, the Yellow Emperor guides the poet through his magnificent palace, a labyrinth of rooms, libraries, gardens, patios, rivers, towers, and straight avenues that in reality are circles. Inspired by these wonders, the poet recites a brief composition consisting of a single line or, perhaps, of a single word. And incredibly "in the poem stood the enormous palace, entire and minutely detailed," with all its glorious, interminable past. Enraged at being surpassed by one of his subjects, the emperor accuses the poet of robbing him of his palace and orders his execution.

This simple, beautifully written parable is another version of "The Aleph," one of Borges's most famous stories. The palace represents the universe, the emperor God, and the poem the ideal but unattainable work of art (the narrator admits his tale is no more than literary fiction). Borges seems to conjecture that if artistic perfection were possible, it would be superior to God's creation, and therefore God, in his wrath, would have to destroy both the artist and his work of art. Borges's esthetic ideas, then, correspond in a sense to his philosophical skepticism. In "The God's Script" Tzinacán succeeds in deciphering the mysteries of the divine mind and loses his identity. In "Parable of the Palace" the poet creates a work of art equal to God's creation and loses his life. Man, Borges suggests, is condemned to his absurd human condition, whether or not he succeeds in his absurd quest for the missing God.

Another version of this same theme is set forth in "The Mirror and the Mask" (1975) (BOS), in which an ancient Irish king commissions his court poet to write a poem extolling his martial exploits. A year later the poet returns with a classical panegyric that greatly pleases the king who, in return, gives the poet a mirror and orders him to compose another piece for the following year. The second composition is not a description of a battle but the battle itself, in all its harshness and chaos. The king lauds his efforts and orders a third poem, this time presenting the poet with a mask. A year later the poet recites to his king a single-line poem so perfect that they both realize they have committed the sin of having known beauty. The poet's third gift is a dagger with which he kills himself. The king becomes a beggar in his own land and never again repeats the perfect poem.

The poet's first composition, which follows all the rules of classical rhetoric, would seem to represent art as an artificial means of expression. The second poem, inspired by the mirror, describes the battle so convincingly that it emerges as a realistic reflection of the world. The poet's third and most remarkable piece, however, is supposedly written while he is masked, a metaphor of his withdrawal from objective reality—and perhaps of Borges's blindness—in order to achieve a perfect subjective beauty. Like the poet in "Parable of the Palace," he must suffer the penalty of death for successfully emulating God.

"The Maker" (1960) (DT) (A) is a tribute to Homer that also conveys some of Borges's fundamental ideas on art. Poetic allusions to Homer's sensitive nature and exploits in battle are followed by a description of his approaching blindness. At first he feels horror but gradually he accepts his fate, facing it with curiosity, hope, and joy as he evokes images of love and war from his youth. These images, enriched by imagination, give rise to the famous epics "it was his destiny to sing and leave echoing concavely in the memory of man." Borges identifies personally with Homer's descent into blindness, but this parable could also be read as a tribute to the creative consciousness, man's best weapon against temporal anguish and spiritual darkness. For Borges art is a product of imagination and solitude, an expression of the intimate self that dreams its own reality and makes life more bearable for all men.

An exceptionally moving tribute to art is the parable "Martín Fierro" (1960) (DT). Borges first mentions the glorious military exploits during the Wars for Independence from Spain, then "two tyrannies" in Argentine history (the Rosas and Perón dictatorships)[2] followed by a reference to "a man" who wrote a vast chronicle about his native land (an allusion to Sarmiento).[3] And after each of these historical references, Borges adds, "These things, now, are as if they had never been." By way of contrast, he tells of a man who, in the 1860s, dreamed of a gaucho who kills a black in a knife fight, throws him down like a sack of bones, and slowly rides away on his horse. This dream of "one man"—José Hernández, author of *Martín Fierro*—unlike the names and events of the historical past, "is part of the memory of all." Borges obviously prefers fiction to history, the former being magically revived with each reading, and the latter having lost its dramatic appeal many years ago. But equally important is Borges's idea of art as a dream, a dream that can seem more real and more alive than reality itself. And as a collective dream, *Martín Fierro* has become transformed into poetic myth.

Something similar occurs in "Parable of Cervantes and Don Quijote" (1960) (DT), in which Borges observes that Cervantes created his famous novel to contrast the fantastic world depicted in books of chivalry with the common, everyday world of seventeenth-century Spain.

However, Borges believes that time has erased the dis-
harmony between these two worlds, Don Quijote and La
Mancha having become just as poetic as, for example,
"Sinbad's haunts or Ariosto's vast geographies." Or, one
might conclude, the real world of Don Quijote and La
Mancha have become just as mythical as the real world of
Martín Fierro and his life on the pampa.

"Narrative Art and Magic" (1932) (D) may be
described as Borges's manifesto on fiction, for it is here
that he contrasts the realistic novel of characters with
fantastic literature. He rejects psychological realism as
"pretentious" and "dishonest," believing that the influences on the life of any human being are too numerous
and complex to depict or analyze. On the other hand, he
favors Coleridge's dictum that all reading of fiction
presumes the willing suspension of disbelief. Thus in a
work of fantasy, the reader should automatically accept the
lucidly defined laws of cause and effect as, for example, in
the case of a character's death soon after the "torture" of
his wax effigy. In Borges's opinion, magical causality also
facilitates the organization of fictional elements into artistically designed structural patterns because, unlike
realism, fantastic literature makes no attempt to conform
to chaotic reality. For Borges fantastic literature is
esthetically superior to realism and, given its symbolic
possibilities, frequently more profound. The basic devices
for fantastic literature, he claims, are four in number: the
work within the work, the contamination of reality by
dream, the voyage in time, and the double. It is interesting
to note that Borges himself utilizes these devices to
undermine assumptions of stability and disintegrate
objectice reality.

As demonstrated by his essay "The Argentine Writer
and Tradition" (L), Borges is vitally interested in
Argentine letters, his focus here being on the question of
what literary elements constitute a national literature. He
disagrees with those who believe the gaucho poem *Martín*

Fierro should serve as a guide for contemporary writers because, although he professes great admiration for this masterpiece, he points out that it and other well-known gaucho poems are replete with "popular" vocabulary and meters never actually used by the gauchos themselves. Thus these works tend to lack the authenticity claimed by many of their admirers.

In Borges's opinion, local color is not a necessary ingredient in a national literature. To prove this contention he reminds his readers that literary giants such as Racine and Shakespeare frequently dealt with foreign themes, that Mohammed never felt compelled to mention camels in the Koran, and that he himself, after writing "those forgettable and forgotten books" of the 1920s abounding in Argentinisms, unintentionally captured the true flavor of the Buenos Aires suburbs in his nightmarish detective story "Death and the Compass."

To those Argentines who claim they are cut off from Europe and therefore should not "play at being Europeans," Borges replies that the Argentine tradition has always included all of Western culture, but that living far from Europe has enabled Argentine writers to handle European themes "without superstition" and "with an irreverence which can have, and already does have, fortunate consequences." His conclusion, then, is that his nation's literature should be universal in its orientation because "anything we Argentine writers can do successfully will become part of our Argentine tradition."

2. THE SYMBOLIC VISION

An exhaustive study of symbolism in Borges's works is beyond the scope of the present study. What is proposed here is a discussion of some of the basic, most frequently recurring symbols Borges utilizes to illuminate his fictional

world. An attempt will also be made to relate these
symbols to the thematic content of his fiction. Like much
modern literature, Borges's stories are enriched by an
abundance of symbolic images that reveal a personal,
intuitive, and often ambiguous reality, impossible to
express conceptually. The symbol has been defined as a
visual sign of something invisible or as an outward sign of
an inward state. Thus it serves not only to unite unconscious with conscious reality but also to arouse emotional
responses and create additional layers of meaning.
Although Borges makes use of archetypal and cultural
symbols, his works are also replete with personal symbolic motifs constituting his unique, private mythology.
Through constant repetition these poetic images create
rhythm and structural harmony, but they also tend to blur
physical reality with an aura of dreamlike subjectivity,
rendering the disturbing impression that our lives are
determined by vague forces operating outside the laws of
cause and effect.

Convinced that literature is similar to myth, Borges
returns, in a sense, to the primordial world of archaic man
prior to rational thought in order to recreate a reality
which, like myth, is apprehended in terms of symbols, free
from intellectual or dogmatic thinking. These symbols
occasionally produce an emotional impact resembling that
of the esthetic reality discussed in the preceding section.
And as we shall see at the end of the present section, a *ficción* in its entirety can also represent something other than
itself.

The two most common symbolic images in Borges's
stories are the mirror and the labyrinth. As indicated in
the preceding chapter, the mirror is utilized at times to
suggest an empty, disintegrating world and at other times
to dramatize various aspects of the double theme. The
labyrinth likewise has several implications, ranging from
the philosophical to the literary. Borges has admitted that
for him the labyrinth signifies "being baffled" and suffer-

ing terror and anguish in the mysterious universe that makes no sense. Thus, in his works it is not surprising that the labyrinth image conveys the epistemological and ontological problems man encounters in coming to grips with an alien world he cannot understand.

Although the vast majority of the mazes depicted in Borges's works merely reflect the human mind, a few of these confusing structures actually do mirror the real world, or at least a portion of it. The most obvious of these are God's maze (the desert) in "The Two Kings and Their Two Labyrinths"; Ts'ui Pên's novel, *The Garden of the Forking Paths,* a complex representation of time described as "a picture, incomplete yet not false, of the universe"; and the remarkable mind of Funes, the Memorious, whose memory of every image that has ever been registered on his consciousness prevents him from thinking. These stories present images of the chaotic, unreasonable world that man vainly attempts to decipher by constructing his own labyrinthine versions of reality.

Perhaps the most literal example of these man-made labyrinths is the one described in "The House of Asterion." Here, it will be recalled, the Minotaur (Asterion) wanders wistfully through his mazelike abode awaiting his redeemer, who will come to him in the form of death. However, the house is not a prison, as it is in the myth, but rather a symbol of culture, an imitation of reality that provides ignorant, alienated man—Asterión is an illiterate monster—with an illusion of understanding the world outside and, at the same time, a refuge from it. A somewhat similar example is found in "The Waiting," whose protagonist enters an imaginary labyrinth consisting of movies, a book, and a recurring dream in order to postpone his encounter with the terrifying finality of death. In "The Library of Babel" the symmetrically structured Library represents logical man's version of the universe, but the illegible books stand for his basic ignorance. And the principles of pantheistic idealism become the basis for an abstract maze "plotted by men . . . destined to be deciphered by men" in "Tlön, Uqbar, Orbis Tertius." The labyrinthine images in all of these tales illuminate the absurdity of human existence.

Another group of Borges's stories treats the modern theme of man's quest for identity, which is revealed to him in a moment of revelation at the center of a symbolic maze. Examples include "Biography of Tadeo Isidoro Cruz (1829–1874)," whose protagonist learns who he is when he meets his mirror image, Martín Fierro, and "The Approach to Al-Mu'tasim," in which the Indian student discovers that God is reflected within himself. In both of these works the mazelike plot structure generates a steadily increasing momentum, intensifying the impact of the denouement.

Other Borgesian labyrinths such as the one in "Ibn Hakkan al-Bokhari, Dead in His Labyrinth" symbolize the travails of creating a *ficción*. This story has for its principal setting Ibn Hakkan's labyrinthine house through which the author—in the guise of two youths—wanders as he fabricates his plot. Ingeniously the labyrinth also reflects the literary form outlined by the confusing chain of events, many of which occur within the structure itself. A fine example of the pure artifice so characteristic of Borges's writings, this tale of a labyrinth with a single room and miles of corridors built by an Arab potentate on the coast of England also implies the absurdity of the artist's endeavor to remake reality on his own terms.

Two additional examples of the labyrinthine creative process are "The Immortal," in which the narrator seeks poetic inspiration in myth, fusing his identity with that of Homer; and "Undr," a medieval tale of the search for the Word embodying an entire nation's poetry. The structural technique of the former delineates the difficulties experienced by the would-be author, who seeks inspiration from the literary past, knowing he can never create an original work. "Undr," meaning "wonder," represents the goal of art reached via the symbolic labyrinth of life, the center of which is an ecstatic moment of intuited beauty.

The best example of the search-for-identity theme is "The South," Dahlmann's dream representing a maze penetrating the depths of his subconscious and culminating with his imminent death in a knife fight on the pampa. The numerous parallels between dream and reality discussed in section 7 of the preceding chapter suggest a maze of nightmarish, reflecting mirrors. In addition, unexpected occurrences such as Dahlmann's having to get off the train at an earlier station bring to mind the random directions taken by one who has lost control over his fate. This impression of helplessness is reinforced by the striking difference between the sanitarium—a symbol of civilization—and Dahlmann's precarious situation expressed by his interior monologue in the final lines of the story: "They would not have allowed such things to happen to me in the sanitarium." Thus Dahlmann is irresistibly propelled toward his destiny, but at the same time it is the very destiny he has subconsciously desired all his life. His emergence onto the plain with a knife in his hand concludes his search for identity, but it also symbolizes the Argentine's subliminal yearning to die fearlessly like the heroic gaucho of the mythical Argentine past.

In a large group of stories the labyrinth emerges as a product of blind reason, pride, or ambition and, consequently, the protagonists as victims of irony. In their entirety these tales also convey man's insecurity and helplessness in a world that inevitably denies him his lofty aspirations. One recalls that in "The Two Kings and Their Two Labyrinths" the intricate labyrinth constructed by the king of Babylon symbolizes excessive pride, bringing about his ruin by God's labyrinth, the desert. Otálora in "The Dead Man" commits a series of ruthless acts designed to win for himself power and glory. At the climactic moment of his murder, however, we realize that he has been trapped in a labyrinth of his own making and, at its center, has been brought face to face with his symbolic, antagonistic self in the form of Bandeira. We also realize that images such as the red-haired woman in the mirror and the ailing Bandeira in bed serve merely to enflame Otálora's desire for power and thus determine the next turn he will take within the symbolic labyrinth in order to achieve his ambition.

It should be recalled that in Borges's work any geometrical figure can become a maze. Thus, in "Death and the Compass" Lönnrot is constantly torn between two mazelike constructs, the triangle and the diamond-shaped figure, both products of his excessive rationalism. However, at least two additional mazes also emerge in this tale. One of these is described when Lönnrot enters the abandoned estate, Triste-le-Roy, in search of the killer. We remember that he perceives a series of mirrors reflecting patios, statues, and stairways, and that all of a sudden he feels anguished by the vastness of both time and space. A symbol of his suppressed and misunderstood inner self ("he was infinitely reflected in opposing mirrors"), this maze foreshadows the defeat of Lönnrot's rational ego as well as his encounter with his double. The other maze, appearing in the final lines of the story, alludes to Zeno's paradox, the straight line of eternity on which Lönnrot challenges Scharlach to look for him after his death. This is an extremely ironic image because it demonstrates once again Lönnrot's obsessive rationalism, even as he faces his absurd destiny determined by an ironic god figure.

Three additional stories delineate symbolic labyrinths in which the reasoning mind flounders in its attempt to find meaning amidst overwhelming confusion. "The Babylon Lottery" describes an institution whose absurd purpose is to organize chance according to rational principles. Gradually the lottery assumes control of every aspect of life, making it a labyrinthine symbol of human destiny. "Averroes' Search" becomes the labyrinth of an

Arab scholar, who attempts to grasp the concepts of tragedy and comedy without ever having seen a theater. His blind rationalism is mocked when, on at least two occasions, he is presented with concrete examples of a theatrical spectacle. And in "The Theologians" two rival clergymen fabricate a labyrinth of theological contradictions symbolizing the absurdities of metaphysics. The center of the labyrinth is reached when the antagonists, having ascended to heaven, discover that in the mind of God they are the same person.

Like the world of myth, Borges's works are fraught with contrasting symbolic motifs that reflect cosmic tensions and enhance the poetic impact of his fictional universe. Of particular notice in this respect are two basic types of symbols he utilizes: those of being, which suggest the order and stability inherent in substantial objects and rigid abstractions, and those of nonbeing, which imply formlessness, instability, or chaos. The symbols of being include light, blood, God, towers, coins, pyramids, tigers, horses, dogs, dreams, bulls, roses, mountains, flags, and red. Among the symbols of nonbeing are the circle, ashes, dust, mud, desert, night, clouds, water, moon, horizon, wheels, sand, stone, swamps, walls, labyrinths, and gray. In addition, a third, smaller group of symbols conveys a state of ambiguity, transition, or change. These include fire, smoke, the color rose, twilight, dawn, afternoon sun, killing, and gray.[1]

Perhaps the two most exaggerated examples of being and nonbeing in Borges's fiction are, respectively, the *Zahir* and the mind of Funes, the Memorious. The former, it will be recalled, is a coin that becomes an obsession to the narrator, symbolizing a dogmatic, petrified "truth" that in his fevered imagination eventually replaces the universe. On the other hand, Funes's mind is so cluttered with random details that he is unable to think or form abstractions. His mind, then, symbolizes the chaotic, quasi-mythical world of sense perceptions prior to the emergence of ideas. As indicated above, the narrator of "The Zahir" is condemned to madness and the unfortunate Funes dies at the age of twenty-one.

Two similarly structured tales, "The Circular Ruins" and "The God's Script," perhaps best illustrate the tension between being and nonbeing, both returning, in a sense, to primordial chaos in order to create reality anew. The principal difference between these two stories is that in "The Circular Ruins" the dreamed man conjured up from the chaos of nothingness symbolizes artistic creation, whereas the secret sentence deciphered on the tiger's back in "The God's Script" represents an abstract "truth" produced by thought. Inasmuch as for Borges dreaming and thinking are synonymous—both involving the creative imagination—the end results of these two activities also bear certain resemblances. The setting of "The Circular Ruins" symbolizes the fluid, formless consciousness that existed in the prelogical, mythopoetic age prior to thought or mental concepts. Other symbols of nonbeing in this tale include the gray wizard kissing the mud of the riverbank; the "unanimous night" of his arrival at the ruins; the dilapidated wall in which he conceals himself to dream; his vision of a circular amphitheater filled with a "vast illusory student body"; his barren, dreamless sleep described as a "viscous desert"; and, after his bout with insomnia, his ritual of purifying himself "in the waters of the river" under a full moon before he actually can begin to dream. Also interwoven throughout the story are symbols of concrete being or abstractions representing the dreamer's (the artist's) creative impulses that lead to the realization of his "work of art." Included among these symbols are the reified student the wizard instructs; the dreamed man's heart and skeleton; the god of Fire with the combined features of a tiger, a colt, a bull, a rose, and a storm; the god's promise to animate the dreamed phantom; the god's orders regarding the upbringing of the dreamed man; and once the latter comes to life, his trek to a faraway mountain to place a flag on its peak.

The story's denouement is sprinkled with symbolic images reinforcing the theme of artistic creation. After a long drought, we are told, the sky takes on the "rose color of leopard's gums"; clouds of smoke rust the "metal of the nights" and panic-stricken wild animals flee. Then, like centuries before, the ruins are again enveloped in a circular wall of flames, and at dawn, as the wizard advances into the inferno, he realizes the awful truth—that he too is a dream. The rose-colored sky, the image of rusting metal, the clouds of smoke, the dawn, and the circular wall of flames suggest the imminent dissolution of the wizard's reality. However, fire and circularity also symbolize regeneration, indicating that, as in the past, the ruins will be left "fertilized" for a new creative cycle. In addition, the wizard's son emerges as a symbol not only of artistic creation but also of the idealist concept of reality, i.e., a product of mental activity. And the wizard, who represents the artist, ironically finds himself just as unsubstantial—and just as absurd—as the world he has created. The circle, then, becomes a symbol of endless futility.

In "The God's Script" a series of tension-creating, symbolic contrasts also leads to a climactic moment of illumination when the Aztec priest discovers the meaning of the universe. Here Tzinacán's dark, circular, stone-walled prison represents his submersion into a state of nonbeing, while the tiger pacing back and forth in the adjacent cell, the stream of midday light let in by the jailer, and Tzinacán's recollections of his youth and of the pyramid erected to the god Qaholom constitute images of order, creativity, and being. Tzinacán's initial efforts to decipher the magical sentence contained in the tiger's spots (the god's script) also represent an impulse toward being, but his recurring nightmare in which he is almost suffocated by heaps of sand indicates his descent once again into a state of nonbeing. This condition is further emphasized by his vision of the magic wheel, a symbol of pantheistic unity that reveals to him his minute role in the universe and, perhaps as a result of this revelation, enables him to decipher the god's script. The omnipotence gained from this discovery is meaningless, however, because his individual identity has been dissolved into the circular, universal whole, plunging him into a permanent state of nonbeing.

Tzinacán's moment of illumination and subsequent descent into nonbeing illustrate Borges's concept of the esthetic reality discussed in the previous section, for the reader is left with the "imminence of a revelation" as he ponders over this enigmatic conclusion. The esthetic value of the story is also determined to a great extent by the dialectical interplay between the symbolic motifs representing light and dark, enlightenment and ignorance, reality and dream, youth and old age, and divine power and human wretchedness. Enhanced by the exotic setting, these mythically based opposites render a poetically conceived universal reality balanced by dramatic tension and contrapuntal elements.

In both "The Circular Ruins" and "The God's Script" the cyclical pattern of nonbeing-being-nonbeing concludes with the destruction of the individual personality. The wizard emerges as a dream, perhaps a dream of a god, and Tzinacán as an insignificant thread embedded in the total universal fabric. The limited success and ultimate defeat of both protagonists convey symbolically the theme of absurdity so common in Borges's work.

A final example of this dialectical interplay between being and nonbeing is provided by a passage from "Death and the Compass." Here the supremely confident Lönnrot has just gotten off the train on his way to arrest the culprit in the abandoned villa, Triste-le-Roy, where he will meet his doom. The implication of each symbol is indicated in brackets in order to emphasize the dynamic fluctuation between symbols of substance or vitality and those of destruction. These striking contrasts augment dramatic tension, thus anticipating the story's climactic conclusion.

The train stopped at a silent loading platform. Lönnrot descended. It was one of those deserted afternoons [nonbeing] which seem like dawn [change]. The air over the muddy plain [nonbeing] was damp and cold. Lönnrot set off across the fields [nonbeing]. He saw dogs [being], he saw a wagon [being] on a dead road [nonbeing], he saw the horizon [nonbeing], he saw a silvery horse [being] drinking the crapulous water of a puddle [nonbeing]. Dusk [change] was falling when he saw the rectangular belvedere [being] of the villa of Triste-le-Roy, almost as tall as the black eucalypti [being] which surrounded it. He thought of the fact that only one more dawn [change] and one more nightfall [change] (an ancient splendor in the east, and another in the west) separated him from the hour so much desired by the seekers of the Name [being].

Color symbolism also lends meaning to a large number of Borges's stories, the most common colors being gray and red. As mentioned above, gray signifies nonbeing, but occasionally it foreshadows death, thus also representing a symbol of transition. Red, on the other hand, alludes to vitality and passion, whereas a faded red or rose color indicates a state of ambiguity or change. Several of many examples follow.

The surname of Herbert Ashe* ("Tlön, Uqbar, Orbis Tertius") evokes grayness, but the fact that his beard "had once been red" also foreshadows his demise, as well as the change that will occur when the world becomes Tlön. Likewise Cartaphilus ("The Immortal"), Albert ("The Garden of the Forking Paths"), and Yarmolinsky ("Death and the Compass") are described as gray, a prefiguration of their deaths. The gray wizard in "The Circular Ruins" and the gray troglodytes of "The Immortal," however, convey a state of nonbeing, the wizard emerging as an unsubstantial dream and the troglodytes as primitives submerged in apathy.

The color red evoked by the names "Scharlach" and "Lönnrot" ("Death and the Compass") reflects the bitter

* An Englishman, Herbert Ashe is patterned after Borges's father.

rivalry between the two men. Somewhat similarly, the long red hair of the Nilsen brothers ("The Intruder") suggests their vitality and passion for living. Blood also symbolizes passion or instinctual behavior, as demonstrated by the English "Indian" woman ("Story of the Warrior and the Captive"), who drinks the blood of a slaughtered animal. At the moment of the death of Loewenthal ("Emma Zunz") we are told that "a gush of rude blood flowed from . . . [his] obscene lips," indicating his fury when Emma shoots him. And in "The South," the red sun of nightfall and the faded red of the general store are prefigurations of the dramatic change destined to affect Dahlmann's existence when he meets his alter ego. In connection with this tale, we are reminded that the south represents a cultural symbol of Argentina's national past, a region evoking instinctual freedom and courage. Other geographical areas holding special meanings for Borges include Uruguay, a symbol of primitivism and savagery, and India, the embodiment of a dreamlike unreality or the universe.

Another form of symbolism in Borges's works emerges from his persistent desire to depict linguistically a total, simultaneous representation of reality, or a considerable segment of it. Of course, this is impossible because language is a linear medium, whereas sight and imaginary visions are instantaneous and intuitive. A few examples of works illustrating this aspect of Borges's esthetics are "The God's Script," in which a formula of fourteen random words on the back of a tiger unlocks the secrets of the universe; "Parable of the Palace," about a poet who composes a brief poem replacing the universe; "Undr," whose title constitutes the entire body of poetry of the Urns; and "The Mirror and the Mask," the tale of a poet who captures in one verse an image of such overwhelming beauty that he must die.

Borges's most brilliant fictional presentation of this linguistic problem is his masterpiece "The Aleph" (discussed in Chapter 1, Section 2). It will be recalled that in this tale, the insufferable Carlos Argentino discovers the Aleph (a point in space containing all points) in his cellar and is inspired to write his long, pedantic poem entitled "The Earth." The fictional Borges (the narrator), on the other hand, upon viewing the Aleph, expresses his frustration because of the difficulties that arise when he attempts to depict it verbally. "I arrive, now, at the ineffable center of my story. And here begins my despair as a writer. All language is an alphabet of symbols whose use presupposes a past shared by all the other interlocutors. How, then, transmit to others the infinite Aleph, which my fearful mind scarcely encompasses? . . . What my eyes saw was simultaneous: what I shall transcribe is successive, because language is successive."

And so Borges launches into his long description of the small iridescent sphere that appears to be rotary because of the "vertiginous sights" it encloses:

I saw the heavy-laden sea; I saw the dawn and the dusk; I saw the multitudes of America; I saw a silver-plated cobweb at the center of a black pyramid; I saw a tattered labyrinth (it was London); I saw interminable eyes nearby looking at me as if in a mirror; I saw all the mirrors in the planet and none reflected me; . . . I saw clusters of grapes, snow, tobacco, veins of metal, steam; I saw convex equatorial deserts and every grain of sand in them; I saw a woman at Inverness whom I shall not forget. . . . I saw tigers, emboli, bison, ground swells, and armies; I saw all the ants on earth; I saw a Persian astrolabe; in a desk drawer I saw (the writing made me tremble) obscene, incredible, precise letters, which Beatriz had written Carlos Argentino; . . . I saw an atrocious relic of what deliciously had been Beatriz Viterbo; I saw the circulation of my obscure blood; I saw the gearing of love and the modifications of death; I saw the Aleph from all points; I saw the earth in the Aleph and in the earth the Aleph once more and the earth in the Aleph; I saw my face and my viscera; I saw your face and felt vertigo and cried because my eyes had seen that conjectural and secret object whose name men usurp but which no man has gazed on; the inconceivable universe.

The above description of the Aleph, approximately one-half of which has been eliminated, is important for several reasons. The use of the anaphoric "I saw" to convey the series of poetic images attempts to render the illusion of simultaneity and rotary movement. Nevertheless, unlike Carlos Argentino, the fictional Borges is never inspired to publish a work of art based on the fabulous Aleph and even strives to erase it from his memory. His desire to forget the Aleph can perhaps be explained by his realization that his description of it, though illuminated by striking poetic imagery, is utterly futile, consisting of random scraps of visible reality far inferior to the magnificent, all-encompassing vision he saw in Argentino's cellar.

Just as important as the Aleph are the unexpected images of Beatriz that Borges catches sight of within it: the obscene letters she has written to Carlos Argentino and her "atrocious relic." There would seem to be a relation between the Aleph and the enigmatic role of Beatriz, for like the Aleph, Beatriz is seen in some detail and then, eroded by the passing of time, fades from the fictional Borges's memory at the end of the story. She is first presented through the many pictures of her in Carlos Argentino's home, then described by the fictional Borges, and finally the total vision of her is rounded out in his mind when he sees her obscene letters and her "atrocious relic" in the Aleph. The "atrocious relic" represents an adroitly conceived oxymoron, a relic being a sacred, venerated object (Borges loved her) as well as a corpse, now "atrocious" because of her obscene letters.

Although the total vision of Beatriz is lost by the fictional Borges, it retains its totality and acquires a special significance for both the real Borges (the author) and the reader. The real Borges, realizing that he can never capture the simultaneous vision of the Aleph (the world) in sequential language, creates the total vision of Beatriz within the story as a symbolic version of the Aleph. But it is a version that the reader, once having finished the story, must grasp intuitively by combining all its parts into a simultaneous vision of the whole. Thus the total fictional impression of Beatriz conveyed to the reader by the story corresponds to the impression of totality conveyed to the fictional Borges by the Aleph in Carlos Argentino's cellar. However, the symbolic Aleph (the story) is superior to Argentino's Aleph, which is destroyed when his house is torn down, because as a work of art it overcomes the limitations of language and conveys a permanent, simultaneous reality that transcends the barriers of logic. For this reason "The Aleph" emerges as a symbol of all literature, whose purpose, according to Borges, is to subvert objective reality and recreate it through the powers of imagination. In his fiction this creative process is realized to a great extent through the adroit manipulation of symbols.[2]

3. IRONY AND THE POINT OF VIEW

Irony has played an ever-increasing role in twentieth-century literature, its complex, multifaceted nature making it a highly controversial concept. It has been said that irony was born of doubt, marked by skepticism, and governed by negation. Because it tends to undermine clarity by destroying dogmas and suggesting multiple interpretations of experience, it has also been called the mother of confusion. It is, then, intrinsically a somewhat pessimistic, negative attitude that often sets the tonal quality of a literary work and, at the same time, tends to throw the reader off balance. Although irony conveys no answers or solutions, it does provide the ironist with a measure of relief from a world he finds more and more incomprehensible. Verbal irony has been defined as saying one thing and meaning another, but irony can also be situational, in which case it involves the occurrence of the unexpected, often at the expense of a confident, unwary victim. Irony frequently stems from the contrast between appearance and reality as presented by a detached observer who tends to look upon his subject with a combination of amusement and superiority. The juxtaposition of opposites also characterizes much ironic literature, its purpose being not only to reveal the contradictions and incongruities in the world but also to enhance the esthetic elements of balance, tension, and ambiguity. In addition to being verbal or situational, irony may be stable or unstable. Stable irony is more easily understood, the reader usually detecting the author's implied meaning and sharing his attitude toward the fictional material. Unstable irony, however, is characterized by a greater degree of ambiguity, often due to the author's inscrutability or to his utilization of more than one unreliable narrative voice.[1]

Like many of his contemporaries, Borges uses irony to present his vision of a paradoxical world devoid of absolutes. In the preceding chapter allusions were made to the ironic elements in his fiction. The present section attempts to deal more systematically with the subject, concentrating first on situational irony, then on Borges's manipulation of the point of view, and finally on his use of verbal irony, which frequently stems from the point of view.

SITUATIONAL IRONY

In a rather large number of Borges's tales, the discrepancy between appearance and reality brings about a totally unexpected outcome, often victimizing the unwary protagonist, the reader, or even the narrator. We recall, for example, that in "The Circular Ruins" the wizard, so proud of his "son" and so eager to prevent him from becoming aware of his humiliating phantom condition, ultimately discovers that he too has been dreamed by another. The narrator of "Man on the Threshold," while searching for the missing Glencairn in an Indian city, interrogates an old man. The latter's tale about a similar occurrence in the past engrosses the narrator, but the surprise ending—Glencairn's execution by a mad judge—suggests that the narrator has been led into a labyrinth of temporal repetitions invalidating his efforts from the very beginning. And "The Approach to Al'Mu-tasim" emerges as a metaphor of man's search for the missing God, the student-protagonist's strange odyssey through India leading him to the discovery of his own soul, the only source of the clarity and tenderness he has sought so vainly in others.

Another victim of irony is Baltasar Espinosa, the free-thinking medical student in "The Gospel According to Mark," who finds himself about to be crucified after innocently seeking to entertain the ignorant Gutres with the legend of Christ's suffering on the cross. Somewhat differently, the narrator of "Guayaquil" falls victim to his own complacency when his antagonist, a strong-willed Jewish professor named Zimmerman, usurps his role as Argentina's representative on a mission to study some of Simón Bolívar's unpublished papers. The parallels between this situation and the historic meeting of Bolívar and San Martín enhance the irony of the denouement.

Sometimes logic can lead to erroneous or preposterous conclusions. Emma Zunz, we assume, will never be punished for the murder of her employer because her alibi is irrefutable. Zur Linde ("Deutsches Requiem") resorts to German philosophy in order to justify the crimes of Nazi Germany and explain Hitler's defeat. And Nils Runeberg ("Three Versions of Judas"), through theological reasoning, transforms Christ's betrayer into mankind's redeemer. Ironically, instead of suffering the martyrdom for which he yearns, Runeberg dies of a ruptured aneurysm and is remembered only by the heresiologists.

The reader occasionally becomes a victim of irony as, for example, in "The Sect of the Phoenix," the puzzling story that turns out to be a series of veiled allusions to the sex act. Once he guesses the story's meaning, the reader can laugh at the seriousness with which he read that the sacred rite is "clandestine" and "somewhat ridiculous," that sectarians "conserve only the obscure tradition of some cosmic punishment," and that a certain scholar "marveled at the ease with which . . . [the sectarians] became Spanish-Americans." The revelation of the protagonist's identity in "The House of Asterion" jolts the reader onto a new level of awareness; the terrible Minotaur of Greek mythology emerges as a symbol of frightened, alienated man. And in "Streetcorner Man" the reader finds himself identifying with the young, inexperienced narrator who, after pretending to be a mere bystander to the dramatic events described, turns out to be a ruthless killer.

Metaphysical irony, resulting from the clash between reasoning man and the incomprehensible divinity, is one of Borges's principal themes. A concept similar to the absurd, this theme is evident in tales such as "The Dead Man" and "The Two Kings and Their Two Labyrinths." The most memorable victim of metaphysical irony, however, is the "pure thinker" Lönnrot ("Death and the Compass"), who rejects the correct conjectures of Police Commissioner Treviranus in order to pursue the killers through a geometrical labyrinth of rigid logic. The center of this symbolic structure is reached when the pursuer Lönnrot discovers that all along he has been manipulated and pursued by the ironic god figure Scharlach. Metaphysical irony also prevails in "The Babylon Lottery," in which men foster the illusion that they are in control of their destiny by patterning their lives according to a bureaucratically operated game of chance. Similarly, the narrator of "The Library of Babel," in a final attempt to reconcile the "limitless" and "periodic" universe symbolized by the Library, expresses his "elegant hope" of discovering some kind of order in the repetition of disorder. Two additional examples of metaphysical irony are "The Theologians" and "The God's Script." In the former Aureliano spends most of his life refuting the metaphysics of John of Pannonia, only to discover after his death that for the "unfathomable divinity" he and his rival, supposedly diametrical opposites, form a single identity. The Aztec priest Tzinacán, we recall, finally succeeds in deciphering the god's script on the tiger, but divine knowledge so overwhelms him that instead of wielding the worldly power for which he has yearned, he renounces his petty human condition and passively waits for time to obliterate him.

Occasionally, the reader's discovery of the discrepancy between appearance and the reality of a given situation gives rise to dramatic irony, the result being that he shares the author's condescending view of the protagonists' human weaknesses. For example, in "Emma Zunz" we are told that when there are rumors of a strike at the factory, Emma "declared herself, as usual, against all violence." The following evening she murders Loewenthal. In "Death and the Compass" the police commissioner Treviranus guesses what really happened on two occasions, but his suggestions are rejected by Lönnrot, whose mental gyrations prove to be as futile as they are fascinating. Although Captain Nolan is introduced as a practical joker in "The End of the Duel," he conceives the fiendish scheme of having the two prisoners of war run a race after their throats have been slit. And in "The Theologians," when John of Pannonia's learned refutation of the Monotones leads to the execution of the heresiarch Euphorbus, the latter's words prefigure the irony of fate awaiting his accuser. "This has happened and will happen again. . . . You are not lighting a pyre, you are lighting a labyrinth of flames."

Borges often implies the juxtaposition of concepts or situations in order to create ironic incongruities and thus invalidate any absolute point of view by presenting its opposite. The idealist world set forth in "Tlön, Uqbar, Orbis Tertius" contrasts ironically with the modern world of exaggerated materialism. Another contrast emerges from the story's postscript, which explains the origin of the secret society and its creation of the mysterious planet. We recall that an American freethinker-millionaire named Ezra Buckley (a kind of inverted mirror image of the idealist bishop-philosopher George Berkeley) proposes a systematic encyclopedia of the planet. For this purpose, he leaves his gold mines and brothels to the society on the condition that "the work will have no truck with the imposter Jesus Christ." The result is a planet conceived by mortal men that eventually will replace the real world created by God. Additional examples of juxtapositions appear in "Dr. Brodie's Report" and "Utopia of a Tired Man." In the former the primitive customs of the Yahoos contrast ironically with those of the reader's world, often satirizing common practices in modern society. For example, unlike the carefully guarded leaders of the civilized nations, who declare war so that others may die, the Yahoos' kings are carried into battle to face certain death from the stones hurled at them by the Ape-men. And in "Utopia of a Tired Man" the aged citizens of a future Utopia end their days voluntarily in the lethal gas chamber of a crematory built, so they believe, by a renowned philanthropist named Adolph Hitler.

Three additional examples of juxtaposition suggest, ironically, the failure of reason to control instinct despite scientific progress. In "The Garden of the Forking Paths" a labyrinthine novel by a deranged nineteenth-century philosopher bears the same title as a twentieth-century labyrinthine short story about a world wrenched by the madness of World War I. "Story of the Warrior and the Captive" depicts a barbarian dazzled by Roman civilization and a nineteenth-century European woman attracted to the barbarism of the pampas. And the librarian protagonist of "The South" rejects modern culture and technology for the primitive gaucho's machismo cult.

As mentioned above, irony may derive from the narrator's attitude toward his fictional material or from the mask donned by the author to relate his tale. A common attitude is one of detachment, often resulting in a flat style that contrasts ironically with the shocking events presented. This is the case in both "The Intruder," which relates the murder of a likeable young woman in order to preserve the friendship of two ruffians, and "The End of the Duel," whose protagonists compete in a race after having had their throats cut. Borges's straightforward, matter-of-fact style in each of these stories gives him the aspect of a god far removed from the imperfect humans he has created. The narrator of "Tlön, Uqbar, Orbis Tertius" also reveals an attitude of detachment, but his irony is more apparent. We recall that in the closing lines we are told that eventually the world we know will become Tlön, but the skeptical narrator adds, "I take no notice. I go on revising . . . a tentative translation into Spanish, in the style of Quevedo, which I do not intend to see published, of Sir Thomas Browne's *Urn Burial*."

Some of Borges's most effective dramatized personas include the narrators of "Dr. Brodie's Report," "Streetcorner Man," and "The House of Asterion." The nineteenth-century Scottish missionary of "Dr. Brodie's Report" sets forth his Swiftian commentaries on customs of the primitive Yahoos in what the original narrator calls "a rather colorless English." The story's irony derives from the discrepancy between his serious tone and the often hilarious content of his report.

In "Streetcorner Man" Borges dons the mask of a boastful but insignificant *compadrito* whose posturing and stylized speech patterns were meant to parody the machismo myth and create an artificial, theatrical atmosphere. The fact that many readers considered it realistic, however, demonstrates that his ironic intention escaped them, probably because they became caught up in the gripping events and surprise ending. Borges's mischievousness becomes even more evident in "The House of Asterion," in which he assumes the point of view of a docile Minotaur, the diametrical opposite of the terrible mythical monster. The Minotaur's emergence as an ironic representation of man enclosed in a world of his own creation illustrates Borges's ability to invert virtually any myth or doctrine to suit his own esthetic or philosophical purposes.

Borges not infrequently displays touches of romantic irony, i.e., a consciousness of his own work that ranges from detachment to playful ambivalence and parody. A notable example is his portrait of Pierre Menard, the French symbolist poet whose rewriting of *Don Quijote* can be read as an ironic metaphor of Borges's reworking of authors such as Stevenson, Kipling, and Chesterton. A somewhat similar attitude emerges from "The Immortal," in which Cartaphilus, Borges's persona and author of the manuscript comprising this story, is accused of plagiarizing Pliny, Thomas De Quincey, Descartes, and George Bernard Shaw. Like Pierre Menard, Cartaphilus demonstrates Borges's theory that literature is an elaboration of other literatures. Borges's concluding statement regarding Cartaphilus's anguish shortly before death expresses his own anguish as a creative artist. "Words, displaced and mutilated words, words of others, were the poor pittance left him by the hours and the centuries." And Averroes's search for the meaning of comedy and tragedy without ever having seen a theater parallels Borges's vain attempts to imagine the Arab scholar's life from the meager knowledge available about him. In the final lines of the story Borges realizes the absurdity of his endeavor and resolves his predicament by effecting an abrupt disappearance of his protagonist, "as if fulminated by an invisible fire."

Two outstanding examples of romantic irony are "The Aleph" and "Ibn Hakkan al-Bokhari, Dead in His Labyrinth." In the former Borges laments his inability to depict the magical Aleph via the medium of language and then proceeds to create his own symbolic Aleph in the form of Beatriz, whose ingeniously conceived "total" portrait emerges in the mind of the reader. Borges's ironic view of his own work is perhaps best set forth in "Ibn Hakkan . . ." This absurd tale of an Arab king's murder in a labyrinth on the coast of England conveys the mental processes involved in creating a plot (symbolized by the labyrinth), giving it the proper form, and breathing life into it. The description of Rector Allaby, one of the narrators, as a man with "out-of-the-way reading habits" who dabbles in oriental literature, clearly marks him as Borges's fictional double. And the reversal of identities of Ibn Hakkan and Zaid, a subject debated by Dunraven and Unwin at the end of the story, demonstrates Borges's "divine power" to manipulate his characters to suit his purpose.

POINT OF VIEW

Because of its effect on tone, distance, and dramatic impact, the narrative point of view is an extremely important element of any literary work. Although Borges makes use of this crucial element to convey theme and enhance esthetic expression, his experiments with the point of view often suggest his desire to flout long-standing literary tradition as well as more recent practices among men of letters. The result is a wide variety of narrative perspectives that, in their entirety, reinforce Borges's denial of absolute values and help to inject irony and ambiguity into his writings. Though difficult to classify because of deliberate inconsistencies, these perspectives range from that of a distant, third-person omniscient narrator to that of a fictional first-person narrator identified as Borges.

The small group of stories told by an omniscient narrator who never intervenes to express his own sentiments includes "The Circular Ruins," "Death and the Compass," "The Secret Miracle," "The South," and "The End." In these stories the events are often reflected through the minds of the protagonists, causing the reader to identify more closely with them and, in a sense, to share their destinies. Thus in "The Circular Ruins" we wonder if, like the horrified wizard, we too are mere dreams of others; in "Death and the Compass" we see ourselves in Lönnrot, logically pursuing our goals, only to discover that logic itself can bear the seeds of destruction; Hladík's reprieve of one year in "The Secret Miracle" reminds us that although time can be twisted and reshaped by the artist, it can also be inexorably cruel; Dahlmann's dream in "The South" expresses our desire to participate in some kind of epic beyond our reach; and in "The End," Borges filters Martín Fierro's last knife fight through the mind of the paralyzed Recabarren, thus arresting the flow of time and generating the aura of myth evoked by the legendary gaucho.

In contrast with the above examples of the nonintervening omniscient narrator, the vast majority of Borges's tales utilize a first-person narrator, even if only briefly. "Emma Zunz" is related in the third person until approximately midway through the story, when we are told, "It is my belief that she did think once, and in that moment she endangered her desperate undertaking." After this brief interjection, the previous perspective is resumed and maintained throughout the rest of the story. Somewhat similarly, the narrator of "The Gospel According to Mark" speaks in the first person only when he introduces his protagonist, Baltasar Espinosa ("We may describe him, for now, as one of the common run of young men from Buenos Aires . . ."). And the use of the first-person narrator in the concluding sentence of "Avelino Arredondo" ironically undermines the flat, objective tone characterizing the rest of the story: "This is the way it probably happened, although in a more involved fashion;

this is the way I imagine it happened." In all of these tales Borges deliberately abandons what he considers the false pretense of objective reality, reminding his readers that literature is not a mirror of the world, but the product of a subjective imagination.

Other stories told by what seems to be an omniscient third-person narrator contain more significant first-person commentaries. In "Biography of Tadeo Isidoro Cruz (1829–1874)," for example, this technique sets a false tone of factual authenticity, which is ironically subverted in the closing sentence, when Cruz emerges as Martín Fierro's antagonist and the reader discovers that Borges has created fiction out of fiction. On the contrary, the first-person narrator in the postscript of "Averroes' Search" serves to set forth the theme of absurdity, Averroes's vain efforts to understand Aristotle being seen as analogous to Borges's efforts to depict Averroes.

The omniscient narrator's presence is felt throughout several tales as, for example, in "The Challenge," which describes a bloody duel between Wenceslao Suárez and a stranger. Although immediacy and suspense are initially conveyed by the narrator's conjectures ("They eat and drink and talk at length. About what? I suspect about subjects involving blood and cruelty—but with each on his guard, wary"), the first-person perspective ultimately becomes a vehicle for a philosophical commentary on the "blind religion of courage" displayed by men like Suárez. A similar degree of omniscience is displayed in "The Approach to Al-Mu'tasim," the story about an Indian novel Borges discusses in the guise of a literary critic. His occasional first-person observations on the exotic book render the impression that it exists, but the fact that it is apocryphal contributes to the paradox of an essay about a nonexistent subject. The narrator of "Pedro Salvadores" also intervenes from time to time, apparently to lend plausibility to the protagonist's nine-year self-incarceration during the dictator Rosas's reign of terror. The historic flavor of this story is ironically eclipsed, however, when Salvadores's tragic fate at last emerges as a symbol of the esthetic moment, i.e., "something we are about to understand, but never quite do."

Borges narrates the majority of his stories from beginning to end in the first person, giving this technique a number of variations. One of these is the dramatized narrator-protagonist, a means by which the author allows his protagonist to speak directly to the reader. The result can be a closer identification between reader and narrator, but if the author's ironic attitude toward his protagonist is detected, the reader will ally himself with the author and view the protagonist with a similar ironic detachment. Such is the case in "Deutsches Requiem," the tale related by the Nazi fanatic, Zur Linde, whose distorted political theories expose the fallacies of reason and parody the Nazi sympathizers in Argentina during World War II. The narrator of "Streetcorner Man" is also dramatized for ironic effect, his exaggerated histrionics serving to parody the values imposed on society by the machismo cult.

"Guayaquil" represents one of Borges's best examples of irony conveyed via the narrator-protagonist technique. The snobbish, condescending Argentine historian (the narrator) becomes the victim of irony when the lesser-known but stronger-willed Professor Zimmerman convinces him that he (Zimmerman) should undertake the mission to examine Bolívar's unpublished papers. However, Zimmerman's overriding ambition and cunning make him just as unattractive to the reader as the narrator. The result is an example of unstable irony that conceals the author's sentiments and leaves the reader torn between two possible reactions.

In "The House of Asterion" and "The God's Script" the effect of the dramatized first-person narrator is to arouse the reader's sympathy and intensify his emotional involvement. The intimate, doleful tone of Asterion becomes highly ironic when, in the final lines, he emerges

as a kind of inverted mirror image of the terrible
Minotaur, i.e., a symbol of man awaiting death as the only
form of deliverance from his mortal condition. The fact
that we are confined to the Aztec priest's point of view in
"The God's Script" reinforces the mystique surrounding
the events and also heightens the impact of the priest's loss
of identity.

In several stories the first-person narrator is either
referred to as Borges or reveals many of his traits. The
narrator of "The Other," which describes the elderly
Borges's encounter with his youthful double in Cambridge,
Massachusetts, perhaps bears the closest resemblance of all
to the real author. A narrator referred to as Borges also
relates "The Aleph" and "The Zahir," but whereas in the
former the narrator's esthetic preoccupations and his role
on the Argentine literary scene link him with Borges, in
the latter the narrator becomes obsessed with the coin and
ultimately loses his sanity. And although the narrator of
"Tlön, Uqbar, Orbis Tertius" never refers to himself by
name, his references to his friend Bioy Casares and his
English father clearly identify him with the real author.

One of Borges's favorite techniques is to present his
tale in the words of a first-person narrator-witness.
Although these narrators are occasionally dramatized—we
recall the child-witness to the duel in "The Meeting"—
they are usually more impersonal and sufficiently remote
to view their subject matter ironically. "The Sect of the
Phoenix" and "The Babylon Lottery" perhaps best
illustrate this point of view, both narrators conveying their
absurd messages with a kind of tongue-in-cheek attitude
that gradually undermines objectivity. Thus, upon
deciphering the symbolic meaning of the "Sect of the
Phoenix," the reader joins the narrator in viewing the sex
act ironically. And when the reader learns that Babylon is
nothing but an "infinite game of chance," he can better
understand why the narrator apparently lives somewhere
"far from Babylon," where he can "think of the lottery

with some astonishment and ponder the blasphemous conjectures murmured by men in the shadows at twilight."[2]

The first-person narrator-librarian of "The Library of Babel" also looks upon his subject matter with ironic detachment, his perspective of the enormous, symmetrically designed edifice being analogous to Borges's view of the universe that man mistakenly thinks he understands. "Funes, the Memorious" conveys man's inability to decipher the universe when the narrator's initial, anaphoric "I remember . . ." is overshadowed by Funes's fabulous, infallible memory, which mirrors the world but limits his powers of reason.[3] In "Utopia of a Tired Man" the narrator suddenly finds himself transported into a future Utopian society, where he gains insight into the absurdities of the world he has left behind.

The technique of narrating a story within a story, often referred to as a Chinese-box structure, characterizes a large number of Borges's works. This type of structure usually consists of a short introduction by a first-person narrative voice and a main plot told by a first-person narrator-protagonist or a narrator-witness. The result is an increase in the narrative distance, which underscores the fictive nature of the events. This pattern is illustrated by such tales as "The Man on the Threshold," which is told to the original narrator by a British official; "Rosendo's Tale," whose protagonist meets Borges in a bar and presents his version of "Streetcorner Man"; "The Unworthy Friend," the story of a Jewish storekeeper who confides in one of his customers; "Juan Muraña," told by a nephew of the famous knife fighter Muraña to a former school chum; and "The Form of the Sword," a tale Borges hears from an Irishman living in Argentina.

Two of the most notable examples of the Chinese-box structure are "The Immortal" and "Undr," both of which present a story within a story within a story. Thus in "The Immortal" the original narrator tells of the discovery of a manuscript written by the antique dealer

Cartaphilus, who then introduces the Roman Marcus Flaminius Rufus as the narrator. Similarly, in "Undr" the original narrator translates a seventeenth-century manuscript which, we learn, is a revision of an eleventh-century work. The narrator of the manuscript initiates the description of the Urns, but he soon presents the Icelander, Ulf Sigurdsson, who in turn assumes the role of narrator. The narrative distance and fictive quality derived from this type of structure not only reflect Borges's preoccupation with the creative process—a major theme in both of these tales—but also demonstrate his contention that literature cannot, and should not, attempt to mirror objective reality.

One might conclude that Borges refuses to follow any rules regarding the point of view except that as the creator of his own fictive world he does as he pleases. His first-person narrators tend to be his most typical as well as his most interesting, perhaps because they are more readily identified with mankind in general attempting to come to grips with uncertainty or chaos.

VERBAL IRONY

In the preface of his book *In Praise of Darkness*, Borges lists some of his esthetic principles, which include: "to feign slight uncertainties, for, although reality is exact, memory is not," and "to narrate events . . . as if I did not fully understand them." Thus in many of his stories a first-person narrator emerges as a kind of bungler who implies or frankly admits his lack of information on certain details. Often a purveyor of verbal irony, this device serves several purposes. It reflects Borges's ironic attitude toward the search for absolute knowledge or truth; it creates a bond of intimacy between the narrator and the reader, encouraging the latter to believe the story, but, paradoxically, it also casts doubt on the veracity of what has been said and thus tends to mislead the reader; and it mocks the modern tradition of the concealed narrator, suggesting that the subjective nature of language invalidates the so-called objective point of view. Examples are legion. In "An Examination of the Work of Herbert Quain" the narrator initiates his commentary on one of Quain's books as follows: "At the end of seven years, it is impossible for me to recuperate the details of the action. But I will outline its plot, exactly as my forgetfulness now impoverishes (exactly as it now purifies) it." In the midst of his tale about a revolution in Ireland, the narrator of "The Form of the Sword" recalls, "We entered (I seem to remember) through the back part of the house." "Theme of the Traitor and Hero" begins with the narrator's admission that under the influence of "the flagrant Chesterton" and Leibnitz he has imagined his tale, "which I shall doubtless develop . . . on profitless afternoons." He then refers to his limited knowledge of details on his subject but concludes his introduction by stating that "today . . . I dimly perceive it thus." Here Borges's frank admission that he is still in the process of creating pure fiction out of fiction and philosophy (the writings of Chesterton and Leibnitz) flaunts the literary conventions of the realistic slice-of-life storytellers who, in Borges's view, believe so naively that they are transcribing reality.

We are told in "The Captive," the story of the white boy carried off by Indians, that "at long last they traced him (the circumstances of the search have not come down to us and I dare not invent what I don't know) and they thought they recognized him." "Pedro Salvadores" begins with the narrator's statement that his tale is a written record, "perhaps the first to be attempted," of one of the strangest and grimmest happenings in Argentine history. He then asserts that "to meddle as little as possible in the telling, to abstain from picturesque details or personal conjectures is, it seems to me, the only way to do this." "The Intruder" is introduced by doubts regarding the source of the story, which, though supposedly true, becomes more fiction than fact due to the narrative perspective. "People

say (but this is unlikely) that the story was first told by
Eduardo, the younger of the Nilsens, at the wake of his
elder brother Cristián. . . . The fact is that someone got it
from someone else during the course of that drawn-out and
now dim night . . . and told it to Santiago Dabove, from
whom I heard it. Years later . . . I heard it again . . . with
the usual minor variations and discrepancies. I set down
the story now. . . . I hope to do this in a straightforward
way, but I see in advance that I shall give in to the writer's
temptation of emphasizing or adding certain details." The
unreliability of the narrator of "The End of the Duel" is
similarly suggested when he admits that the events were
collected by a ranch foreman "from oral accounts" that "I
transcribe now with a good deal of misgivings, since both
forgetfulness and memory are apt to be inventive." And
after relating the strange occurrences surrounding Pedro
Damián's demise, "The Other Death" ends with the narrator's confession that in his story "there are a few false
memories." Indeed, he suspects that Pedro Damián never
existed, that his story derives from his recollections of a
medieval clergyman named Pier Damiani.

Borges's verbal irony often takes the form of poking
fun at himself, his narrator, his fictional material, or even
literature in general. "An Examination of the Work of
Herbert Quain" ends with an allusion to the apocryphal
Quain's belief that since many would-be men of letters are
incapable of invention, they must content themselves with
sham. For these "imperfect writers" Quain wrote a collection of eight stories entitled *Statements*. Borges alludes to
his own lack of originality—an idea he has expressed on
many occasions—when he asserts that he was ingenious
enough to "extract" from Quain's collection his own story
of "The Circular Ruins." Borges also playfully refers to
himself in "The Unworthy Friend," when his narrator-
protagonist Santiago Fischbein tells his unnamed interlocutor, "Maybe you can make some use of this story—
which, of course, you'll dress up with daggers."

Borges delights in satirizing various aspects of upper-middle-class Argentine society, often focusing on artistic and literary circles. In "The Zahir" Clementina Villar always "appeared at the correct places, at the correct hour, with the correct appurtenances and the correct boredom; but the boredom, the appurtenances, the hour and the places would almost immediately become passé and would provide Clementina Villar with the material for a definition of cheap taste." Marta Pizarro and Clara Glencairn, the wealthy antagonists of "The Duel," dabble in painting out of boredom with their purposeless lives. When the First Congress of Inter-American Painting and Sculpture is to be convened in Cartagena, Clara would like to be named the Argentine delegate, but Marta is awarded this honor. The themes of the conference, we are told, are "of burning interest: Can the artist disregard the indigenous? Can he omit or slight flora and fauna? Can he be insensitive to problems of a social nature? Should he not join his voice to those suffering under the yoke of Saxon imperialism? Et cetera, et cetera."

As indicated previously, Borges's portrait of Carlos Argentino in "The Aleph" is fraught with irony, but Argentino's foibles also parody the absurdity of literary endeavor and the clichés it spawns. "His [Carlos Argentino's] ideas seemed so inept to me, their exposition so pompous and so vast, that I immediately related them to literature: I asked him why he did not write them down. Foreseeably he replied that he had already done so: these concepts, and others no less novel, figured in the Augural Canto, or more simply, the Prologue Canto, of a poem on which he had been working for many years, without publicity, without any deafening to-do, putting his entire reliance on those two props known as work and solitude. First, he opened the floodgates of the imagination; then he made use of a sharp file. The poem was titled *The Earth*; it consisted of a description of the planet, wherein, naturally, there was no lack of picturesque digression and elegant apostrophe."

Borges's most ironic view of literature and literary circles emerges from "Pierre Menard, Author of *Don Quijote*." Here the caustic first-person narrator assumes the stance of an indignant friend of the recently deceased, apocryphal writer, whose accomplishments have been reported erroneously by the press. "The *visible* works left by this novelist [Menard] are easily and briefly enumerated. It is therefore impossible to forgive the omissions and additions perpetrated by Madame Henri Bachelier in a fallacious catalogue that a certain newspaper, whose Protestant tendencies are no secret, was inconsiderate enough to inflict on its wretched readers—even though they are few and Calvinist, if not Masonic and circumcised." After listing Menard's esoteric works, the narrator initiates his discussion of the principal subject at hand. "Now I will pass over to that other part, which is subterranean, interminably heroic, and unequalled, and which is also—oh, the possibilities inherent in man!—inconclusive. This work, possibly the most significant of our time, consists of the ninth and thirty-eighth chapters of Part One of *Don Quijote* and a fragment of the twenty-second chapter. I realize that such an affirmation seems absurd; but the justification of this 'absurdity' is the primary object of this note." The real absurdity, of course, is that the product of Menard's arduous endeavor is identical to the passages written by Cervantes.

Occasionally Borges's irony leads him afield to issues unrelated to the subject at hand. In "The Elderly Lady," for example, his mention of the Battle of Big Hill triggers the following comment: "Always envious of our glories, the Venezuelans attribute this victory to General Simón Bolívar, but the impartial observer, the Argentine historian, is not easily taken in and knows only too well that the laurels rightfully belong to Colonel Mariano Rubio."

The German philosopher Martin Heidegger, who supported the Hitler regime, becomes a target of irony in
"Guayaquil," when the narrator alludes to Professor Zimmerman's contention that government should be neither
visible nor emotional.

This proposal drew the unanswerable refutation of Martin
Heidegger, who, using newspaper headlines, proved that the
modern chief of state, far from being anonymous, is rather the
protagonist, the choragus, the dancing David, who acts out the
drama of his people with all the pomp of stagecraft, and resorts
unhesitatingly to the overstatement inherent in the art of oration.
He also proved that Zimmerman came of Hebrew, not to say
Jewish, stock. Publication of this essay by the venerated
existentialist was the immediate cause of the banishment and
nomadic activities of our guest [Zimmerman].

A final example of Borges's verbal irony appears at the
end of "Dr. Brodie's Report," when the Scottish missionary
condescendingly compares the institutions of the barbarous
Yahoos with those of their mirror image, modern civilized
man.

Only too well do I know the Yahoos to be a barbarous nation,
perhaps the most barbarous to be found upon the face of the earth,
but it would be unjust to overlook certain traits which redeem
them. They have institutions of their own; they enjoy a king; they
employ a language based upon abstract concepts; they believe, like
the Hebrews and the Greeks, in the divine nature of poetry; and
they surmise that the soul survives the death of the body. They also
uphold the truth of punishments and rewards. After their fashion,
they stand for civilization much as we ourselves do, in spite of our
many transgressions.

4. STYLISTIC ELEMENTS

As many critics have pointed out, the essence of Borges's
prose style is its brevity, clarity, compactness, and rigorous
precision, qualities that have contributed to an overall
impression of classical purity and slightly mannered

elegance. Borges has repeatedly expressed his distaste for rare words and ornate language, striving instead for economy, polish, and even invisibility. He is a meticulous craftsman who writes draft after draft of each tale before he is satisfied with the final product. Thus his style emerges as highly functional, the perfect vehicle for dramatizing the archetypal situations of his atemporal, cerebral universe. As indicated previously, it also contrasts strikingly with the banal documentation of realism and the ornate linguistic vehicle of modernism.

Although the youthful Borges sought to impress his readers with striking metaphors and vocabulary chosen from the Argentine vernacular, he eventually outgrew these tendencies. The stories of *A Universal History of Infamy* (1935) represent a relatively unimportant portion of his *oeuvre,* but they demonstrate his ability to fuse fact with fiction in a highly appealing manner and, in a sense, lay the groundwork for the brilliant style of his cosmic *ficciones* of the 1940s and 1950s, still the mainstay of his renown. Sometime after the mid-1950s he tired of labyrinths and reflecting mirrors, evolving instead a more straightforward and realistic mode of expression inspired by, in his words, the "laconic masterpieces" of the young Kipling. The most successful result of this new orientation is *Dr. Brodie's Report* (1970), several stories of which depict episodes involving the *compadrito,* or hoodlum. Borges's most recent collection, *The Book of Sand* (1975), is also characterized by linguistic directness and simplicity, but it marks a shift to the more philosophical and esthetic themes reminiscent of his earlier writings. Mention should be made of *Dreamtigers* (1960) and *In Praise of Darkness* (1969), both of which contain poetically conceived vignettes and parables on literary, philosophical, and esthetic topics. In these works the style is uncomplicated but highly evocative.

Unlike Borges's ultraist poetry of the 1920s, in which he utilizes the metaphor to alter the meaning of words and create esthetic tension, his prose seldom contains metaphors that function as figures of speech. Nevertheless, many of Borges's stories can be read as sustained metaphors of esthetic or metaphysical ideas. An outstanding example is "The Aleph," in which the total portrait of Beatriz Viterbo becomes a substitute for the Aleph, the magically compressed universe Borges is unable to depict in lineal language. "The Circular Ruins" not only gives symbolic expression to the idealist tenet of life as a dream, but in addition constitutes a phantasmagorical metaphor of the creative process. This theme is also developed metaphorically in "Pierre Menard, Author of *Don Quijote*" and "The Immortal," both of which dramatize Borges's well-known assertion that his fiction is, in reality, a reworking of his favorite authors. The most ingenious treatment of the creative process, however, is "Ibn Hakkan al-Bokhari, Dead in His Labyrinth," an absurd conceit* of the thematic and structural preoccupations that plague the storyteller as he weaves his plot and develops his characters within its framework.

In "Theme of the Traitor and Hero" the dual character of the Irish conspirator, Kilpatrick, can be read as a metaphor, not only of the disunity of the human personality traditional psychology attempts to analyze and explain, but also of the utterly fictitious nature of history. "Death and the Compass" and "Averroes' Search" might be described as metaphoric representations of rational man's vain quest for knowledge. "The Library of Babel" and "Tlön, Uqbar, Orbis Tertius" are elaborate conceits of universal culture, the former emerging as a man-made symmetrically designed library whose illegible volumes reflect the impenetrable divine mind, and the latter as an encyclopedic labyrinth destined to become, though provisionally, the accepted view of the world. Somewhat simi-

---

* A conceit is an elaborate metaphor in which a writer describes an idea by use of an analogy that often seems farfetched.

larly, "The House of Asterion" conveys modern man's fear, ignorance, and alienation in the face of the vast, incomprehensible universe. The chaotic world of chance is institutionalized in "The Babylon Lottery," another metaphor of man's absurd search for order. And "Funes, the Memorious" underscores the abyss between man and the world by demonstrating that if the human mind could mirror reality, it would be so cluttered with details that thought—and, indeed, human life itself—would become impossible.

Critics have stated that, like Kafka, Borges writes realistically about fantasy, and indeed his concise, classical language and his allusions to recondite but seemingly factual material, do tend to make his unsuspecting reader accept what would ordinarily be rejected. Still, following his oft-quoted dictum that unreality is the condition of art, Borges utilizes a wide variety of stylistic devices to blur concrete reality and create a shadowy, hallucinatory world that somehow preserves the underlying essence of the human condition. His writings are sprinkled with understatements, affirmations by negation, parenthetical corrections or commentaries, and doubts or denials of information previously stated as truth. On the other hand, he bolsters the credibility of his tales by introducing the scholarly footnote, often documented with page numbers and precise dates, and by alluding to maps, atlases, dictionaries, encyclopedias, and real people. The uncertainty created by this adroit juxtaposition of fiction and objective reality reflects his belief that intellect and truth are no less illusory than imagination and art.

Three of Borges's best known tales will serve to illustrate the above-mentioned stylistic devices. "Funes, the Memorious" contains numerous parenthetical phrases that contradict or cast doubt on previous statements, thus accentuating the fictional nature of the events. The initial sentence conveys the narrator's admission that his memory of his protagonist may be less than accurate. "I remember

him (I scarcely have the right to use this ghostly verb; only
one man on earth deserved the right, and he is dead)."
Throughout the rest of the story, statements are altered or
corrected (". . . I had the apprehension [the secret hope]
. . .) (He reasoned [or felt] . . .") in order to emphasize
the narrator's limited knowledge of the past and, at the
same time, heighten the effect of his protagonist's remarkable mental processes.

"Pierre Menard, Author of *Don Quijote*" begins
with the narrator's expression of distress over the publication of a "fallacious catalogue" of Menard's works by a
certain Madame Henri Bachelier. Professing to rectify
these errors, he first alludes modestly to his "meager
authority" and then mentions his friendship with two
aristocratic ladies, whose approval of his corrections
provides support for his subsequent affirmation by negation: "These authorizations, I believe, are not insuffi-
cient." The subsequent bibliography of the apocryphal
author includes a wide variety of titles, some of which refer
to well-known figures such as Descartes, Leibnitz, Paul
Valéry, Saint-Simon, and Quevedo, and others to fictitious
men of letters. "Pierre Menard . . . ," like "Funes, the
Memorious," contains many parenthetical phrases qualify-
ing the narrator's statements or conveying his thoughts on
his subject matter. Injections such as "which seems to me
irrefutable," "how shall I say it," "I speak, naturally, of
my personal capacity," "which no one can deny me in
good faith," "word for word and line for line," constantly
disrupt the narrative thread, lending an aura of
authenticity to an author who is not only nonexistent but
whose "rewriting" of *Don Quijote* emerges as an utterly
absurd endeavor.

The use of the footnote and precise dates, so common
in Borges's fiction, is exemplified by "Three Versions of
Judas," the tale of the Swedish scholar Nils Runeberg,
who reasons that Judas, not Jesus, is God's son and the
redeemer of mankind. The main body of the text contains

names of real authors and theologians (Dante, De Quincey, Kemnitz, Hans Lassen Martensen), the mention of whom would seem to imply that the apocryphal Runeberg and the works attributed to him are likewise authentic. This playful juxtaposition of the real and the fictitious is accentuated, moreover, by the story's three footnotes, which supposedly document Runeberg's absurd theories with references to writers such as Almafuerte (a late-nineteenth-century Argentine poet), Euclydes da Cunha and Erik Erfjord (obscure theologians), Maurice Abramowicz (a school chum of Borges's in Switzerland), and Jaromir Hladík (the protagonist of "The Secret Miracle"). The ambiguity resulting from this technique is, of course, a basic ingredient of Borges's *oeuvre*.

Borges's weltanschauung in the face of the indecipherable universe is expressed by a connotative vocabulary designed to evoke a shadowy or hidden side of life and thrust the reader into a realm of uncertainty, mystery, and poetic wonder. Thus his favorite adjectives include *dark, vast, remote, enigmatic, abstract, intricate, secret, chaotic, incoherent, indecipherable, perplexing, mysterious, arcane, reflecting, nebulous, desolate, inexhaustible, deserted, empty, infinite, intimate, illusory, eternal, labyrinthine,* and *vertiginous.* Correspondingly, his writings are replete with abstract or semi-abstract nouns such as *darkness, twilight, solitude, melancholy, chaos, eternity, reflection, fluctuation, expanse, chance, dream, shadow, phantom, enigma, mystery, illusion, conjecture, network, mirror, vertigo,* and *labyrinth.* And, in addition, adverbs and adverbial phrases like *maybe, perhaps, probably, I believe,* and *it seems to me* frequently suggest doubts on the part of the narrator about the authenticity of the material presented.

The following examples illustrate Borges's unique use of vocabulary. In "The Garden of the Forking Paths," Yu Tsun states that he "contemplated the fluctuations of the day which would probably be my last." Soon thereafter he

sees himself as "an abstract spectator" as he approaches
Stephen Albert's home on an evening that is "at once intimate and infinite." In the course of their conversation,
Albert refers to Ts'ui Pên's "invisible labyrinth of time,"
which finds concrete expression in the absurd events of the
story. The narrator of "The Library of Babel" imagines
that "the polished surfaces [of a mirror] feign and promise
infinity." He also alludes to the "formless and chaotic
nature of almost all books" in the library, adding that the
certainty of everything having already been written
"nullifies or makes phantoms of us all." In "Death and
the Compass," Gryphius is described as a man with "a
nebulous grey beard." En route to Triste-le-Roy, Lönnrot
gets off the train on a "deserted afternoon," and once
inside the estate, he catches sight of a two-faced Hermes
that casts "a monstrous shadow" in a "desolate garden."
After seeing himself "infinitely reflected in opposing mirrors," he imagines the house to be "infinite and growing,"
"made larger by the penumbra, . . . the mirrors, . . . the
solitude." The project of dreaming a man in "The Circular Ruins" exhausts "the entire expanse" of the
wizard's mind. The uninhabited, ruined temple is the
appropriate site for his project because it contains "a
minimum of visible world." Gazing at "the vast illusory
student body" in an amphitheater, he seeks to redeem one
of the students from his condition of "empty illusion" and
interpolate him into the real world. And following his bout
with insomnia, he understands that "modeling the
incoherent and vertiginous matter of which dreams are
composed" is the most difficult task that a man can
undertake.

As suggested previously, paradox constitutes a fundamental element of Borges's work, his most coherent statement on the subject having been set forth in his essay on
Zeno of Elea, "Avatars of the Tortoise."[1] Borges's fascination with the paradoxical would seem to stem, at least in
part, from his conviction that intellectual systems are
doomed to fail because they can never marshall all the

necessary information. The perception of paradox, however, serves not only to undermine the reader's complacent belief in order, but also to reveal some of the enigmatic aspects of the universe. For Borges, who relishes ideas for their esthetic value, these revelations have both cerebral and esthetic rewards. His famous statement on the subject is worth repeating. "We . . . have dreamed the world. We have dreamed it strong, mysterious, visible, ubiquitous in space and secure in time; but we have allowed tenuous, eternal interstices of injustice [paradoxes] in its structure so that we may know that it is false."

Many of Borges's stories give concrete form to paradoxical situations. Both "The Zahir" and "The Aleph," for example, depict the world condensed into a small spherical object. In "Death and the Compass" reason brings about Lönnrot's destruction, having transformed him from the pursuer into the pursued. "Deutsches Requiem" and "Three Versions of Judas" demonstrate how logic can lead to utterly absurd conclusions. Pierre Menard creates an "infinitely richer" version of *Don Quijote,* which is identical to Cervantes's original work. The pantheistic idealism of Tlön is hailed as absolute truth by the gullible inhabitants of Earth despite their history of "provisional" philosophical systems. Funes, the Memorious's memory is more lucid than that of any man who has ever lived, but he is unable to think. Although the Library of Babel is symmetrically structured and its books are identical in size, the narrator's "elegant hope" of finding order within the edifice lies in the repetition of disorder. The wizard of "The Circular Ruins" dreams a man only to discover that his dream is no less real than he is.

Emma Zunz deftly illustrates how reason can disguise guilt as innocence. Kilpatrick, the Irish conspirator, emerges as a traitor who signs his own death decree in order to become a hero. His descendant, a historian named Ryan, seeks the truth only to find both Kilpatrick and himself enveloped in a web of fiction. A game of chance becomes a rationally conceived bureaucratic institution governing all phases of life in Babylon. The Indian student's labyrinthine search for God leads back to himself in "The Approach to Al-Mu'tasim." "The South" portrays a cultured librarian who relishes death in a knife fight with a gaucho hoodlum. And in "The Garden of the Forking Paths" a Chinese spy sacrifices his own life by killing an Englishman he admires in order to help the Germans, whom he despises.

These paradoxical situations depicted in Borges's *ficciones* are reinforced stylistically by the extensive use of oxymoron, a figure of speech that might be defined as a concise paradox.* Examples abound in most of the above-mentioned tales. Sciences exist "in countless numbers" on the planet of Tlön, which offers "minute and vast evidence" of being an ordered planet. Pierre Menard's "private archives" are carefully examined by the story's narrator who finds in them a reference to "an authentic effigy" of a certain Countess of Bagnoregio. Menard is said to have stated that Cervantes was "swept along by inertias of language and invention" as he composed his immortal work. In "The Circular Ruins" the wizard's canoe sinks into the "sacred mud" as he debarks near the ancient temple. After his initial efforts to dream a man, he discovers that people of the region have been "spying respectfully" on his sleep.

The Company sponsoring the lottery of Babylon provides "sacred privies," a "dusty aqueduct," and an "alphabetical archive of variable veracity" for the citizenry. The narrator of "The Library of Babel" states that, in order to find the elusive Man of the Book, someone proposes adopting a "regressive approach." In this same tale youths are said to prostrate themselves before books and "barbarously kiss" the pages. Yu Tsun ("The Garden of the Forking Paths") sees a "wounded, happy soldier"

---

* An oxymoron consists of two contradictory words or phrases combined to produce a rhetorical effect. "Eloquent silence" is an example of an oxymoron.

in a railroad station and experiences a state of "abject happiness" as a result of the "precious accident" of the train schedule. Stephen Albert subsequently informs him that he, a "barbarous Englishman," has acquired the key to the "transparent mystery" of Ts'ui Pên's labyrinth. As he concludes his last conversation with Funes, the Memorious, the narrator sees his face in the "equivocal clarity" of the dawn. He also recalls the "stammering greatness" of Funes's senseless efforts to catalogue the images of his memory and create a new system of enumeration. At the beginning of "Theme of the Traitor and Hero," a reference is made to Leibnitz, who "invented pre-established harmony"; this tale concludes with Ryan's resolution, after some "tenacious caviling," not to reveal the discovery he has made about his ancestor.

In "Death and the Compass," one of Borges's most paradoxical stories, the murders are referred to as "frugal pogroms"; the "mystery" of the strange events becomes "almost crystalline" to Lönnrot; the gate to Triste-le-Roy, which abounds in "superfluous symmetries," opens with "laborious passivity"; after his capture Lönnrot detects a "fatigued triumph" in Scharlach's voice; and a moment before his death Lönnrot feels an "impersonal, almost anonymous sadness." In his dream at the beginning of "The Secret Miracle," Hladík runs across the sands of a "rainy desert," and after his arrest he resorts to "perverse logic" in order to prevent his execution. Nils Runeberg, the protagonist of "Three Versions of Judas," is a man of "intellectual passion," who proposes "an extravagant and even limitless asceticism" as an explanation of Judas's conduct. In "The End" Recabarren's guitar is described as a "meager labyrinth infinitely winding and unwinding."

The paradoxical theme of "Emma Zunz" is strengthened stylistically when, pretending to be a prostitute, Emma chooses a coarse, unattractive seaman so that "the purity of the horror might not be mitigated." In "Deutsches Requiem" Dietrich zur Linde, reasoning that everything that can happen to a man is preordained, declares that "every negligence is deliberate, every chance encounter an appointment, every humiliation a penitence, every failure a mysterious victory." He also considers "insidious, deceitful mercy" to be "the greatest of sins" and finds an "almost terrible flavor of happiness" in Nazi Germany's defeat. We are told in "The Aleph" that the deceased Beatriz Viterbo walked with "a kind of gracious torpor"; her cousin, Carlos Argentino, corrects his poem in accordance with a "depraved principle" of verbal ostentation; in the "gigantic instant" in which he gazes at the Aleph, Borges catches sight of the "atrocious relic" of his beloved Beatriz; and after he is interrupted by Argentino's "hateful, jovial voice," he refuses with "suave energy" to discuss the Aleph.

Additional examples of oxymoron in Borges's work include such phrases as "pompous frivolity" and "physical humiliation" ("The Theologians"), "rude supplication" ("The House of Asterion"), "monotonous barbarity" and "luminous, fundamental night" ("Biography of Tadeo Isidoro Cruz"), "humiliated and gratified" ("The Dead Man"), "invisible presence" and "He had spoken fiercely, joyfully" ("The Man on the Threshold"), "harmless knife play" ("The Challenge"), "maliciously and cheerfully" ("The Intruder"), "unseen presence" ("Pedro Salvadores"), "diffused splendor" ("The Duel"), "melancholy and pompous tone" and "more or less unanimous vote" ("Guayaquil"), and "well-constructed nightmares" and "I felt an intruder in the chaos" ("There Are More Things").

The transferred epithet* and hypallage† are two additional stylistic devices utilized extensively by Borges.

* A transferred epithet is an adjective used to limit grammatically a noun it does not logically modify, though the relation is so close that the meaning is clear. Examples are Shakespeare's "dusty death" and Milton's "blind mouths."

† Hypallage is a figure of speech in which an adjective is applied to a noun other than the more appropriate one. An example is Keats's "The murmurous haunt of flies" rather than "the haunt of murmurous flies."

More meaningful in his works than ornamental, these devices serve several purposes. By underscoring effect rather than cause, they tend to enhance verbal economy and accelerate narrative progression. Equally important, the juxtaposition of ordinarily unrelated nouns and adjectives disrupts the traditional use of language, thrusting the reader onto more abstract, ambiguous, or irrational levels of reality. Examples of the transferred epithet are legion in most of Borges's fiction, especially in the stories published during the 1940s and 1950s. "The Approach to Al-Mu'tasim" abounds in striking word combinations that contribute to its mysterious oriental flavor and reflect the paradoxical chain of events. The novel discussed in the story is viewed as an "uncomfortable combination" of allegorical Islamic poetry and the murder mystery. The Sirkar police attempt to break up a riot with "impartial lashes," causing the student-protagonist to scale the wall of an "entangled garden." Subsequently the student sees with "miraculous consternation" a tenderness in the facial expression of an evil man, a revelation that initiates his "insatiable search" for a soul equivalent to God. The first sentence of "The Circular Ruins" ("No one saw him disembark in the unanimous night") is likely to puzzle the reader, but the story's thematic representation of life as a dream makes the "unanimous night" a metaphor of the blindness characteristic of all men. The exotic, nightmarish setting is enhanced, moreover, by phrases such as "the vertiginous matter" of which dreams are composed and the "incessant trees" threatening to strangle the ruins of a "propitious temple."

The reader of "The Babylon Lottery," one of Borges's most absurd tales, encounters a multitude of transferred epithets reflecting the irrational theme of institutionalized chaos. These include "vertiginous country," "blasphemous conjectures," "indignant agitation," "mysterious monotony," and "divine modesty." The deceased protagonist of "An Examination of the Work of Herbert Quain" is allotted a half-column of "necrological piety"

by the *Times Literary Supplement*. Quain introduces
characters of "ancient blood," one of whom favors her sui-
tor with a "distracted kiss." The "febril" Library of Babel
contains a "miniature" room for the satisfaction of "fecal
necessities" and "hazardous volumes" providing a
"minute history of the future." The narrator of "Funes,
the Memorious" initiates his tale by stating that he
scarcely has the right to use the "ghostly verb" *remember*.
He then demonstrates that the "ferocious splendor" and
"surging avenues" of Babylon, London, and New York
cannot compare with the pressures of reality that leave
their mark on Funes's "implacable memory."

The erosion of rigid logic in "Death and the Compass" is effected by the repeated use of the transferred
epithet long before Lönnrot's downfall. The scene of the
first murder is the Hôtel du Nord, a prism-shaped edifice
which the Hebrew scholar Yarmolinsky views with
"ancient resignation." When Commissioner Treviranus
explains Yarmolinsky's murder on the basis of chance,
Lönnrot states that he prefers "a purely rabbinical explanation." The second victim is found in a remote slum
whose rose-colored mud walls reflect the "disordered setting" of the sun. Lönnrot finds a "violent star of blood" on
the floor of the hotel room occupied by Gryphius, the man
believed to be the third victim. An "anonymous triangle
and a dust-laden Greek word" are the principal clues that
induce the ill-fated Lönnrot to journey along a "dead
road" on a "deserted afternoon" to Triste-le-Roy. In his
explanation of how he trapped Lönnrot, Scharlach refers
to the "reverent fear" of pronouncing the name of God
and the "perverse cubicle" where he spent a week under
his assumed name, Gryphius. And just before his death,
Lönnrot hears the "useless cry" of a bird, a symbol not
only of his helplessness but also of the impotence of reason,
which has led him to his destruction.

"The Secret Miracle" is also sprinkled with transferred epithets that lend tension and ambiguity to the

strange sequence of events. An "effusive catalogue" issued by Hladík's publishers exaggerates his renown, bringing about his arrest by the Nazis. During his nights in prison he strives to hold fast the "fugitive substance" of time as he thinks about his "equivocal and languid past." And after having been granted a year to finish his play, he eagerly weaves his "lofty invisible labyrinth in time," a metaphor of the complex creative process that takes the artist outside the realm of chronological progression. Similar stylistic effects are achieved in "The Theologians," the story of two rival ecclesiastics. Aurelian considers revising his treatise on the Monotones, but upon reading John of Pannonia's brilliant discussion of the same subject, he decides "with resentful integrity" to send his own to Rome unmodified. Reference is also made to the "hermetic books" the theologians read as well as to the "contemplative deserts" and "arduous limits" of the empire Aurelian seeks in order to meditate in solitude.

The labyrinth of reason traced by Emma Zunz begins with her feelings of "blind guilt" upon learning of her father's death. On the Paseo de Julio she wanders unnoticed through an "indifferent portico." After the "arduous events" of her "desperate undertaking" with a sailor she becomes aware of the "insipid movement" of the streetcar taking her through the "opaque suburbs" to Loewenthal's residence. And when she shoots Loewenthal, the gush of "rude blood" flowing from his "obscene lips" captures the immediate results of her deed along with her victim's reaction.

Although hypallage is not as prevalent in Borges's fiction as the transferred epithet, it also is used frequently as a subtle rhetorical device to undermine the order of language and underscore the chaotic reality rational man strives to organize and analyze. In "The Approach to Al-Mu'tasim," for example, we are told that the Indian student kills a Hindu "with desperate hands," the adjective desperate obviously referring to the student's state of

mind. In a literary commentary, the narrator of the same
story states that the "punctual itinerary of the hero"
represents the progress of the soul in its mystic ascent.
Similarly, the wizard of "The Circular Ruins" is
awakened by the "inconsolable shriek of a bird" and, just
before approaching the wall of flames, he watches "the
panic-stricken flight of wild animals."

In "The Babylon Lottery" the narrator's "atrocious
variety" of fate includes his recollection of once having
found himself faced with the "silent handkerchief of a
strangler." Borges's apocryphal author, Herbert Quain,
never considered himself a genius, even on his "extravagant nights of literary conversation." The Library of
Babel is provided with "indefatigable ladders for the
voyager." As Yu Tsun ("The Garden of the Forking
Paths") flees from Captain Richard Madden on a train
bound for Ashgrove, he chooses a seat as far as possible
from the "fearful window." Funes, the Memorious, we are
told, remembers every detail of the "tempestuous mane of
a stallion."

The use of hypallage in the initial sentence of "The
Form of the Sword" ("His face was crossed with a ran-
corous scar.") delineates the fundamental physical and
mental traits of this protagonist with maximum brevity.
The Hôtel du Nord in "Death and the Compass" displays
the "hateful whiteness of a sanitorium." While investigating the murder of Yarmolinsky in this building, the prag-
matic Commissioner Treviranus brandishes "an imperious
cigar." The terrified Jaromir Hladík ("The Secret
Miracle") anticipates his execution on the "tremulous
eve" and the "sleepless dawn" of his death. In the
postscript of "The Immortal," the reader is told of a
critical commentary on the story by the "most tenacious
pen of Doctor Nahum Cordovero." Prior to the murder of
Loewenthal, Emma Zunz resolutely imagines herself
"wielding the firm revolver" in order to elicit a confession
from him. And in "The Intruder" the Nilsen brothers are

described as hoodlums who attend "dingy parties held in tenements on Saturday nights."

In addition to oxymoron, the transferred epithet, and hypallage, Borges utilizes a variety of other poetic devices to capture an ambiguous vision of reality and to convey his sense of wonder in the face of a world he can never hope to understand. Some of these devices are asyndeton* ("the Library will last on forever: illuminated, solitary, infinite, perfectly immovable, fitted with precious volumes, useless, incorruptible, secret."); alliteration, which is often difficult to render in translation ("I felt visible, vulnerable."); antithesis ("a banal and atrocious reality"); and the unusual, metaphoric use of verbs ("From the far end of the corridor, the mirror was spying on us.").

Another striking rhetorical device utilized by Borges is the juxtaposition of words denoting physical and mental, or concrete and abstract, qualities. The end result is frequently the creation of a subversive, dreamlike atmosphere that undermines objectivity and expands fictional dimensions. For example, in "Death and the Compass" Black Finnegan is said to be "crushed, annihilated almost, by respectability." As he climbs the spiral staircase to the belvedere of Triste-le-Roy, Lönnrot is overpowered by two "ferocious and stocky" men. Immediately thereafter he detects in Scharlach's voice "a hatred the size of the universe, a sadness no smaller than that hatred."

The deceased Beatriz Viterbo ("The Aleph") is described as having had long, lovely, tapered hands. While having sexual intercourse with a sailor Emma Zunz "took refuge, quickly, in vertigo." The protagonist of "The Waiting" discovers that each day brings a "translucent network of minimal surprises." "Intoxicated with insomnia and with vertiginous dialectic," Nils Runeberg wanders through the streets of Malmö in the final lines of

---

* Asyndeton is a condensed expression in which words or phrases are presented in a series, separated only by commas, without the use of conjunctions.

"Three Versions of Judas." The Princess of Faucigny Lucinge ("Tlön, Uqbar, Orbis Tertius") receives "fine, immobile pieces" of her silver table service in a crate from Europe. As Yu Tsun approaches Albert's home in "The Garden of the Forking Paths," he hears Chinese music, "blurred by the leaves and by distance." The narrator of "The Form of the Sword" pursues his enemy "down the dark corridors of nightmare and the deep stairs of vertigo."

In his efforts to subvert concrete reality through the creation of an unsubstantial dreamworld, Borges relies heavily on abstract nouns, a technique that also enhances verbal precision and economy. Many examples are found in "Emma Zunz," whose protagonist's cerebral labyrinth is reflected in phrases such as "she . . . noted the routine or technique of the other women [prostitutes]"; "in order that the purity of the horror might not be mitigated"; "she thought of it with weak amazement"; "her fear was lost in the grief of her body, in her disgust"; "the grief and the nausea were chaining her"; and "her fatigue was turning out to be a strength." The narrator of "The Form of the Sword" recalls the Englishman's "energetic thinness." The Hôtel du Nord in "Death and the Compass" unites the "whiteness of a sanitorium, the numbered divisibility of a prison, and the general appearance of a bawdy house." Just before he is murdered, Yarmolinsky tries to ring a bell, which would arouse all the hotel's "forces." The narrator of "The Immortal" refers to the "urgency of my thirst," "my covetousness to see the Immortals"; "the humility and wretchedness of the troglodyte"; and "the perfection of tolerance and almost that of indifference" among the Immortals. And the accumulation of abstract nouns in the final, climactic sentence of "The Circular Ruins" underscores the dissolution of the wizard's concrete reality. "With relief, with humiliation, with terror, he understood that he also was an illusion, that someone else was dreaming him."

After leaving Buenos Aires, Otálora ("The Dead Man") lived a "life of farflung sunrises." Nils Runeberg, the protagonist of "Three Versions of Judas," adds "the complexities of calamity and evil" to the concept of the Savior. He is convinced, moreover, that the "treachery of Judas . . . was a predestined deed which has its mysterious place in the economy of the Redemption." For Droctulft, the Lombard barbarian in "The Story of the Warrior and the Captive," the city of Ravenna represents "a whole whose multiplicity is not that of disorder." In "The South" we are told that "the dash and grace of certain music, the familiar strophes of *Martín Fierro,* the passing years, boredom and solitude" fostered Dahlmann's "voluntary, but never ostentatious nationalism." The narrator of "The Form of the Sword" states that John Vincent Moon's "cowardice was irreparable." And Funes, the Memorious, was capable of detecting "the tranquil advances of corruption, of caries, of fatigue."

Occasionally Borges accentuates the abstract, cerebral nature of his fictional universe through the use of metonymy,* a device that serves to focus more sharply on the situation than on the character, thus tending to fragment, depersonalize, or weaken the latter. Some of the best examples of this technique are found in "The Garden of the Forking Paths," the absurd spy story whose abstract theme of man trapped in labyrinthine time is reflected by phrases such as "Now that my neck hankers for the hangman's noose"; "if only my mouth, before it should be silenced by a bullet, could shout this name in such a way that it could be heard in Germany"; "the hand of a stranger assassinated him [Ts'ui Pên]"; and "from the end of the avenue, from the main house, a lantern approached." From the patio in the home of Funes, the Memorious, the narrator hears the young man speaking in

---

* Metonymy is a figure of speech in which the name of one object is used for another to which it is related or of which it is a part. An example is "the crown" when used to refer to the king.

Latin and adds: "the voice (which came out of the obscurity) was reading, with obvious delight, a treatise or prayer or incantation." The wizard in "The Circular Ruins" lectures to his students in an amphitheater where "the faces listened anxiously and tried to answer understandingly." The God of Fire commands the wizard to send his "son" to a temple downstream "so that some voice would glorify him in that deserted edifice." Toward the end of "The Secret Miracle" we are told that "the rifles converged upon Hladík," and exactly a year later "a quadruple blast brought him down."

Metonymy is used repeatedly in "The Meeting" to negate the free will of the participants in the duel and depict the mysterious power of their weapons, which symbolize the lingering strength of the machismo cult. When the dinner host lights a lamp over a display cabinet filled with knives, the boy narrator perceives a "glint of steel." Moments later he morbidly anticipates the duel, imagining it as "a chaos of steel." The climax likewise suggests that the knife has a life of its own. "Suddenly the blade seemed shorter, for it was piercing the taller man's chest." And in the final lines of the story, we learn that Juan Almanza, the possible owner of one of the weapons, "was killed by a stray bullet during some election brawl or other."

In "The Man on the Threshold" the narrator describes the people leaving the trial of an English official in the following terms: "The faces and voices were those of drunkards." The librarian in "The Library of Babel" asserts that when he dies, there will not lack "pious hands to hurl me over the banister." Julius Caesar, whose assassination is referred to in "Theme of the Traitor and Hero," was awaited by "the knives of friends." The father of Tadeo Isidoro Cruz perishes in a ditch, "his skull sliced open by a saber from the Peruvian and Brazilian wars." The narrator of "Pedro Salvadores" imagines that Salvadores, hidden in the cellar of his home, dreamed of that night when "the blade sought his throat." And the protagonist of "The Elderly Lady" is the last victim of "that throng of lances" high on a Peruvian tableland more than a century ago.

Given Borges's poetic treatment of the confrontation between the human consciousness and the mysterious world, it is not surprising that he occasionally resorts to the use of synesthesia* in order to capture sensory experience with greater intensity and vivacity. This technique also disrupts logical thought patterns and makes the reader share Borges's view of a marvelous reality enriched by shades of ambiguity. The "clouds of taciturn students" that fill the amphitheater in "The Circular Ruins" create a hushed, nebulous atmosphere reflecting the tale's idealist negation of concrete reality. After a dreamless night the wizard awakens as if emerging from a "viscous desert," perhaps a metaphor of the frustration felt by the sensitive artist trapped in the sterile, everyday world. At the end of the story the "clouds of smoke which rusted the metal of the nights" prefigure the final dissolution of the wizard's concrete reality. In "The Garden of the Forking Paths" Yu Tsun's arrival at Stephen Albert's home is preceded by striking images that prepare his entrance into the mysterious realm of his Chinese ancestor. As he walks along the road, he hears a high-pitched, "almost syllabic music . . . moving with the breeze," and upon approaching Albert's gate, he observes that the "stuttering sparks of the music kept on."

Borges is more than likely parodying the jargon of art critics when, in "The Duel," he alludes to their condemnation of a painting by Clara Glencairn because it suggested "the tumult of a sunset." The fabulous memory of Funes, the Memorious, is explained in part by the fact that in his mind "each visual image was linked to muscular

---

* Synesthesia is the association of an image or sensation perceived by one of the senses with that received by another. A certain sound, for example, may evoke the sight of a certain color. "Blue note" is an example of synesthesia.

sensations, thermal sensations." The drunken, boastful Otálora's death in "The Dead Man" is foreshadowed by the image of a "dizzying tower," a symbol of his destiny. The narrator of "The Form of the Sword" remembers the Englishman's "glacial eyes." In the final lines of this same story the Englishman describes his pursuit of his enemy down "the dark corridors of nightmare" and "the deep stairs of vertigo." And in "The South" the dichotomy between the primitive and civilized sides of Juan Dahlmann's character is expressed by the original "violent color" of the general store and its present faded condition.

Anaphora* as a stylistic device is significant in Borges's work because it conveys a kind of phenomenological confrontation between the human consciousness and the vast, fluctuating reality of the universe. In "Funes, the Memorious" the narrator's repetition of "I remember" emerges as ironic when his own faltering memory is compared to Funes's incredible ability to recall the most minute details of the past. While Emma Zunz is undergoing her sexual ordeal with a sailor, the repetitious "she thought" introduces clauses depicting, alternately, her physical repugnance and her exalted sense of justice. The phrase "I thought" is used somewhat similarly in "The Immortal" to contrast the Roman narrator's perceptions of reality with those of the primitive troglodyte, one of the Immortals. "I thought that Argos and I participated in different universes; I thought that our perceptions were the same, but that he combined them in another way and made other objects of them; I thought that perhaps there were no objects for him, only a vertiginous and continuous play of extremely brief impressions. I thought of a world without memory, without time."

As Lönnrot ("Death and the Compass") walks from the train to Triste-le-Roy, his imminent fate is fore-

---

* Anaphora is the repetition of a word or words at the beginning of two or more successive lines of verse or prose sentences. This device is used frequently in the works of Walt Whitman, one of Borges's favorite poets.

shadowed by the anaphoric "He saw" and subsequent symbols of dissolution such as "dead road," "horizon," and "the crapulous water of a puddle." In "The South" Dahlmann's metaphoric journey across the empty plains and into the primitive past acquires a haunting, dreamlike quality through the repetition of "He saw." When the barbarian Droctulft arrives in the city of Ravenna ("Story of the Warrier and the Captive"), he is awed by the visual wonders of a culture he never dreamed existed. "He sees the day and the cypresses and the marble. He sees a whole whose multiplicity is not that of disorder; he sees a city, an organism composed of statues, temples, gardens, rooms, amphitheaters, vases, columns, regular and open spaces."

The two most memorable uses of anaphora in Borges's fiction appear in "The Aleph" and "The God's Script." Quoted at length above, the description of the Aleph attempts, in lineal language, to condense a simultaneous, intuitive view of the world through the repetition of "I saw" and a wide variety of striking, poetically conceived images. More conceptual than esthetic, the cosmic vision described anaphorically in "The God's Script" enables the narrator to comprehend the vast scheme of the universe, thus illuminating the writing on the tiger.

O bliss of understanding, greater than the bliss of imagining or feeling. I saw the universe and I saw the intimate designs of the universe. I saw the origins narrated in the Book of the Common. I saw the mountains that rose out of the water, I saw the first men of wood, the cisterns that turned against the men, the dogs that ravaged their faces. I saw the faceless god concealed behind the other gods. I saw infinite processes that formed one single felicity and, understanding it all, I was able also to understand the script of the tiger.

3

A Final Word

The study of Borges's works reveals him to be a highly sophisticated writer who views fiction not as an artistic representation of the real world, but rather as a poetic re-creation of the cultural labyrinths man has fabricated throughout history. Borges readily admits that his fictional universe stems from his varied and often esoteric readings in literature, philosophy, and theology, fields of human endeavor that, in his opinion, have analyzed and explained the world in fascinating but purely fictitious terms. As a result of these basic ingredients, his tales exude an aura of unreality that for him constitutes the very nature of art. Borges considers man's quest for truth as an utterly vain endeavor; philosophy and theology represent "provisional" systems of thought destined to be discredited and replaced by others; history evolves as a product of the imagination tempered by time; and psychology is downgraded as fakery because individual behavior depends on phenomena far too numerous and complex to be systematized and understood. Thus Borges limits himself to the portrayal of faceless characters in archetypal situations that serve to conceptualize as well as to formalize his fictional world. Not infrequently his stories can be read as allegories or parables rich in poetic insights and metaphysical implications.

Like many twentieth-century authors, Borges depicts the absurdity of mortal man's search for meaning

and transcendence in an infinite universe beyond his
intellectual comprehension. The absurd is illustrated not
only by the vain quest for truth but also by the artist's
persistent, though futile efforts to achieve esthetic perfection. Borges utilizes a symbolically evocative vocabulary
and poetic devices such as the oxymoron, the metonym,
and the transferred epithet in order to disintegrate concrete
reality and thrust his reader into an abstract, hallucinatory
world fraught with irony and paradox. He also frequently
dons the mask of the bungling narrator, contradicting
himself at every turn or frankly admitting that he does not
know all the facts surrounding the events he is relating.
The result is the collapse of certainties and an ever-
increasing awareness that beneath outward appearances
there exists an uncharted realm of endless contradictions,
the probing of which is a major facet of Borges's fiction.

One of Borges's most haunting images is the
labyrinth, a symbol of chaos and confusion that usually
takes the form of a mental structure designed to explain
the incomprehensible. The labyrinth of time is frequently
set forth in similar but not identical cycles, a device that
serves to capture the basic realities of human experience in
patterns reminiscent of universal myths. Indeed, Borges's
typical story represents a symbolic, self-contained micro-
cosm, in which chaos is pitted against order, ignorance
against knowledge, or illusion against reality. This endless
confrontation of opposites, actually the obverse and the
reverse of the same coin, produces the overall impressions
of circularity, timelessness, and compositional unity so
characteristic of Borges's entire work.

Another major element in Borges's work is the mirror
image, often a symbol of the dissolution of concrete reality
or the implication of the divided self. Several of his protagonists turn out to be his ironic fictional doubles, resulting in the kind of self-mocking style so common in
twentieth-century fiction. For Borges, literature is a
form of verbal artifice that reflects the author's state of

mind while he is immersed in the creative process. As demonstrated in "Pierre Menard, Author of *Don Quijote*," it is also a living organism that acquires new meanings and esthetic qualities with the passing of time and with each reading. In this connection, one might speculate that in a future world of sexual equality "The Intruder" could be read as a parody of male chauvinism.

Borges's negative attitude toward reason has perhaps enhanced his ability to create a truly fictive universe that replaces, as art should, objective or everyday reality. Which of his tales best fulfill this function? In my opinion, "Death and the Compass" and "The South" are Borges's two most memorable *ficciónes,* the former for its deft combination of an exciting, impeccably drawn plot, metaphysical irony, and nightmarish ambience, and the latter for its universal theme, fusion of reality and dream, and reflecting-mirror structure. In view of their philosophical speculations, "Tlön, Uqbar, Orbis Tertius," "The Circular Ruins," and "The Library of Babel" are surely among Borges's most intriguing works. "The Aleph" comes to grips with esthetic preoccupations perhaps better than any other story. And "The Garden of the Forking Paths," because it is the most gripping, is probably the most popular.

Borges's vision of the world has been referred to as "subversive" for several reasons. He makes us acutely aware that all doctrines, whether they appear on the shifting political scene of American life or on the wall posters of Peking, will inevitably be replaced by others. His ingenious parodies of human reason erode conventional modes of thinking, leaving us with the propensity to regard the most far-fetched idea as possible or even plausible. And his ability to fuse objective, concrete reality with the illusory world of dreams creates disturbing doubts about the nature of existence.

Few living writers enjoy the universal esteem accorded Borges by the sophisticated reading public, critics, and other men of letters. The essence of his weltanschauung and literary genius can perhaps be synthesized in two of his prose masterpieces, "The Babylon Lottery" and "New Refutation of Time." In the former an ironically detached narrator depicts life as a labyrinth through which man wanders under the absurd illusion of having organized and understood a chaotic, meaningless world; in the latter Borges makes an elaborate attempt to overcome the temporal anguish he shares with all men, but ultimately he is forced to admit the reality of lineal time, the objective world, and his own mortality. Although these two works repeat the existential theme of futility, they also illustrate the triumph of art over the absurd human experience. For this reason Borges, the creator of unique *ficciónes,* will continue to live long after Borges, the man, has ceased to exist.

Notes

Introduction

1. Juan Domingo Perón (1895–1974) governed Argentina
    from 1946 until 1955 and again from 1973 until his death
    the following year. Borges despised him, especially during
    his first nine years as head of state.
2. Alicia Jurado, *Genio y figura de Jorge Luis Borges,* Edi-
    torial Universitaria de Buenos Aires, Buenos Aires, 1964.
3. Alicia Jurado, p. 14.
4. Alicia Jurado, p. 18.

1. Borges and the absurd
Human condition

1. The Philosophy of the Absurd

1. Sartre calls conscious reality Being-for-itself and noncon-
    scious reality Being-in-itself. Being-for-itself is free to make
    choices and is subject to dynamic change whereas Being-in-
    itself is represented by the static permanence of things in
    nature. According to Sartre, man desires both the surety of
    things in nature and the free choice of consciousness, or he
    wants to escape the responsibility of Being-for-itself and
    still remain superior to Being-in-itself. Sartre concludes
    that man attempts to achieve absolute Being by vainly
    pursuing the impossible "in-itself-for-itself," or the missing
    God.
2. D. P. Gallagher, *Modern Latin American Literature,* p.
    113.

2. The Negation of Reason

1. In his essay entitled "From Allegories to Novels" (OI), Borges discusses two contrasting opinions on the art of allegory, that of the Italian critic Benedetto Croce, who rejects allegory, and that of the English novelist G. K. Chesterton, who favors it. Although Borges tends to agree with Croce, much of his work has an allegorical flavor.

2. Pantheism is discussed at the beginning of section 4 of this chapter.

3. Idealism is discussed at the beginning of section 3 of this chapter.

4. A literary and artistic movement founded in Zurich, Switzerland, in 1916, dadaism was devoted to the negation of all traditional values in philosophy and the arts. Its chaotic form was a protest against what its leaders felt to be the insane destruction of civilized life and thought during World War I. The leader of dadaism was Tristan Tzara.

5. Borges has suffered from insomnia all his life. This condition was probably instrumental in his creation of "Funes, the Memorious," which can be read as a metaphor of insomnia or total lucidity.

6. General Simón Bolívar of Venezuela (1783–1830) was the flamboyant and ambitious liberator of the northern part of South America from Spanish rule. General José de San Martín of Argentina (1778–1850), the liberator of the southern part of South America, was a more modest and less ambitious man. The two men met briefly in Guayaquil, Ecuador, in July 1822, but little is known of what was said between them. Soon after this meeting San Martín resigned his command and sailed for Europe, leaving the strong-willed Bolívar free to carry out his plans for the political reorganization of the continent.

7. In "An Autobiographical Essay" (A), Borges wrote of Schopenhauer: "Today, were I to choose a single philosopher, I would choose him. If the riddle of the universe can be stated in words, I think these words would be in his writings."

8. The cabala is an occult system of mystical interpretation of the Bible that was developed by Jewish rabbis and certain medieval Christians. Borges finds the cabalists

particularly intriguing because their belief in a so-called
Holy Book of Knowledge composed of obscure symbols and
dictated word for word by a divine intelligence coincides
with a recurring theme in his own works, i.e., the world as
an impenetrable book in which everything is already written. Borges discusses the cabala in his essay "The Mirror
of the Enigmas" (OI).

9. The labyrinth is a major motif in Borges's work. It can
take almost any form, including that of a geometrical
figure, examples of which are the diamond-shaped figure
and the straight line.

10. These images include the statues of Diana, the Roman god-
dess of the hunt, and Hermes, the Greek god of invention,
trickery, and cunning. The Diana obviously suggests the
role of Lönnrot as the pursuer, enhancing the irony of the
denouement, and the statue of Hermes would seem to
portend the trap into which Lönnrot is about to fall.

11. Actually, metaphysical irony is an important aspect of the
absurd. It stresses man's efforts to succeed in the world only
to be defeated in the end by a Supreme Being, often seen dia-
bolically plotting his defeat

12. D. P. Gallagher's analysis of "Death and the Compass" is
the best I have seen. (See his *Modern Latin American
Literature*, pp. 96–110.)

13. The idea of Scharlach as God is suggested symbolically by
the appearance of the Roman deity Janus in Scharlach's
delirium at the time of his brother's arrest. Because he had
two faces looking in opposite directions, Janus was able to
know the future as well as the past and thus, like
Scharlach, presided over the beginnings and the ends of
events.

14. Zeno of Elea's "Dichotomy" is referred to here. According
to this paradox, before a body in motion can reach a given
point it must first traverse half of the distance; before it can
traverse half it must traverse a quarter; and so on ad
infinitum. Hence, for a body to pass from one point to
another it must traverse an infinite number of divisions.
Theoretically, then, a goal can never be reached. (This
paradox is similar to the one involving Achilles and the
tortoise except that in the "Dichotomy" it is a question of
only one moving body.) When Lönnrot tells Scharlach to

meet him at a certain point in the maze of a straight line, he is implying that Scharlach will never be able to find him. Or Lönnrot is perhaps suggesting that his future death constitutes the ritualistic repetition of an endless cosmic charade. (For a discussion of Zeno of Elea's paradoxes, see *Greek Thinkers*, by Theodor Gomperz [New York: Humanities Press, 1964], Vol. I, pp. 191–207.)

15. Borges's skeptical attitude toward Christianity at times becomes almost Voltairean as, for example, in his attack on the concept of the Holy Trinity, which appears in his essay "History of Eternity" (HE): "Imagined at a stroke, its conception of a father, a son, and a ghost, articulated on one single organism, seems like a case of intellectual teratology, a deformation which only a horrific nightmare could have engendered. Hell is mere physical violence, but the three inextricable persons are a horror of the intellect, an infinity as stifled and specious as that of mutually reflecting mirrors."

16. In Greek mythology the Minotaur was a monster with a bull's head on a human body. Poseidon sent a bull from the sea as a sign to prove Minos's right to become king of Crete, but Minos failed to sacrifice it to him. In revenge, the god caused Minos's wife Pasiphaë to conceive a passion for the bull. Aided in satisfying it by Daedalus, she bore the Minotaur, whose name was Asterius. It was shut up by Minos in the labyrinth. Every ninth year it was fed with fourteen youths and maidens, a tribute exacted from Athens until Theseus killed it with Ariadne's aid.

17. Some critics have suggested that Asterion represents Borges, who has lived much of his life isolated in a labyrinth of books. Although this idea is not without merit, I prefer a more universal interpretation of the story.

18. The Spanish title of this story is "Abenjacán el Bojarí, muerto en su laberinto." The fact that King Ibn Hakkan's name begins with an A in Spanish emphasizes the antithetical *A-Z* hero-villain relationship between him and Zaid.

19. In 1941 Borges failed to win Argentina's National Literary Prize. The details of this incident are discussed in the introduction.

20. For a brief discussion of the cabala, see footnote 8 of this section.

21. The esthetic implications of "The Aleph" are discussed in more detail in chapter 2.

22. The story's title also provides a clue to its meaning. The phoenix was a mythical Arabian bird that at the end of a certain number of years was believed to consume itself in fire and come forth from the ashes with a new life.

23. These topics are discussed in section 5 of this chapter.

24. This essay and pantheism are discussed in section 4 of this chapter.

25. Satire frequently attacks social and political evils for the purpose of effecting reform. In most of his work Borges is far more ironic than satirical, irony being more subtle and often more ambiguous than satire.

26. In Borges's works Uruguay, a less developed country than Argentina, appears to represent the instinctual, primitive side of life. Thus it is ironic that the Congress, which represents an attempt to organize the world, should decide to have its headquarters in Uruguay.

27. Several additional tales by Borges also imply the negation of reason. "Avelino Arredondo" (1975) (BOS), for example, is an imaginary account of a young Uruguayan fanatic's assassination of President Idiarte Borda in 1897. Arredondo, the assassin, spends several weeks in isolation before committing his crime single-handedly. The flat, spare style and lack of details serve to suppress motivation and thus heighten the protagonist's solitude and seemingly irrational behavior.

"The Sect of the Thirty" (1975) (BOS), like "Three Versions of Judas," is a parody of Christian theology. In this story Borges describes the absurd beliefs and rituals of an imaginary sect, an offshoot of Christianity that derives its name from the thirty coins Judas was allegedly paid for his betrayal of Christ. The Sect of the Thirty denies Judas's villainy and worships him, along with Christ, as the son of God.

"The Night of the Gifts" (1975) (BOS) treats two exciting events: the death of the legendary Argentine outlaw Juan Moreira and an Indian raid on an outpost settlement of whites. The two narrators have told their stories so many times, however, that they remember the words more than the events. In this way, one of Borges's favorite themes emerges, namely, that language does not mirror the real world but rather creates its own separate reality.

"The Disk" (1975) (BOS) and "There Are More Things" (1975) (BOS) are two of Borges's minor works. In the former, which recalls "The Zahir," the narrator becomes obsessed with a one-sided disk, a symbol of power. The second story is told by an Argentine who is studying in Texas when he receives the news of his uncle's death. Upon his return to Argentina, he learns that his uncle's home has been sold to a madman. At the story's end the protagonist enters the home and finds himself lost in a labyrinth.

3. *Idealism*

1. L. S. Dembo, "Interview with Jorge Luis Borges," *Wisconsin Studies in Contemporary Literature,* 11 (Summer 1970) p. 317.

2. For additional information on the cabala, see footnote 8, section 2, of this chapter.

3. Macedonio Fernández (1874–1952) was an eccentric Argentine humorist and philosopher whom Borges greatly admired. The two men were intimate friends for many years.

4. For information on Zeno of Elea, see footnote 14, section 2, of this chapter.

5. Adolfo Bioy Casares (b. 1914), it will be recalled, is a well-known Argentine author and a close friend of Borges. Other real people who appear in this fantastic story include the Argentine essayist Ezequiel Martínez Estrada (1895–1964), the Mexican writer Alfonso Reyes (1889–1959), and the Uruguayan novelist Enrique Amorim (1900–1960).

6. This reference to a minor god alludes to Gnosticism, another of Borges's esoteric interests. Gnosticism is a philosophicoreligious doctrine of the pre-Christian and early Christian era that stressed knowledge, rather than faith, as the true key to salvation. Borges's most complete discussion of Gnosticism, which was considered heretical by the Christians, appears in his essay entitled " A Vindication of the

False Basílides" (OI). Born in Alexandria in 100 A.D.,
Basílides was a Gnostic heresiarch whose cosmogony is
described as follows: A superior god of unknown origin
(*pater innatus*) created the first heaven, which is presided
over by angels. Below this realm is a second one identical to
the first, and below the second, a third identical to the
second, etc., until a total of 365 is reached. The demiurge
presiding over the last heaven is the creator of our world
and the deity mentioned in our sacred scriptures. The
Gnostics were eventually suppressed by the Christians, but
Borges reminds us that if Alexandria had defeated Rome,
this strange "provisional scheme" to decipher the mysteries
of the universe would be a "coherent and majestic" part of
our lives today.

7. Pantheism is discussed in more detail at the beginning of
   section 4 of this chapter.

8. Critics have an occasion alluded to Borges as an idealist. I
   believe Borges finds idealism well suited to his purpose of
   depicting a poetic, hallucinatory world of fiction, but I
   suspect that aside from the esthetic possibilities it offers, he
   considers this philosophical system just as absurd as any
   other. The ending of "Tlön, Uqbar, Orbis Tertius" would
   seem to support this opinion.

9. Hladík's "Vindication of Eternity" is probably a reference
   to Borges's essay, "New Refutation of Time," in which
   he too attempts to deny the passing of time. This essay is
   discussed in section 5 of this chapter.

10. For information on Gnosticism, see footnote 6 of this sec-
    tion.

11. Buddhism, which also sees life as a dream, might have
    influenced Borges's thinking when he wrote this story with
    its mystical, oriental flavor. For Borges the East is the
    embodiment of unreality.

12. This well-known view of Borges is expressed in the epi-
    logue of *Dreamtigers*, which is discussed in section 6 of this
    chapter.

4. Pantheism

1. In Borges's essay entitled "From Someone to Nobody"
   Shakespeare is treated as a literary god who is both every-

body and nobody. This essay is discussed at the beginning of the present section.

2. In his portrayal of the Immortals, Borges has also utilized elements of Gnosticism that appeal to him. The irrational gods to whom the City of the Immortals is dedicated recall the Gnostic demiurges, the creators of our inferior world. The Immortals' indifference toward good and evil, which eventually must correct each other, and the numerous identities of the manuscript's narrator reflect the Gnostics' view of time as a long cycle of reincarnations. And the Immortals' rejection of the senses and dedication to "pure speculation" are paralleled by the Gnostics' belief in the evils of physical matter and, consequently, their submersion in meditation. (For more information on Gnosticism, see footnote 6 of section 3 of this chapter.)

3. The jaguar is considered a god by some Mexican Indian tribes. In this story Borges uses the terms *jaguar* and *tiger* interchangeably. As we shall see in chapter 2, the tiger in Borges's works symbolizes a variety of things ranging from instinct, mystery, and passion to adventure and esthetic perfection.

5. *The Treatment of Time*

1. The runic cross was used in Scandinavia and the British Isles between the second and twelfth centuries. It has curved arms enclosed in a circle.

2. "General Quiroga Rides to His Death in a Carriage" (MAW), one of Borges's well-known poems, deals with this subject.

3. Reference is made here to Domingo Faustino Sarmiento (1811–1888), author of *Facundo or Civilization and Barbarism* (1845), a biography of Quiroga and a fascinating description of Argentina. Sarmiento was also president of Argentina (1868–1874).

4. In 1852 Rosas was defeated in the Battle of Caseros by General Justo José de Urquiza. He fled to England and never returned to Argentina. Borges, for some reason, seems to prefer Quiroga to Rosas in this piece. The two men were probably equally unscrupulous.

5. The least successful of the stories in *Ficciones,* "An Exami-

nation of the Work of Herbert Quain" (1941) (F) deals with the bizarre literary experiments of an apocryphal author whose most important work is a "regressive, ramified novel" appropriately titled *April March*. In Quain's remarkable work, which in some respects represents the reverse of "The Garden of the Forking Paths," time moves backward, bifurcating into nine separate novels, one symbolic, one psychological, one communist, and so on. Herbert Quain probably represents Borges's self-caricature, his view of the novel as a symmetrically structured game governed by arbitrary rules corresponding to Borges's view of fiction in general. Although the treatment of time is central to the story, pantheism is implied by the totality of Herbert Quain's work—all novels contained in one—and by Borges's playful concluding remark that one of Herbert Quain's stories is the source of "The Circular Ruins."

6. Time is the principal ingredient in several additional stories. "An Elderly Lady" (1970) (DBR) is the story of María Justina Rubio de Jáuregui, a centenarian and the last surviving offspring of the soldiers who fought in the South American War of Independence. Although once wealthy, she and her family have been reduced to genteel poverty. She has become senile and in recent years has been little more than a vegetable. On her 100th birthday she is honored by a visit by the Minister of War, but she remains totally unaware of the occasion's significance. A few days later she dies. Borges treats the ravages of time ironically through his allusions to the family's lost social prestige and the protagonist's mental and physical deterioration.

    A tale of minor importance, "Ulrike" (1975) (BOS) describes the narrator's brief love affair with a Norwegian girl, Ulrike, in England. The veiled allusions to the Scandinavian cycle of legends known as the *Völsunga Saga* and the vaguely drawn parallels between the protagonists of the story and the ancient legend suggest cyclical recurrence.

6. The Double and the Mirror Image

1. "The Bribe" (1975) (BOS) also portrays doubles, but unlike the vast majority of Borges's tales, it might be

characterized as "psychological." The two protagonists are
Ezra Winthrop, a native New Englander of Puritan ethics,
and Eric Einarsson, a scholarly and ambitious Icelander.
Both are professors of Old English at the University of
Texas (where Borges lectured in 1961). When Winthrop is
assigned the task of choosing the speaker at a symposium of
Old English scholars, he is faced with a dilemma because
there are only two logical possibilities, Einarsson, who has
made himself unpopular, and Herbert Locke, a shy,
taciturn professor with impeccable qualifications who has
collaborated with Winthrop on scholarly projects. Several
days before the choice is to be made, an article by Einarsson
attacking Winthrop's teaching methods appears in a
professional journal. His personal feelings notwithstanding,
Winthrop chooses Einarsson as the speaker.

Borges focuses on the reason for Winthrop's choice,
which he explains by the professor's Puritan ethics and the
American passion for impartiality. Einarsson, a foreigner,
is well aware that Winthrop will be governed by his fair-
mindedness and admits to him that for this reason he
deliberately published his article attacking him just before
he had to make his decision. The scrupulously impartial
Winthrop and the unscrupulous Einarsson would seem to
be mirror opposites, but as Winthrop tells Einarsson in the
final lines of the story, "we aren't so different. One sin is
common to us both—vanity. You pay me this visit to boast
of your clever stratagem; I backed you to boast that I am an
upright man."

7. The Machismo Cult

1. Alicia Jurado, *Genio y figura de Jorge Luis Borges,* p. 82.
2. The "enormous cat" also recalls Borges's obsession with
    the tiger, a symbol of strength, instinct, and beauty that, in
    Dahlmann's fevered imagination, could have been replaced
    by the smaller feline.
3. For additional information on Sarmiento, see footnote 3,
    section 5.
4. "Juan Muraña" (1970) (DBR), like "The Meeting," dra-
    matizes a reincarnated spirit embodied in a dagger. The

uncle of the story's narrator was Juan Muraña, one of the most famous hoodlums of his day. Muraña died somewhat mysteriously when the narrator was a small boy, but his demented widow lived with her sister and nephew (the narrator). When they were threatened by their landlord with an eviction notice for not paying their rent, the aunt went to his house late at night and killed him with Juan Muraña's dagger. Some time later she confided to the narrator that the dagger *was* Muraña, and that he had saved them from being put out on the street.

2. Some Aspects of Borges's Esthetics

1. The Esthetic Ideal

1. Juan Manuel Rosas was a dictator of Argentina (1835–1852). As leader of the Federalist party, he persecuted the Unitarians unmercifully. For more information on Rosas, see footnote 4, section 5, chapter 1.
2. For information on Rosas, see the preceding footnote. For information on Perón, see footnote 1, Introduction.
3. For additional information on Sarmiento, see footnote 3, section 5, chapter 1.

2. The Symbolic Vision

1. For a more complete discussion of symbols of being and nonbeing, see *The Mythmaker* by Carter Wheelock, pp. 63–98. Wheelock's book represents the most complete and scholarly study to date of symbolism in Borges's fiction. Although I have altered some of his ideas, the basic concept of symbols expressing being and nonbeing was first set forth by Wheelock.
2. "The Aleph" can also be read as a parody of *The Divine Comedy,* the second surname of Carlos Argentino Daneri combining the name of the poet, Dante Alighieri. Because Carlos Argentino leads Borges to the Aleph in his cellar, he can also be identified with Vergil, Dante's guide to Hell. Beatriz Viterbo recalls Dante's beloved, not only because of

her name, but also because during her lifetime she treated Borges with disdain, just as Beatrice treats Dante disdainfully in Paradise. These parallels serve to enrich the literary texture of Borges's story which, when read in this light, becomes a vast work of art in miniature just as the Aleph represents the entire world in miniature.

3. Irony and the Point of View

1. For a discussion of stable and unstable irony, see Wayne C. Booth, *A Rhetoric of Irony* (Chicago: University of Chicago Press, 1974), pp. 1–31, 233–277.

2. The fact that the narrator of "The Babylon Lottery" is about to depart by boat could also indicate his approaching death—thus his keen insight into the realities of his native land—and his voyage with the mythical Charon. (In classic mythology Charon ferries the spirits of the dead across the river Styx to Elysium.)

3. The narrator of this story is one of Borges's most developed first-person narrators, Borges's purpose apparently being to create a concrete reality around his narrator in order to make Funes more believable. His use of circumstantial details is a technique he learned from Chesterton and Kipling.

4. Stylistic Elements

1. "Avatars of the Tortoise" is discussed in chapter 1, section 3.

Bibliography

Works by Jorge Luis Borges in Spanish

1. Poetry

Fervor de Buenos Aires. Buenos Aires: Imprenta Serantes, 1923.
Luna de enfrente. Buenos Aires: Editorial Proa, 1925.
Cuaderno San Martín. Buenos Aires: Editorial Proa, 1929.
Para las seis cuerdas. Buenos Aires: Emecé Editores, 1965.
El otro, el mismo. Buenos Aires: Emecé Editores, 1969.
El oro de los tigres. Buenos Aires: Emecé Editores, 1972.
La rosa profunda. Buenos Aires: Emecé Editores, 1975.
La moneda de hierro. Buenos Aires: Emecé Editores, 1976.

The numerous anthologies of Borges's poetry published by Emecé Editores are not listed.

2. Essays

Inquisiciones. Buenos Aires: Editorial Proa, 1925.
El tamaño de mi esperanza. Buenos Aires: Editorial Proa, 1926.
El idioma de los argentinos. Buenos Aires: M. Gleizer, 1928.
Evaristo Carriego. Buenos Aires: M. Gleizer, 1930. (Reprinted with additions by Emecé Editores, 1955, as Vol. IV, *Obras completas*.)
Discusión. Buenos Aires: M. Gleizer, 1932. (Reprinted with modifications and additions by Emecé Editores, 1957, as Vol. VI, *Obras completas*.)
Las Kenningar. Buenos Aires: Colombo, 1933.
Historia de la eternidad. Buenos Aires: Viau y Zona, 1936. (Reprinted with additions by Emecé Editores, 1953, as Vol. I, *Obras completas*.)

Nueva refutación del tiempo. Buenos Aires: Oportet y Haereses, 1947.

Aspectos de la literatura gauchesca. Montevideo: Número, 1950.

Otras inquisiciones (1937–1952). Buenos Aires: Ediciones Sur, 1952. (Reprinted by Emecé Editores, 1960, as Vol. VIII, *Obras completas*.)

La poesía gauchesca. Buenos Aires: Centro de Estudios Brasileiros, 1960.

Macedonio Fernández. Buenos Aires: Ediciones Culturales Argentinas, 1961.

Prólogos. Buenos Aires: Torres Agüero, 1975.

3. Prose Fiction

Historia universal de la infamia. Buenos Aires: Ediciones Tor, 1935. (Reprinted with minor additions by Emecé Editores, 1954, as Vol. III, *Obras completas*.)

El jardín de senderos que se bifurcan. Buenos Aires: Ediciones Sur, 1941.

Ficciones (1935–1944). Buenos Aires: Ediciones Sur, 1944. (Contains the stories of *El jardín de senderos que se bifurcan* plus six new ones.) (Reprinted with addition of three stories by Emecé Editores, 1956, as Vol. V, *Obras completas*.)

El Aleph. Buenos Aires: Editorial Losada, 1949. (Second edition, 1952, contains four additional stories. Emecé Editores reprinted the 1952 Losada edition as Vol. VII, *Obras completas,* 1957.)

La muerte y la brújula. Buenos Aires: Emecé Editores, 1951. (Reprints stories published in previous collections.)

El informe de Brodie. Buenos Aires: Emecé Editores, 1970.

El congreso. Buenos Aires: El Archibrazo Editor, 1971.

El libro de arena. Buenos Aires: Emecé Editores, 1975. ("El congreso" included.)

4. Prose and Poetry

El hacedor. Buenos Aires: Emecé Editores, 1960. (Vol. IX, *Obras completas*.)

Antología personal. Buenos Aires: Ediciones Sur, 1961. (Selected pieces from previously published collections.)

Nueva antología personal. Mexico: Siglo XXI Editores, 1968.
   (Selected pieces from previously published collections.)
Elogía de la sombra. Buenos Aires: Emecé Editores, 1969.

5. Complete Works

In 1974 the nine volumes of *Obras completas* published by
Emecé were consolidated into one volume entitled *Obras com-
pletas.* The original Emecé volumes have been published by
Alianza (Madrid) in the Libro de Bolsillo series.

WORKS BY JORGE LUIS BORGES
TRANSLATED INTO ENGLISH

Labyrinths. Edited by Donald A. Yates and James E. Irby. New
   York: New Directions, 1962. (An anthology taken from
   several collections of Borges's stories and essays.)
Ficciones. Translated by Anthony Kerrigan et al. New York:
   Grove Press, 1962.
Dreamtigers. Translated by Mildred Boyer and Harold More-
   land. Austin: University of Texas Press, 1964. (English ver-
   sion of *El hacedor.*)
Other Inquisitions 1937–52. Translated by Ruth L. C. Simms.
   Austin: University of Texas Press, 1964. (Introduction by
   James E. Irby.)
Fictions. Edited by Anthony Kerrigan. London: John Calder,
   1965.
A Personal Anthology. Edited by Anthony Kerrigan. New York:
   Grove Press, 1967.
The Book of Imaginary Beings. In collaboration with Margarita
   Guerrero. Revised, enlarged, and translated by Norman
   Thomas di Giovanni in collaboration with the author. New
   York: Dutton, 1969.
The Aleph and Other Stories (1933–1969). Translated by
   Norman Thomas di Giovanni. New York: Dutton, 1970;
   London: Cape, 1971. (The contents do not coincide with the
   Spanish-language editions of *El Aleph.*)
An Introduction to American Literature. In collaboration with
   Esther Zemborain de Torres. Translated and edited by L.

Clark Keating and Robert O. Evans. Lexington: University of Kentucky Press, 1971.

Dr. Brodie's Report. Translated by Norman Thomas di Giovanni. New York: Dutton, 1972; London: Cape, 1974.

A Universal History of Infamy. Translated by Norman Thomas di Giovanni. New York: Dutton, 1972; London: Allen Lane, 1973.

Selected Poems 1923–1967. Translated by Norman Thomas di Giovanni et al. New York: Delta, 1973.

In Praise of Darkness. Translated by Norman Thomas di Giovanni. New York: Dutton, 1974.

Chronicles of Bustos Domecq. In collaboration with Adolfo Bioy Casares. Translated by Norman Thomas di Giovanni. New York: Dutton, 1976.

The Book of Sand. Translated by Norman Thomas di Giovanni. New York: Dutton, 1977.

The Gold of the Tigers. Translated by Alastair Reid. New York: Dutton, 1977.

WORKS ABOUT JORGE LUIS BORGES

1. Books

Alazraki, Jaime. *Jorge Luis Borges.* New York and London: Columbia University Press, 1971 (Columbia Essays on Modern Writers, No. 57). (An excellent short introduction to Borges's fiction.)

————. *La prosa narrativa de Jorge Luis Borges.* Madrid: Gredos, 1968. (Second edition, with appendices, 1974.) (The best study to date on the themes and style of Borges's fiction.)

————. *Versiones. Inversiones. Reversiones.* Madrid: Editorial Gredos, 1977. (A good study of Borges's use of the mirror image in his *ficciones.*)

Barrenechea, Ana María. *La expresión de la irrealidad en la obra de Jorge Luis Borges.* Mexico: Colegio de México, 1957. (An excellent study of the principal themes in Borges's work. Very useful bibliography.)

————. *Borges the Labyrinth Maker.* New York: New York University Press, 1965. (Translation by Robert Lima of *La*

expresión de la irrealidad en la obra de Jorge Luis Borges.
A few additions.)

Blanco-González, Manuel. *Jorge Luis Borges: Anotaciones sobre el tiempo en su obra.* Mexico: Ediciones de Andrea, 1963. (Critical and even hostile. Sees Borges as frivolous and inconsistent.)

Christ, Ronald J. *The Narrow Act: Borges' Art of Allusion.* New York: New York University Press, 1969. (Concentrates mainly on allusions in Borges's work to other literatures, especially English literature.)

Cohen, J. M. *Jorge Luis Borges.* Edinburgh: Oliver and Boyd, 1972. (A general introductory study of Borges's life and work.)

Crossan, John Dominic. *Raid on the Articulate.* New York: Harper and Row, 1976. (Concentrates on the metaphysical and play elements in Borges's work.)

Ferrer, Manuel. *Borges y la nada.* London: Tamesis Books Ltd., 1971. (A study of Borges's rejection of the real world for the illusory world of fiction.)

Garcilli, Enrique. *Circles Without Center.* Cambridge, Mass.: Harvard University Press, 1972. (A discussion of the labyrinth theme in Borges's works.)

Gertel, Zunilda A. *Borges y su retorno a la poesía.* Mexico: Ediciones de Andrea, 1968. (A study of thematic and structural elements in Borges's poetry.)

Jurado, Alicia. *Genio y figura de Jorge Luis Borges.* Buenos Aires: Ed. Universitaria de Buenos Aires, 1964. (Interesting and informative presentation of Borges's personal life by a close friend.)

Murillo, L. A. *The Cyclical Night. Irony in James Joyce and Jorge Luis Borges.* Cambridge, Mass.: Harvard University Press, 1968. (Interpretations of "The Garden of the Forking Paths" and "Death and the Compass.")

Rest, Jaime. *El laberinto del universo: Borges y el pensamiento nominalista.* Buenos Aires: Librerías Fausto, 1976. (Emphasis on Borges's doubt of language as a means for expressing reality.)

Rodríguez Monegal, Emir. *Borges: Hacia una lectura poética.* Madrid: Guadarrama, 1976. (Three essays on Borges, the best of which compares his work with that of Octavio Paz.)

—————. *Jorge Luis Borges. A Literary Biography*. New York: Dutton, 1978. (A lengthy examination of the private and professional facets of Borges's life.)

Shaw, D. L. *Borges Ficciones*. London: Grant & Cutler, 1976. (Brief, perceptive analysis of Borges's seventeen stories in *Ficciones*.)

Stabb, Martin S. *Jorge Luis Borges*. New York: Twayne, 1970. (A very good introduction to Borges's work as a whole.)

Stark, John O. *The Literature of Exhaustion: Borges, Nabokov, and Barth*. Durham, North Carolina: Duke University Press, 1974. (A discussion of modern literary techniques in three avant-garde writers of fiction.)

Sturrock, John. *Paper Tigers*. London: Oxford University Press, 1977. (Focuses principally on the overriding concern in Borges's work for the nature of literature and the process of creating it.)

Sucre, Guillermo. *Borges el poeta*. Mexico: Universidad Nacional Autónoma de México, 1968. (Useful study of Borges's poetry that also illuminates thematic elements in his prose.)

Wheelock, Carter. *The Mythmaker: A Study of Motif and Symbol in the Short Stories of J. L. Borges*. Austin: The University of Texas Press, 1969. (The most detailed study of Borges's symbolism. Somewhat controversial.)

2. Articles

Alazraki, Jaime. "Aproximación a la prosa narrativa de Jorge Luis Borges." *Symposium* 24 (1970): 5–16. (Fine study of classical and lyrical aspects of Borges's style.)

—————. "Borges and the New Latin American Novel." In *Prose for Borges*. Ed. Charles Newman and Mary Kinzie. Evanston, Illinois: Northwestern University Press, 1974, pp. 331–350. (Good discussion on thematic and stylistic elements in Borges's fiction that have influenced the writings of Cortázar, García Márquez, and others.)

—————. "Kabbalistic Traits in Borges' Narration." *Studies in Short Fiction* 5 (1971): 78–92. (Very useful in understanding some of Borges's esoteric references to the cabala.)

—————. "Oxymoronic Structure in Borges' Essays." In *The Cardinal Points of Borges*. Eds. Lowell Dunham and Ivar

Ivask. Norman, Oklahoma: University of Oklahoma Press, 1972, pp. 47–53. (Very perceptive analysis of Borges's style and structure in his essays.)

————. "Tlön y Asterión: anverso y reverso de una epistemología." *Nueva Narrativa Hispanoamericana* 1, 2 (1971): 21–33. (An excellent study of some parallels between "Tlön, Uqbar, Orbis Tertius" and "The House of Asterion.")

Anderson-Imbert, Enrique. "Un cuento de Borges: 'La casa de Asterión.'" *Revista Iberoamericana* 25, 40 (1960): 33–43. (Analyzes structural and mythical elements in the story, concluding that Borges sees himself as Asterion.)

————. "El éxito de Borges." *Cuadernos Americanos* 207 5 (1976): 199–212. (Demonstrates that Borges's success stems from his ability to create an imaginary world free from dogmatic concepts.)

————. "El punto de vista en Borges." *Hispanic Review* 44, 3 (1976): 213–21. (A careful listing of the various points of view used in Borges's fiction.)

Arango, Guillermo. "La función del sueño en 'Las ruinas circulares' de Jorge Luis Borges." *Hispania* 56, Special Issue (1973): 249–54. (Very fine essay explaining the story as an allegory of esthetic creation.)

Ayora, Jorge. "Gnosticism and Time in 'El inmortal.'" *Hispania* 56, 3 (1973): 593–96. (Contributes to a better understanding of one of Borges's most complex *ficciones*.)

Barth, John. "The Literature of Exhaustion." *Atlantic Monthly* 220, 2 (1967): 29–34. (Perceptive commentary on Borges's works and contemporary literature in general.)

Berlitt, Ben. "The Enigmatic Predicament: Some Parables of Kafka and Borges." In *Prose for Borges*. Eds. Charles Newman and Mary Kinzie. Evanston, Illinois: Northwestern University Press, 1974, pp. 212–37. (Borges's works are viewed as parables of man's search for knowledge and the artist's search for esthetic perfection.)

Berg, Mary. "Review." *Modern Fiction Studies* 19, 3 (1973): 469–74. (Good comments on *Dr. Brodie's Report*.)

Bickel, Gisèle. "La alegoría del pensamiento." *Modern Language Notes* 88 (1973): 295–316. ("Tlön, Uqbar, Orbis Tertius" is seen as a kind of allegorical key to Borges's entire work.)

Botsford, Keith. "The Writings of Jorge Luis Borges." *Atlantic*

Monthly 219, 1 (1967): 99–104. (A general article introducing Borges to readers of English.)

Dauster, Frank. "Notes on Borges' Labyrinths." *Hispanic Review* 30 (1962): 142–48. (Useful remarks on the meaning of the labyrinthine symbol in Borges's work.)

Enguídanos, Miguel. "Imagination and Escape in the Short Stories of Jorge Luis Borges." *Texas Quarterly* 4 (1961): 118–127. (Stresses the elements of reality in Borges's fiction.)

————. "Correspondencia: A propósito de Jorge Luis Borges." *Revista Universidad de México* 26, 11 (1962): 31. (Defense of Borges against the charge of "McCarthyism.")

Faris, Wendy B. "Laberintos, Retruecanos, Emblemas: Borges' Dissatisfaction with Labyrinths." *Studies in Short Fiction* 12, 4 (1975): 351–60. (Sets forth examples of Borges's shift from his labyrinthine vision of the world to a more emotional approach to reality.)

Flores, Angel. "Magical Realism in Spanish American Fiction." *Hispania* 38, 2 (1955): 187–92. (Borges seen as an early practitioner of magical realism.)

Foster, David William. "Borges and Structuralism: Toward an Implied Poetics." *Modern Fiction Studies* 19, 3 (1973): 341–51. (Borges's work seen in terms of cultural constructs.)

————. "Borges' 'El Aleph'—Some Thematic Considerations." *Hispania* 47, 1 (1964): 56–59. (Interesting comments on "El Aleph" and "The Immortal." Also compares Borges with Kafka.)

Frank, Roslyn M. "Lo profano y lo sagrado en 'La muerte y la brújula.'" *Nueva Narrativa Hispanoamericana* 5 (1975): 127–35. (Views the story as a cosmic drama that repeats itself infinitely.)

Gallagher, D. P. "Jorge Luis Borges." In *Modern Latin American Literature.* New York: Oxford University Press, 1973, ppl 94–121. (The best introductory article on Borges that I have found. Also contains an excellent discussion of "Death and the Compass.")

Gallo, Marta. "El tiempo en 'Las ruinas circulares' de Jorge Luis Borges." *Revista Iberoamericana* 73 (1970): 359–78. (Stresses the dreamlike atmosphere and circular nature of time in the story.)

Gertel, Zunilda. "'El sur,' de Borges: Búsqueda de identidad en el laberinto." *Nueva Narrativa Hispanoamericana* 1, 2 (1971): 35–55. (A careful analysis of the story's thematic and structural relationships.)

Giordanno, Jaime. "Forma y sentido de 'La escritura del Dios,' de Jorge Luis Borges." *Revista Iberoamericana* 78 (1972): 105–15. (Views the story as a kind of solipsistic labyrinth.)

Gordon, Ambrose, Jr. "A Quiet Betrayal: Some Mirror Works in Borges." *Texas Studies in Literature and Language* 17 (1975): 207–18. (Treatment of the mirror image in several of Borges's prose works.)

Gyurko, Lanin A. "Borges and the 'Machismo' Cult." *Revista Hispánica Moderna* 36 (1970–71): 128–45. (Excellent study of Borges's ambivalent attitude toward the code of the Argentine macho.)

————. "Rivalry and the Double in Borges' 'Guayaquil.'" *Romance Notes* 15 (1973): 37–46. (A very good analysis of the story.)

Harss, Luis. "Jorge Luis Borges, or the Consolation by Philosophy." In *Into the Mainstream.* New York: Harper & Row, 1966, pp. 102–136. (General introductory essay on Borges's life and work.)

Hart, Thomas R., Jr. "The Literary Criticism of Jorge Luis Borges." *Modern Language Notes* 78, 5 (1963): 489–503. (A discussion of Borges's ideas on esthetics.)

Irby, James E. "Introduction" to *Labyrinths.* Ed. Donald A. Yates and James E. Irby. New York: New Directions, 1962. (Very good introductory comments on Borges's life and fiction.)

Isaacs, Neil D. "The Labyrinth of Art in Four *Ficciones* of Jorge Luis Borges." *Studies in Short Fiction* 6 (1969): 383–94. (Good essay on the role of the labyrinth in "The Babylon Lottery," "The Library of Babel," "Tlön, Uqbar, Orbis Tertius," and "The Garden of the Forking Paths.")

Kadir, Djelal. "Borges the Heresiarch Mutakallimun." *Modern Fiction Studies* 19, 3 (1973): 461–68. (Discusses the philosophical implications of Borges's shadowy world.)

Kellerman, Owen L. "Borges y *El informe de Brodie:* Juego de voces." *Revista Iberoamericana* 81 (1972): 663–70. (Stresses the ironic effect of Borges's narrative techniques in *Dr. Brodie's Report.*)

Levy, Salomón. "El 'Aleph,' símbolo cabalístico, y sus impli-
caciones en la obra de Jorge Luis Borges." *Hispanic Review*
44, 2 (1976): 143–61. (Stresses style as an esthetic device to
capture an absolute reality.)

Lewald, H. Ernest. "Borges: His Recent Poetry." *Chasqui* 4, 1
(1974): 19–33. (Stresses the themes of resignation, self-
abnegation, and death in Borges's recent poetry.)

————. "The Labyrinth of Time and Place in Two Short
Stories by Borges." *Hispania* 45 (1962): 630–36. (Borges's
labyrinth of time and space is seen as the only certainty in
his work.)

Lusky, Mary H. "Père Menard: Autor." *Texas Quarterly*
18, 1 (1975): 104–116. (Utilizes Freudian psychology to
analyze several of Borges's stories.)

Lyon, Thomas E. "Borges and the (Somewhat) Personal Narrator." *Modern Fiction Studies* 19, 3 (1973): 363–72.
(Enlightening comments on Borges's manipulation of the
point of view.)

Maloff, Saul. "Eerie Emblems of a Bizarre, Terrifying World."
Saturday Review, 2 March 1970, p. 34. (Review of English
translations, *Labyrinths* and *Ficciones.*)

McBride, Mary. "Jorge Luis Borges, Existentialist: 'The Aleph'
and the Relativity of Human Perception." *Studies in Short
Fiction* 14, 4 (1977): 399–401. (Analyzes the existential
idea implied in "The Aleph" that absolute truth is forever
elusive.)

Mellizo, Carlos. "Dos héroes borgeanos: Tadeo Isidoro Cruz y
Juan Dahlmann." *Chasqui* 2, 3 (1973): 43–51. (Good com-
parison of two of Borges's heroes with the protagonist of *Dr.
Jekyll and Mr. Hyde.*)

Merivale, Patricia. "The Flaunting of Artifice in Vladimir
Nabokov and Jorge Luis Borges." *Wisconsin Studies in
Contemporary Literature* 8, 2 (1967): 294–309. (Compares
the narrative techniques utilized by the two authors to create
their fictitious versions of reality.)

Murillo, L. A. "The Labyrinths of Jorge Luis Borges. An
Introduction to the Stories of the *Aleph.*" *Modern Language
Quarterly* 20 (1959): 259–66. (Views Borges's fiction as an
expression of twentieth-century man's existential crisis.)

Natella, Arthur A. "Symbolic Colors in the Stories of Jorge Luis
Borges." *Journal of Spanish Studies Twentieth Century* 2, 1

  241

(1974): 39–48. (Gray seen as a symbol of eternity and vague-
ness.)

Paley de Francescato, Marta. "Borges y su concepción del
universo en *Otras inquisiciones.*" *Kentucky Romance
Quarterly* 20 (1973): 469–81. (A good discussion of the
themes in Borges's best collection of essays.)

Phillips, Allen. "Notas sobre Borges y la crítica reciente."
Revista Iberoamericana 22, 43 (1957): 41–59. (Very good
review of the Borges criticism up to 1957.)

————. "'El sur' de Borges." *Revista Hispánica Moderna* 29
(1963): 140–47. (One of the best analyses of "El sur.")

Rasi, Humberto M. "The Final Creole: Borges' View of
Argentine History." In *Prose for Borges.* Ed. Charles
Newman and Mary Kinzie. Evanston, Illinois:
Northwestern University Press, 1974, pp. 143–65. (Dis-
cusses the evolution of Borges's attitudes toward prominent
figures from the Argentine past.)

Rest, Jaime. "Borges y el pensamiento sistemático. *Hispamérica*
1, 3 (1973): 3–23. (Stresses the playful nature of Borges's
philosophy and his infinite search for reality.)

————. "Borges y el universo de los signos." *Hispamérica* 3, 7
(1974): 3–24. (Discusses Borges's view of language as a
means to verbalize, systematize and deform the real world.)

Rodríguez Monegal, Emir. "Borges: The Reader as Writer." In
Prose for Borges. Ed. Charles Newman and Mary Kinzie.
Evanston, Illinois: Northwestern University Press, 1974,
pp. 96–137. (Explains how Borges's art as a writer is based
on his art as a reader.)

————. "Borges: Una teoría de la literatura fantástica."
Revista Iberoamericana 95 (1976): 177–89. (Discusses why
Borges prefers fantastic to realistic literature.)

————. "Symbols in Borges' Works." *Modern Fiction Studies*
19 (1973): 325–40. (A discussion of the more common
symbols in Borges's work.)

Sábato, Ernesto. "Borges y Borges." *Revista Universidad de
México* 18, 5 (1964): 22–26. (A discussion of Borges the
poet and Borges the writer of fiction.)

Sawnor, Edna A. "Borges y Bergson." *Cuadernos Americanos*
185 (1972): 247–54. (Compares Bergson's and Borges's
concepts of time.)

Scari, Robert M. "Aspectos realista-tradicionales del arte narra-

tivo de Borges." *Hispania* 57, 4 (1974): 899–907.
(Demonstrates how several of Borges's tales create an aura
of abstract unreality based on concrete reality.)

Scholes, Robert M. "A Commentary on 'Theme of the Traitor
and the Hero.'" In *Elements of Literature.* New York:
Oxford University Press, 1978, pp. 174–77. (Very fine discussion of Borges's story-telling techniques in this story and
their implications.)

Sosnowski, Saúl. "'The God's Script'—A Kabbalistic Quest."
Modern Fiction Studies 19, 3 (1973): 381–94. ("The God's
Script" viewed as an affirmation of the intrinsic values of
man and the historical process.)

Updike, John. "Books: The Author as Librarian." *New Yorker,*
31 October 1965, pp. 223–46. (Perceptive general discussion
of Borges's work.)

Weber, Frances W. "Borges' Stories: Fiction and Philosophy."
Hispanic Review 36, 2 (1968): 124–41. (Very good dis-
cussion of the philosophical and conjectural nature of
Borges's fiction.)

Wheelock, Carter. "The Committed Side of Borges." *Modern
Fiction Studies* 19, 3 (1973): 373–79. (Denies that Borges's
work represents an escape from reality.)

————. "The Subversive Borges." *Texas Quarterly* 18, 1
(1975): 117–26. (Emphasizes how Borges's readers change
their traditional ways of looking at the world.)

Yates, Donald A. "Behind 'Borges and I.'" *Modern Fiction
Studies* 19, 3 (1973): 317–324. (Borges's duality of consciousness is explained by various incidents from his personal life.)

3. Special Issues of Periodicals and Collections of Essays (listed in chronological order)

"Discusión sobre Jorge Luis Borges," *Megáfono,* No. 11 (August
1933). (Opinions on Borges's work by various Latin
American critics.)

"Desagravio a Borges," *Sur,* No. 94 (July 1942). (Statements by
various Latin American writers in support of Borges after
he fails to win the 1941 National Literary Prize.)

"Los escritores argentinos: Jorge Luis Borges," *Ciudad,* Nos. 2–

3 (1955). (Articles on Borges by writers of the younger generation.)

"Jorge Luis Borges," *L'Herne* (1964). (Collection of articles and interviews by French, American, and Hispanic writers. All translated into French.)

Dunham, Lowell, and Ivar Ivask. *The Cardinal Points of Borges.* Norman, Oklahoma: University of Oklahoma Press, 1970. (Essays presented at a symposium at the University of Oklahoma. Uneven quality.)

Prose for Borges (a *TriQuarterly* book, ed. Charles Newman & Mary Kinzie). Evanston, Illinois: Northwestern University, Fall 1972. (Collection of essays on Borges. Varied in quality.)

"Jorge Luis Borges Number," *Modern Fiction Studies,* 19, 3 (Autumn 1973). (Good essays on various aspects of Borges's work.)

Alazraki, Jaime. *Jorge Luis Borges.* Madrid: Taurus, 1976. (Volume of good essays on various aspects of Borges's work. Edited by Alazraki.)

"Todo Borges y . . . la vida, la muerte, las mujeres, la madre, la política, los enemigos," *Gente,* 27 January 1977. (Magazine edition with information and pictures about Borges's personal and public life.)

"40 inquisiciones sobre Borges," *Revista Iberoamericana,* 43, 100–101 (July–December 1977). (Forty essays on Borges's work, generally of high quality.)

4. Interviews and Statements by Borges (listed according to names of interviewers)

Botsford, Keith. "About Borges and Not about Borges." *Kenyon Review* 26 (Autumn 1964): 723–37. (Borges speaks candidly about his work.)

Burgin, Richard. *Conversations with Jorge Luis Borges.* New York: Holt, Rinehart and Winston, 1969. (A series of interesting conversations revealing much about Borges's life and works.)

Chica Salas, Susana. "Conversación con Borges." *Revista Iberoamericana* 96–97 (July–December 1976): 585–91. (Borges talks of time, the rationale for suicide, and his pro-Semitism.)

Christ, Ronald. "The Art of Fiction: Jorge Luis Borges." *Paris Review* 40 (Winter–Spring 1967): 116–64. (Borges remarks on how he began writing fiction.)

Dembo, L. S. "Interview with Jorge Luis Borges." *Wisconsin Studies in Contemporary Literature* 11, 3 (Summer 1970): 315–23. (Revealing statements by Borges about ideas and symbols in his works.)

Di Giovanni, Norman T., Daniel Halpern, and Frank MacShane. *Borges on Writing*. New York: Dutton, 1973. (Contains enlightening statements by Borges on his works.)

Di Sovico, Aurelio, "Interview with Jorge Luis Borges." *Hispania* 59, 3 (September 1976): 527. (Portion of interview taken from the April 26, 1976, issue of *Atlas*. Borges discusses some of the symbols in his work and denies he has any philosophy.)

Fernando Moreno, César. "Harto de los laberintos." *Mundo Nuevo* 18 (December 1967): 5–29. (Long, interesting discussion in which Borges reveals a new orientation in his works. Introduction by Emir Rodríguez Monegal.)

Guibert, Rita. "Jorge Luis Borges." In *Seven Voices*. New York: Alfred A. Knopf, 1973, pp. 77–117. (Valuable discussion of a wide range of topics: literature, philosophy, religion, and Borges's personal likes and dislikes.

Irby, James E. "Encuentro con Borges." *Revista Universidad de México* 16, 10 (June 1962): 4–10. (Interesting information revealed about Borges's life and possible influences on his work.)

Milleret, Jean de. *Entretiens avec Jorge Luis Borges*. Paris: Belfond, 1967. (Informative remarks by Borges on his works.)

Rodman, Selden. *Tongues of Fallen Angels*. New York: New Directions, 1972, pp. 5–37. (Interesting conversation on subjects including politics, Borges's stories, contemporary literature, and his divorce.)

Sorrentino, Fernando. *Siete conversaciones con Jorge Luis Borges*. Buenos Aires: Pardo, 1974. (Good discussion of Borges's ideas on both literature and politics.)

5. Bibliography

Becco, Horacio J. *Jorge Luis Borges: Bibliografía total 1923–73*. Buenos Aires: Casa Pardo, 1973.

Fiore, Robert L. "Critical Studies on Jorge Luis Borges."
    Modern Fiction Studies 19, 3 (Autumn 1973): 475–80.
—————. "Toward a Bibliography on Jorge Luis Borges
    (1923–1969)." In *Cardinal Points of Borges,* Ed. Lowell
    Dunham and Ivar Ivask. Norman, Oklahoma: University of
    Oklahoma Press, 1971, pp. 83–105.
Foster, David W. *A Bibliography of the Works of Jorge Luis
    Borges.* Tempe, Arizona: Center for Latin American
    Studies, Arizona State University, 1971.
Lucio, Nodier, and Lydia Revello. "Contribución a la bibliografía
    de Jorge Luis Borges." *Bibliografía argentina de artes y
    letras* 10–11 (April–September 1961): 45–111.
Ríos Patrón, José Luis, and Horacio Jorge Becco. "Bibliografía
    de Borges." *Ciudad* 2–3 (April–September 1955): 56–62.

6.   *Autobiography*

Borges, Jorge Luis. "Autobiographical Notes." *New Yorker,* 19
    September 1970, pp. 40–99. Also published in *The Aleph
    and Other Stories, 1933–1969.* New York: Dutton, 1970;
    London: Cape, 1971. (Borges relates many interesting
    events about his life.)

Index

MODERN LITERATURE MONOGRAPHS

In the same series: (continued from page ii)